Duelism

Confronting Sport Through Its Doubles

Edited by
Brittany Reid
Taylor McKee

Duelism

Confronting Sport Through Its Doubles

Edited by
Brittany Reid
Taylor McKee

First published in 2021
as part of the *Sport & Society* Book Imprint
doi:10.18848/978-0-949313-49-2/CGP (Full Book)

Common Ground Research Networks
60 Hazelwood Dr.
University of Illinois Research Park
Champaign, IL
61820

Library of Congress Cataloging-in-Publication Data

Names: Reid, Brittany, editor. | McKee, Taylor, editor.
Title: Duelism : confronting sport through its doubles / edited by Brittany
  Reid & Taylor McKee.
Description: Champaign, IL : Common Ground, 2021. | Includes
  bibliographical references. | Summary: "In Duelism: Confronting Sport
  through Its Doubles, we adopt a consciously interdisciplinary approach
  to sport that accounts for its centrality and multiplicity of meaning in
  society. Together, we assert that sport is best understood alongside
  broader issues or concepts that can be thought of as its doubles, since
  each helps to define the parameters of what it means to critically
  consider sport in society. By inviting critical attempts to treat sport
  studies as an evolving, interdisciplinary field of research, we have
  endeavored to create a collection of emerging sport scholarship that
  reflects the multifaceted, contentious, and vital nature of sport, both
  in society and as an area of study"-- Provided by publisher.
Identifiers: LCCN 2020050285 (print) | LCCN 2020050286 (ebook) | ISBN
  9780949313478 (hardback) | ISBN 9780949313485 (paperback) | ISBN
  9780949313492 (adobe pdf)
Subjects: LCSH: Sports--Sociological aspects.
Classification: LCC GV706.5 .D84 2021 (print) | LCC GV706.5 (ebook) | DDC
  306.4/83--dc23
LC record available at https://lccn.loc.gov/2020050285
LC ebook record available at https://lccn.loc.gov/2020050286

Cover Photo Credit: Taylor McKee (London, Ontario. 2017)

Table of Contents

Contributors

Phillip Chipman is a PhD candidate in the Department of Human Kinetics at the University of Ottawa. He has published an article analyzing the development of bodybuilding in Montreal. He continues to study questions regarding masculinity, identity, and nation in the context of Quebec.

Nevada Cooke is a PhD candidate at the University of Western Ontario and an Assistant Professor in the Sport and Recreation Management department at Keystone College.

Tom Fabian is an Assistant Professor of Sport Management at St. Francis Xavier University. His primary research areas are centered around globalization and sport, university sport, and volleyball. Current projects include the marginalization of traditional games, a global history of volleyball, and an anthology about Canadian university sport reform.

Steve Greenfield is a Professor of Sports Law and Practice at the University of Westminster where he is Co-Director of the Centre for Law, Society and Popular Culture and joint editor of the Entertainment and Sports Law Journal: https://www.entsportslawjournal.com/. Steve has written widely on a range of sport and law issues including child protection, injuries, and coach liability.

Conor Heffernan is an Assistant Professor of Physical Culture and Sport Studies at the University of Texas at Austin.

Tiago J. Maranhão holds a PhD in History from the Vanderbilt University. He is currently a Mellon Partners for Humanities Education postdoctoral fellow and a Visiting Professor of Latin American History at Tougaloo College (HBCU), USA. His interests relate to racial relations, public health, physical culture, and the processes of nationalism and nation-building.

Taylor McKee is an Adjunct Assistant Professor in Sociology at Western University and an Instructor in the Department of Philosophy, History, and Politics at Thompson Rivers University. His research focuses on media, violence, and Canadian history.

Lukasz Muniowski holds a Ph.D. in American Literature from the University of Warsaw, Poland. He is the author of *Three-Pointer!: A 40-Year NBA History* (2020), *Narrating the NBA: Cultural Representations of Leading Players after the Michael Jordan Era* (2021), and *The Sixth Man: A History of the NBA's Best Off the Bench* (2021).

Andrew Pettit is a PhD Candidate in Kinesiology at the University of Western Ontario with specialization in Transitional Justice and Post-Conflict Reconstruction. His research focuses on questioning how sport has been historically understood as a peace-promoting endeavor by peoples and nations, while also problematizing the practical and ethical issues concerned with the application of sport for development and peace initiatives.

Brittany Reid is an Assistant Teaching Professor in the Department of English and Modern Languages at Thompson Rivers University. Her research and teaching explore a broad variety of topics, including Sport Literature, Romanticism, Theatre History, Shakespearean Studies, and Gothic Literature.

Jamie Ryan is a Ph.D. candidate in English Literature at Queen's University in Kingston, Ontario. He studies sports literature and gender, specifically women's hockey narratives. His dissertation explores the representation, or lack thereof, of women in sports novels and films along with the personal stories of professional women's hockey players.

David Scott is a Lecturer in Sport Development at Abertay University. His primary research interest is the role sport plays in everyday society through the use of microsociology, existential-phenomenology, and individuals' lived experiences.

Hendrik Snyders is the head of Department of History at the National Museum (Bloemfontein) and a research associate at the Department of History at the University of the Free State. His research focuses on race, sport, masculinity, memory, heritage, and public history as well as colonialism in South Africa. Hendrik graduated with a PhD (history) from the University of Stellenbosch.

Christoph Wagner lives in Paris where he works as a teacher for English and German. His PhD covers the Anglo-German football rivalry in the 20th century and how it was covered in the sports press in England and Germany. He is also editor of 120minuten.net, an award winning football long read website in Germany.

Kevin B. Witherspoon is the Dr. Benjamin E. Mays Endowed Chair in the Department of History & Philosophy at Lander University in Greenwood, SC. He has received numerous awards at Lander, including the Distinguished Professor Award in 2014. His first book, *Before the Eyes of the World: Mexico and the 1968 Olympics* won the 2009 North American Society for Sport History Book Award. His most recent book, *Defending the American Way of Life: Sport, Culture and the Cold War*, co-edited with Toby Rider of Cal State-Fullerton, was published in 2018. His current research focuses on the U.S./Soviet sports rivalry during the cold war.

Ashley Woodiwiss is chair of the Department of Government, Criminology, and Sociology at Lander University in Greenwood, SC. As a political theorist his areas of specialization include contemporary democratic theory, political theology, and civic engagement. Currently team-teaching a "sports and politics" course at Lander, Woodiwiss is widely published and co-editor of the volume, *The Re-enchantment of Political Science.* He has won numerous teaching awards and was 2013 winner of the South Carolina Independent Colleges and Universities faculty of the year award.

Boccioni, Umberto (1882-1916). Dynamism of a Soccer Player. 1913.
Oil on canvas, 6' 4 1/8" x 6' 7 1/8" (193.2 x 201 cm). The Sidney and Harriet Janis Collection.
Digital Image © The Museum of Modern Art/Licensed by SCALA / Art Resource, NY

Introduction: Sport, Duality, and "Duelism"

Brittany Reid and Taylor McKee

In his work "Dynamism of a Soccer Player" (1913), Italian Futurist painter Umberto Boccioni produced an unconventional rendering of an athlete in action. In line with Modernist techniques, and the principles outlined in the "Futurist Painting: Technical Manifesto," Boccioni eschewed mimetic realism by working to re-create the "dynamic sensation" produced when "movement and light destroy the materiality of bodies" (Boccioni et. al, 1910, 30). Through the "dynamic sensation" evoked through the painting, Boccioni re-created the kinetic and material realities of sport in practice. What resulted is an image that is both fractured and multifaceted, revealing the chaotic and often cataclysmic dynamism of both sport and the sporting body in motion. Although the titular soccer player is the work's subject, the painting depicts a swirling cacophony of colour, shape, and texture, with a disembodied calf as the only discernible human remains. In line with Boccioni and his coterie's view that movement and light "destroy" the corporeal form, this apparent act of artistic violence reveals the many influences acting on, or against, the physical body in sport.

Viewed as a metaphor for sport in society, this painting harnesses the reality of sport as eternally at war with itself and the world around it. While the human experience is its fixed center, sport can be characterized as an ever-changing and multifarious set of practices, activities, and institutions. Although sports have significantly changed since its creation in 1913, the painting's explosive quality represents the multifaceted character of sport, from its depths, to its points of lightness, to its unexplored shadows, and troubles traditional expectations of sport as merely a form leisure. In this way, "Dynamism of a Soccer Player" symbolizes the prismatic, combative, and conflicted nature of sport by capturing the violent convergence of its many disparate dimensions.

But although efforts to define or regulate sport have been historically contentious, popular treatments often elide these complex histories, instead offering linear, progressivist sporting narratives. Consequently, sport history is often reframed as a form of Whig history, with the apparent march of humanity towards enlightenment passively resulting in more inclusive, accessible, and safe forms of sport. Dislocated from their circumstances, stories of athletic empowerment from throughout sport history can obfuscate the complicated conditions from which they emerged. For example, sporting icons such as Tommie Smith and John Carlos, Ned Hanlon, Jackie Robinson, Tom Longboat, or the members of the All-American Girls Professional Baseball League must be resituated in their original contexts, and their accomplishments understood in relation to the trials and tribulations with which they were forced to contend. Each of these examples help demonstrate how the development of sporting culture and studies have been marked by a series of conflicts, centering on issues such as the organization and purpose of activities, who can and cannot play them, or how they should be integrated into people's lives.

As Coakley and Donnelly observe in *Sports in Society*, sport history can be viewed as the "study of certain people at different times and in different places struggling over and coming to terms with what they wanted their physical activities to be and how they wished to include them in their lives" (2009, 56). Critically analyzing the history of sport through its many struggles, and tentative resolutions, can offer a more holistic understanding of sport as a crucible for society's broader issues. As with Boccioni's painting, the intricacies of sport can be revealed by shattering them and exploring the remaining wreckage. To assess these complex relationships more accurately, it is necessary to explore both the embodied world of sport, as well as the world that sport embodies. It is this treatment of sport in context that has informed our development of this scholarly collection.

"Defining 'Duelism'"

This collection critically interrogates sport by observing how sports and sporting culture are defined through their relationships to diverse facets of life and society. From nationhood to gender, to class and politics, we have gathered critical readings from sport scholars across the globe that explore sports' connections with their significant doubles: an approach we have termed "duelism." Our treatment of sport in this collection is not rarified and abstract, but instead treats sport in, through, and in relation to the societies that continue to shape its development. As each chapter demonstrates, these relationships between sport and the outside world reveal both the deep intrenchment of these connections, as well as their oft-conflicted nature. We coined the term "duelism" to capture these two essential phenomena observable within modern sport: sports as sites of struggle, and sports as defined in relation to their many "doubles."

First, the term "duelism" captures the spirit of combat and conflict that has so long defined the role of sport in society. As previously acknowledged, the development of modern sport, and the academic legitimatization of sport studies, has been defined by intense periods of adversity and conflict. Through our overarching notion of "duelism" as a theoretical construct, we have built on Coakley and Donnelly's characterization of modern sport's development as a history of struggle (2009, 56). Responding to this call, our authors have made concrete observations about the way sport and sport history remain embattled fields of contestation. Second, "duelism" carries with it an understanding of sport's inherent duality. Because sports are directly connected to the world in which they are played, they must be situated in context to understand how they respond to and inform their circumstances. These connections are best expressed through the metaphor of the double: two entities or concepts that share an irrevocable bond between them and can only be understood in relation to each other. As *Duelism* demonstrates, sport is defined by many instances of doubling, and these mutualistic relationships illuminate how sport and the broader world interact. Tracing these connections helps reveal the true character of sports, as well as the societies that inform their development. Our treatment of sport through its relationships with other concepts, issues, or institutions necessitates a critical foundation in the interrelated notions of doubles, duality, and the Doppelgänger. As cultural concepts, these three ideas have shared and ancient origins that have informed our conception of this collection's central theme.

Doubles, Duality, and the Doppelgänger: Critical Context

Twins, couples, duplicates, and pairs make frequent appearances in Classical writing and often carry great symbolic significance. In Roman mythology Janus, the god of transitions and new beginnings, is depicted with two faces: one looking back to the past and another ahead to the future. In both Greek and Roman mythology, the eternal link between twin brothers, Castor and Pollux, led to their immortalization as the Gemini, one of the zodiac constellations. Similarly, throughout the tradition of Judeo-Christianity, pairings such as Adam and Eve, Cain and Abel, or Jacob and Esau are described as mirrored opposites transfigured through familial love.[1] Closer than kin, these biblical doubles exemplify the elevated risks and rewards of such innate interpersonal connections by extending beyond the expectations of a typical husband/wife or brother/brother relationship.

Although each depiction is unique, they all contribute to the rich collective mythology of the double. Whether appearing as dual personalities, kindred spirits, or character complements, these early doubles transcend the confines of prototypical human relationships to forge a complex bond with each other. At their most foundational level, these relationships can be attributed to a preternatural sense of "sameness" wherein the two individuals are distinct yet inseparable. Although they are each autonomous and function individually, doubles are inextricably linked, and their symbolic significance is manifested through the ties which bind them. Continuing to expand the concept of doubles, Debra Walker explores how the double can transcend a character archetype to become a complex counterpart for any individual, entity, or even concept. In her introduction to *Body Politics and the Fictional Double*, she remarks that, in our contemporary context, "Although this double is created and maintained most often by forces beyond ourselves (television, magazines, cultural mandates and myths), we bear its markers on our bodies, particularly those of age, race and gender" (King, 2000, viii). This leads her to conclude that, in this way, the fictional double is always with us" (viii).

---

[1] For more information on these early doubles see, Ovid *Fasti* I 126-7, Pseudo-Hyginus *Fabulae* 224, Genesis 2: 15-24, Genesis 4:8, Genesis 25:19-34, respectively.

But although the double relationship often implies a sense of symbiosis and mutual benefit, this is not always the case. Since its earliest conceptions, the double presented dangerous potential. In "The Shadow Within: The Conscious and Unconscious Use of the Double," Claire Rosenfield describes the double relationship's dual potential as beneficial or parasitic: "duality inspires both terror and awe whether that duality be manifested in a twin birth, or man and his shadow, or in one's reflection in water or in a mirror, or in the creation of an artifact resembling the exterior self" (1963, 326). Rosenfield's characterization of doubles confounds a simplistic reading of Classical examples. Her inclusion of a "twin birth, or man and his shadow, or in one's reflection in water or in a mirror, or in the creation of an artifact resembling the exterior self" extends the initial paradigm of doubles and allows for a much broader definition that persists to the present.

Moreover, her assertion that the double has always inspired both "terror and awe" encourages further critical inquiry: Are all doubles true equals? Do both individuals or aspects mutually benefit from this shared connection? And, philosophically speaking, must both of these individuals, concepts or entities in a doubling exist on the same ontological level or be valued the same in society? What would it mean if they did not? Although these questions are timeless and carry with them the double's universal appeal, no one has been more preoccupied with answering them than the Romantics, and their response came through the conception of the Doppelgänger.

In contemporary colloquial expression, the term "Doppelgänger" has come to mean a close physical likeness between individuals. However, this simplification does not account for the ideological context that gave birth to the Romantic Doppelgänger, nor does it capture its emblematic use in literature from the late-eighteenth through the nineteenth century. The term Doppelgänger, directly translated as "double-goer," was first introduced by Johann Paul Friedrich Richter in his 1796 novel, *Siebenkäs*.[2] In its Romantic-era conception, and our own application of the term in this collection, the Doppelgänger refers to only one half or member of a particular kind of double relationship. Operating on a different ontological level than his or her counterpart, the Doppelgänger is a secondary antitype of an individual. Unlike doubles in general, the Doppelgänger is literally or figuratively created by the dominant individual. Consequently, the existence of the Doppelgänger depends on an unequal privileging within the pairing. From the implicit hierarchy of this bond, the Doppelgänger is most frequently represented as a phantom double, evil twin, or abject opposite of its corresponding counterpart. Compared to the equal balance of power possible in a double/double union, in a Doppelgänger relationship the Doppelgänger is necessarily subjugated by the more socially privileged individual. For this reason, while "double" is a blanket term for any pairing or partner offering completion through an innate

---

[2] For Richter's original conception of the Doppelgänger see *Flower, Fruit, and Thorn Pieces; or the Married Life, Death, and Wedding of Siebenkäs, Poor Man's Lawyer*, trans. Alexander Ewing (London: George Bell and Sons, 1897).

connection, the term "Doppelgänger" is applied to only one member of the relationship, specifically, the one considered secondary to the actions and behaviors of the other.

This disparity in the Doppelgänger relationship results from an understanding of the Doppelgänger as the physical manifestation of the subconscious, whether of the individual or the collective. As exemplified through William Blake's spectre or James Hogg's preternatural lookalike,[3] the Doppelgänger was created to represent some darker drive or impulse. The hierarchy implicit within the relationship therefore reflects the privileging of the conscious over the subconscious. Considered in this way, the Doppelgänger is literally the repressed or latent urges of an individual, group, or society brought to life. As such, these secondary entities are not fettered by the same social and moral codes as their corresponding dominant counterparts. While this allows the Doppelgänger greater freedom, it also means that he or she is not as socially normative as the individual and therefore marginalized as an aberration, marked as a preternatural being, or sidelined as a questionable presence. As Andrew Webber notes in *Doppelgänger: Double Visions in German Literature*, the hierarchy between the individual and the Doppelgänger is often challenged or questioned in Romantic fiction because "in the case of the *Doppelgänger* the 'real' is duplicated as phantasm in such a way as to defy distinction" (1996, 9). The resulting power struggle between an individual and his or her Doppelgänger is an essential aspect of this relationship and presents the primary source of conflict between them.

Although the figure of the Doppelgänger was born out of literature, like the double, the figure has also transcended the limitations of literary representation to become a metaphor for destructive duality. In *the Doppelgänger: Literature's Philosophy*, Dimitris Vardoulakis explains how "the Doppelgänger has escaped from the confines of the printed page and has entered into the realm of a historical development. Thus, the expansion of the Doppelgänger ineluctably leads from literature, to criticism, to philosophy" (Vardoulakis, 2010, 107). For this reason, the Doppelgänger can be employed as a symbol for any relationship that is preternaturally close, in dissolvable, self-forged, and ultimately marked by a mutual destruction.

In "Grimaces of the Real, or When the Phallus Appears" Slavoj Žižek further elucidates this modern conception of the Doppelgänger by delineating its root cause and function:

> He is the subject's double who accompanies him like a shadow and gives body to a certain surplus, to what is in the subject more than subject himself. This surplus represents what the subject must renounce, sacrifice even—the part in himself that the subject must murder in order to start to live as a 'normal' member of the community. (1991, 54)

---

[3] See James Hogg's 1824 novel *The Private Memoirs and Confessions of a Justified Sinner* and the relationship between Robert and Gil-Martin (Oxford: Oxford UP, 2010).

Even though Žižek relocates this paradigm from its initial Romantic context, the power dynamic remains the same and the conceit carries through into contemporary critical perspectives. As a "certain surplus of the individual" and "what is in the subject more than subject himself," the Doppelgänger is both a distinct entity and direct effusion from a group, concept, or individual. While doubles in general can be two autonomous individuals strengthened by an innate bond, the Doppelgänger is created by his or her corresponding individual—or society at large. Representing what we must "renounce," "sacrifice," or "murder" to become a "normal member of society," the Doppelgänger is forced into a combative relationship with their dominant counterpart. This sense of conflict and struggle reverberates through the Romantic conception of the Doppelgänger and carries forward into our critical reading of sport.

From Duality to "Duelism"

The essays in this collection evoke these many and nuanced understandings of doubles, Doppelgänger, and duality by exploring sports in relation to other key concepts. Most especially though, we have drawn together works that treat sport's duality, or more specifically its "duality," by considering sport in combat with specific ideas, concepts, institutions, or peoples. This approach has not only resulted in interdisciplinary and collaborative research, but also required authors to consider historical and/or contemporary instances of sport in practice to demonstrate precisely *how* sport can be thought of as "dueling" their chosen entities.

This critical framework requires an acknowledgement of sport as a central fixture of modern life that is constantly interacting with, responding to, or informing many diverse facets of existence. As such, sports are deeply imbricated within society and can only be comprehended in relation to the seemingly "outside" world and the many forms of "doubling" that these myriad relationships take. In *Canada Learns to Play,* Alan Metcalfe acknowledges the significance of sport in our world and its broader social function by arguing that "Sport is not peripheral to society, it is indeed central to life and reflects the dominant social and political concerns" (1987, 13). This centrality can be viewed in nucleic terms, as modern sport is not distinct from society, but instead entangled with "dominant social and political concerns" at a quasi-molecular level.

Metcalfe's point, that sport "reflects the dominant social and political concerns," has often been rearticulated when the barrier between sports and society is seen to be especially permeable. For example, Montreal's Richard Riots in 1955, the 1976, 1980, and 1984 Summer Olympics boycott, or the Black Lives Matter player strikes of 2020 have all revealed the natal bond between sport and our broader world. Through such instances, it is apparent that sport is often representative of, and responding to, societal conditions, with the instability of the world frequently mirrored through the instability of sport itself.

Extending the analogy, sport is not only a mirror to society: passive, stagnant, and replicating. Instead, its relationship to society is complex, dynamic, and marked by constant interpenetration. Sport thus reflects and refracts its societal influences, producing a double, or *Doppelgänger*, of itself. Alternatively, as many of this collection's chapters reveal, sport often takes on the role of society's Doppelgänger: socially unacceptable and representing our darker, less civilized impulses that each of us "must renounce, sacrifice even" to proceed as a "'normal' member of the community" (Žižek, 1991, 54). The Doppelgänger relationship captures the inherent duality of someone or something, as their "excess" is incarnated in a separate entity that continues to haunt them so long as both exist. The Doppelgänger is the physical embodiment of anything that contradicts or undercuts the perceived identity of whomever or whatever creates it. But although they appear to be distinct, the subject and their Doppelgänger are intrinsically and irrevocably linked in a biological sense, and the connection between them cannot be severed, since they both create and sustain each other.

In the case of sport, the Doppelgänger metaphor suggests that it is impossible to critically analyze sport without accounting for its many doubles that continue to inform its evolution, and that many of these double relationships have destructive potential. For example, studying the role of hockey violence in Canada allows the researcher to better understand the ethos of the nation itself. According to Ryan Edwardson, "The Dominion of Canada, based upon a British inheritance, was replaced or more accurately, reimagined into a Peaceable Kingdom of multiculturalism, civic rights, and a social safety net" (2012, 281). However, although Canada is often self-promoted as a peaceful country, the sanctioned violence seen in hockey represents a direct challenge to this constructed identity. In line with Žižek's conception of the Doppelgänger as the embodiment of "excess," hockey represents Canada's excess, existing outside accepted notions of pacifism (1991, 54). As Gruneau and Whitson argue in *Hockey Night in Canada: Sport, Identities and Cultural Politics*, "hockey has a level of physical confrontation beyond that of most other sports hockey is a continuous physical contest in which the use of force to neutralize speed and skill is a matter of course" (1993, 175). In this way, hockey, and specifically hockey violence, can be thought of as Canada's sporting Doppelgänger, as it is both born of its underlying impulses, yet treated as distinct from its collective identification. Examples, such as this, demonstrate how the double or Doppelgänger relationship collapses the binary opposition between sport and any other aspect of life. Rather than being diametrically opposed to society, sport *is* society on a foundational, elemental level.

By interrogating sport through its doubles, it becomes clear that sport is defined through a multiplicity of relationships, allowing it to be considered in the context of many critical fields, foci, or areas of interest. For this reason, sports are inherently politicized, just as they are psychologized, fictionalized, historized, gendered, or racialized. Accordingly, in the more than thirty years since Metcalfe's assertion that sport is "central to life," many authors, scholars, and researchers have investigated the many and varied ways that sports relate to the world at large. Their interdisciplinary efforts, which collectively constitute "sport studies," are commonly classified under the subgenres of sport psychology, sociology, literature, history, and more. But although interdisciplinarity is a defining feature of sport studies, critical efforts to acknowledge sports' many points of entanglement by crossing genre, approach, or discipline remain relatively scant. Consequently, while individual branches of sport studies continue to grow and develop through strong research, the possibility of considering sport through a more holistic critical approach that is representative of its conflicted and contested boundaries, have so far been underexplored. With *Duelism*, we sought to bring authors into "direct conversation" by encouraging co-authorship or collaborative submissions, especially those across traditional disciplinary lines. These efforts resulted in two interdisciplinary, co-authored chapters, as well the co-editing of this manuscript by two researchers from different areas of sport studies. We believe this collaborative and interdisciplinary approach not only reflects the collection's emphasis on dialogical exchange, but also distinguishes *Duelism* in interesting ways from existing work in the field.

This view of sport as a multifaceted area of study carries into our chosen focus: confronting sport through its doubles. Although many may agree that sports are indeed "central to life," as Metcalfe suggests, this claim is frequently proven through studies that seek to legitimize sport through focused analysis, but fail to account for the innumerable ways that sports define, and are defined through, other areas of our individual and collective experiences.

In *Duelism: Confronting Sport Through Its Doubles*, we adopt a consciously interdisciplinary approach to sport that accounts for its centrality and multiplicity of meaning in society. To that end, this collection mirrors the many corollaries of sport studies through diverse critical viewpoints that explore a broad range of sports and their relationships. Instead of simply treating sport in the abstract or theoretical, our theme has required authors to engage with sport in practice and to consider how it relates to their chosen double. Resultantly then, by discussing sport in relation to other intersecting concepts, i.e. racial relations, gender politics, or nationhood, our authors have grounded their analysis through specific instances of combat, conflict, and contestation in sport. In this way, each chapter necessarily takes the form of sport praxis by employing historical and/or contemporary sporting events or conditions to explain how sport can be understood in relation to its doubles.

Together, we assert that sport is best understood alongside broader issues or concepts that can be thought of as its doubles, since each helps to define the parameters of what it means to critically consider sport in society. Furthermore, as revealed by the metaphor of the Doppelgänger, these pairings are often mutually destructive, as sports are not always positively aligned with broader concepts, peoples, or entities. In these contexts, the Doppelgänger relationship is a fitting conceit, as the sometimes parasitic, chaotic, and fractured nature of these connections is laid bare. Employing Žižek's description of the Doppelgänger allows us to explore sport in context and consider how it is often conceived of as a "shadow" of our more civilized natures that "gives body to a certain surplus" (1991, 54).

For example, do we have an ethical responsibility to intervene in the current concussion crisis and does this intervention necessitate eradication of certain sporting practices, or even entire sports? Additionally, what is the changing role of sport in the wake of Covid-19? And furthermore, how are traditional understandings of the relationships between sport and race, gender, or nation being variously collapsed or expanded in contemporary society? In *Duelism*, we collectively seek to answer such questions and others like them. By inviting critical attempts to treat sport studies as an evolving, interdisciplinary field of research, we have endeavored to create a collection of emerging sport scholarship that reflects the multifaceted, contentious, and vital nature of sport, both in society and as an area of study.

Chapter Breakdown

Each chapter in *Duelism* explores a different issue in sport through duality, doubles, or the figure of the Doppelgänger. These case studies cover many diverse topics from across the world of sport and introduce methodologies, epistemologies, or critical lenses from throughout sport studies.

In Chapter One, "The Games Must Go On': Politics and the Olympic Games, from Mythos to Management," Witherspoon and Woodiwiss critically expound on the evolving "mythos" of the Modern Olympic Movement. Together, they contend that sports and politics exist in "duelism" within the Olympic Games by interrogating key examples that reflect how the Olympics have been influenced by external politics and, conversely, how the politics of the Olympics have informed the outside world.

Chapter Two confronts the human costs associated with the complex "duality" of sport/law. In "Safeguarding Children When Playing Sport: An Abject Failure of Sport and Law," Greenfield investigates child safeguarding in sport law and addresses the evolving, and often contentious, relationship between sport and liability.

Chapter Three, "De-anglicized: Sport and Nationhood in a Transatlantic Brazilian Perspective," traces the impact of cultural colonialism on Brazilian sport. Specifically, Maranhão acknowledges the spectre of British football, and how it continues to haunt Brazilian football today.

Chapter Four critically assesses the interrelationship between sport and emotions. In "That Feeling When…What? Sport, Society, and Emotions," Scott advances current conceptions of the role emotions play in sport through key instances of emotional effusion, such as in-game celebrations.

Chapter Five, "Shuffling Sideways: The Arrested Development of (Girl) Hockey Goaltenders in Hockey Films," offers a comparative character study of the role of girl goaltenders in hockey movies. Through critical discussion of the goaltender archetype, both in practice and in hockey fiction, Ryan situates this argument within the larger context of sport and gender studies.

Chapter Six, "Jocks and Nerds: The Role of Sport in the North American Education System," explores the historical "duelism" between sports and education in North America. Evoking Cartesian dualism and the history of physical education, Fabian makes a case for a holistic approach to education that fosters both the body and the mind.

In Chapter Seven, Muniowski uses the figure of the Doppelgänger to explore the relationship between two sporting icons in the Argentinian cultural imagination. "Messi and Maradona: The Best Player in Football History as the Doppelgänger?" casts Lionel Messi as Diego Maradona's Doppelgänger to describe how the former continues to live in the latter's shadow.

In Chapter Eight, "Combating War? Joe Weider, Bodybuilding, and the Korean War," Chipman, Cooke, and Heffernan examine how Joe Weider's fitness magazines employed militarism, amid the Korean War, to promote a particular paragon of muscular masculinity. This strategy supplanted the magazine's previous mandate of encouraging a healthy lifestyle with the jingoistic advertisement of American military supremacy.

Chapter Nine investigates the complex doubling of race and sport. In 'For Both Language Groups to Feel at Home Either as Participants or Sightseers': Sport, Memory, Resistance and Nation at the 1952 Van Riebeeck Sports Festival" Snyders offers a historical, critical study of the 1952 Van Riebeeck Tri-centenary Festival, discussing how the continuing legacy of Dutch colonialism in South Africa has informed the relationship between sport, race, and nationhood.

Chapter Ten explores the "duelism" between sporting communities and nationhood. In "The Rusedski Affair: Treason, Nationhood, and the Making of a Canadian Tennis Traitor," Pettit examines how the complexities of national and sporting allegiances can produce the character archetype of the athlete as traitor.

Finally, Chapter Eleven traces the conflict between two rival sporting nations in the late-twentieth century. Wagner's "England Versus Germany in the Sports Press: Mistrust and Glorifying the Past" uses media studies and content analysis to comparatively discuss how Germany's football team was depicted in the English press, and vice versa.

REFERENCES

Balla, G., U. Boccioni, C. Carra, L. Russolo, G. Severeni. (2001). "Futurist painting: Technical manifesto 1910," *Futurist Manifestos*. (U. Apollonio, Ed.). MFA Publications.

Boccioni, U. (1913). Dynamism of a soccer player [oil on canvas]. Museum of Modern Art, New York City, New York, United States. https://www.moma.org/collection/works/80009.

Coakley, J., and P. Donnelly. (2009). *Sports in society: Issues and controversies*. (2nd Canadian ed.) McGraw-Hill.

Edwardson, R. (2008). *Canadian content: Culture and the quest for nationhood*. University of Toronto Press.

Gruneau, R. and D. Whitson. (1993). *Hockey night in Canada: Sport, identities, and cultural politics*. Garamond Press.

King, D. Walker. (2000). "Introduction: Body fictions." *Body politics and the fictional double*. (D. Walker King, Ed.). Indiana University Press.

Metcalfe, A. (1987). *Canada learns to play: The emergence of organized sport*. McClelland and Stewart.

Rosenfield, C. (1963). "The shadow within: The conscious and unconscious use of the double." *Daedalus*, vol. 92. https://www.jstor.org/stable/20026781?seq=1#metadata_info_tab_contents.

Vardoulakis, D. (2010). *The doppelgänger: Literature's philosophy*. Fordham University Press.

Webber, A. (1996). *Doppelgänger: Double visions in German literature*. Clarendon.

Žižek, S. (1991). "Grimaces of the real, or When the phallus appears." *October*, vol. 58. https://www.jstor.org/stable/778797?seq=1#metadata_info_tab_contents.

Chapter 1

"The Games must go on": Politics and the Olympic Games, from *"Mythos"* to Management

Kevin Witherspoon and Ashley Woodiwiss

"The Games must go on," declared International Olympic Committee President, Avery Brundage (Guttmann, 1984, p. 254). This came in the immediate aftermath of the slaughter of Israel's Olympic team during the 1972 Munich Olympics. Brundage's appeal to the Games as a vehicle for the overcoming of political difference stood in the tradition of Baron de Coubertin's late-nineteenth-century revival of the Olympics and the founding of the IOC as an idealized international athletic event populated by aristocratic young men, pursuing individual excellence as sporting amateurs (Guttmann, 1984; Llewellyn and Gleaves, 2016). The *mythos* of the modern Olympic movement embodies the prejudice of modernity writ large: that politics are problematic but also eliminable. The Games must go on, in this sense, because they are essential to achieving the "end of history," with history here understood as the realm of conflict and violent difference. In this account *sports*, and especially the idealized Olympic Games, stands opposed to *politics*, with the former the realm of imagined cosmopolitan brotherhood, and the latter, the realm of agonistic difference. In this modern *mythos* sports and politics exist in *duelism*.

In this chapter we claim the modern *mythos* cannot be sustained. In the spirit of this volume, we undertake a critique of the "duelism" between sports and politics through the critical analysis of the modern Olympic Games. Our thesis: The Olympic Games must be understood as themselves political projects replete with agendas, mechanisms, and powers that seek to control what goes on inside as well as outside Olympic Stadia, and all to serve a *mythos* as unpersuasive as it is impracticable. We develop this argument in five sections. In a brief introduction, we document how recent scholarship sets the stage for our account through its depiction of the antique Olympic Games as an expression of the *agonistic* competition between Greek city-states. The original Olympics did not hold sports and politics in duelism; sports simply *were* politics (the concern of the *polis*) carried on by other means. The second section chronicles the rise of the modern Games and how the *mythos* of a Games beyond politics was developed by Coubertin and the rise of the IOC. Throughout this section we document the pervasive presence of the political. We extend our analysis in sections three and four where we analyze the 1968 and 1972 Summer Games as two sides of a single development: the Games as global media events that invite the arrival of political forces from within (1968) and from without (1972), which threaten the "purity" of athletic competition.[1] In our fifth and concluding section we arrive at Los Angeles Olympic Organizing Committee Chairman Peter Ueberroth's by now self-evident 1984 declaration, "The Olympics are a political event" (Amdur, 1983, p. V, 1). The modern *mythos* of the duelism between Olympics and politics has given way to the post-modern acceptance that the Olympics are indeed political "all the way down." Now all that is left is the management of the ineradicable political problem. Whether in the selection of host country, the development of the rules for the Olympic program events and ceremonies, or in crowd control (in and out of Olympic Village and Stadium) the goal is to "minimize the damage" that could happen if "pure politics" were to erupt during the corporately-sponsored global mega-media events that are the Olympics Games of our day.[2] This management mission requires the establishment of a vast and intricate bureaucratic apparatus of surveillance and securitization to continue the illusion of purity within and without (Handelman, 2016). For the post-Modern Olympics, preserving the duelism of sports and politics comes at a very high price indeed.

The Greek Olympics: *Agon* **and** *Polis*

Scholars have examined a myriad of themes related to our understanding of the social, economic, and political aspects of the original Greek Olympic Games. What comes into view from this scholarly vantage point is the link that existed in the Greek Olympics between *agon* and *polis*. *Agon* is translated with a number of meanings, among them "contest," "competition at games," and "gathering." So, the Games themselves were expressions of *agon* by nature of there being contests between athletes. But these athletes competed on behalf of, and in service to, rival *poleis* (cities), achieving public glory and rewards from those cities as a result of their victories (Kouřil 2019). The *agon* of the Games replicated, through athletic competition, the already existing *agon* between Greek city-states.

As such, the Greek Olympic Games were ineliminably bound up with explicit political concerns. From Thucydides we learn of Alcibiades, who in 416 BC boasted of his success in the recent Olympiad and how his victory justified his claim to leadership of a proposed Athenian military expedition. Claims Alcibiades:

---

[1] Our focus on the Summer Olympics does not suggest that the Winter Olympic games are beasts of a different kind. The limitation of space, and drama of Mexico City and Munich, set the boundaries of what can reasonably be carried off here. For excellent accounts of specific Winter Games, see Findling and Pelle, 2004; also, Guttmann, 2002.

[2] What Helen Lenskyj has dubbed the "Olympic Industry." See, Lenksyj (2000).

Athenians, I have a better right to command than others and at the same time I believe myself worthy of it. The Hellenes, after expecting to see our city ruined by war, concluded it to be greater even than it really is, by reason of the magnificence with which I represented it at the Olympic Games. Custom regards such displays as honorable and they cannot be made without leaving behind them an impression of power. [VI.16.]

Here note how Alcibiades claims that his success in the individual athletic *agon* (of chariot-races) also served as a victory for Athens, with his personal magnificence being understood by rival cities as a sign of Athens' own power. This linkage of *agon* and *polis* lies at the heart of Allen and Latinvoa's *The Ancient Olympics as a Signal of City-State Strength* and their claim:

[T]he ancient Olympics acted as one substitute for violent confrontations between city-states by producing a signal of city-state strength; that is, it provided everyone in the region a cheap source of information that was correlated with military prowess. Once relative strengths were known with some acceptable probability, the outcome of violence was better known, and as a result, costly battles could be avoided (2012:3).

In Ancient Greece, *agon and polis* were inextricably linked. The well-known peace of the Olympics simply allowed for city-state struggle to continue, just set in a different key. It was inconceivable, indeed nonsensical, to think that the Olympic *agon* could be thought of as non- or un- or anti-political. So, in the antique context, no duelism between Olympics and politics existed because it was all about the *polis*.

Could modernity sunder the *agon* of athletic competition from the signaling of the *polis* and thereby achieve a post-political ideal?

The Modern Olympics: The *Mythos* of Athletics without *Polis*

The modern Olympics, as conceived and developed by their creator, Baron Pierre de Coubertin, were intended to be above political influence. Coubertin, a physical educator of French aristocratic origin, saw in sport not only a means to strengthen French youth physically, but also morally and emotionally. Motivated initially by a desire to help the French people overcome a disgraceful defeat in the Franco-Prussian war of 1870-1871, Coubertin traveled widely, adopting what he perceived to be the best elements of sporting programs and competitions throughout Europe and the United States, but he was most deeply impressed by sports as played at the British Rugby School. As his sporting ethos evolved in the 1880s and '90s, he began preaching a new pseudo-religion, which he called "Olympism," inspired and motivated by the ancient Greek Olympics. Though rooted in European aristocratic values, Olympism could be embraced by all, as it relied not on wealth or noble bloodlines, but rather on two interwoven doctrines: "the cult of effort;" and "the cult of eurythmy" (Boykoff, 2016, p. 13). The latter might be described as a life-balance, a synergy perhaps suggested in another phrase, *mens sana in corpore sano*, "a sound mind in a sound body." Such harmony of mind and body could be achieved by anyone.

European elites embraced Coubertin's vision, along with its message of peace and harmony. As Coubertin wrote in 1912,

> You promote happy relations between peoples, bringing them together in their shared devotion to a strength which is controlled, organized, and self-disciplined. From you, the young world-wide learn self-respect, and thus the diversity of national qualities becomes the source of a generous and friendly rivalry (Boykoff, 2016, 10).

This early messaging of the Olympics as a harbinger of peace and understanding became a key element in the Olympic image, remaining so even today. Thus, as the current IOC website explains,

> Olympism is a philosophy of life, exalting and combining in a balanced whole the qualities of body, will and mind. Blending sport with culture and education, Olympism seeks to create a way of life based on the joy of effort, the educational value of good example, social responsibility and respect for universal fundamental ethical principles. (IOC, 2020).

The IOC, the site continues, "is a not-for-profit independent international organization that is committed to building a better world through sport" (IOC, 2020). This is the image and message that the IOC presents to the world.

And yet, from the beginning, the lofty ideals and rhetoric of Coubertin and the other Olympic founders came with striking limitations. While anyone might engage in athletic activity sufficiently to improve their fitness and health, to Coubertin only the "pure" athlete might attain the highest levels of achievement. Competing for money or prizes demeaned the "pure" athlete, who competed solely for the honor of his country. Thus, as Coubertin wrote, the Olympic athlete became "a sort of priest, an officiating priest in the religion of the muscles" (Boykoff, 2016, p. 13). The necessity of amateurism was instilled from the outset. Eliminated from consideration for Olympic competition were any "professional" athletes, who competed for money or prizes, or perhaps as a vocation. With this simple declaration, the Olympic founders all but eliminated anyone outside of their comfortable sphere of wealthy, white men of Euro-American origin. Indeed, all of the key decisions made by the Coubertin group in those early years, where to host the games, what sports to play, and who is allowed to participate (only men, only amateurs), established a pattern of including an elite, western few and excluding the great majority of the world's population (Llewellyn and Gleaves, 2016).

The internal politics of Olympic leadership, amateurism, and elitism were further muddied by the overt intrusion of global politics upon the early Olympics. Even, and perhaps especially, the first Olympics, held in Athens in 1896, revealed the complications involved in one city and nation hosting a global event, as Greek organizers disagreed with IOC officials on a number of organizational matters. Most pointedly, the Greeks hoped to become permanent Olympic hosts; Coubertin and the IOC had no intentions of establishing a single host city (Bijkerk, 2004; Lennartz and Wassong, 2004). The 1904 Olympics, held in St. Louis, staged as an athletic appendage to the World's Fair also being held in St. Louis that year, were so disastrous that they nearly extinguished the nascent Olympic movement (Barnett, 2004). Few international competitors were able or inclined to make the arduous journey to the middle of North America, and a variety of organizational difficulties threatened the viability of the Games. They stretched out over several months, included all manner of strange events, and, most troublesome, incorporated a demeaning sideshow called the Anthropology Days, in which Aboriginal peoples from nations all over the world "competed" in events they often barely understood (Bijkerk, 2004; Barnett, 2004). Overt political dissent made its first appearance at the 1906 Intercalary (Olympic) Games in Athens. Irish track athlete Peter O'Conner, forced against his will to compete for the British squad, wore a green jacket and distanced himself from the British team during the Opening Ceremonies. More boldly, as the British flag was raised after O'Conner's silver medal performance in the long jump, he shimmied up the flagpole and unfurled a large Irish flag (Boykoff, 2016).

The presence of global politics in the Olympic movement became even more evident in the inter-war years. The 1916 Olympics, awarded to Berlin, were cancelled as World War I consumed Europe; the IOC would extend an olive branch of reconciliation to Germany twenty years later with the 1936 Berlin Olympics. In the aftermath of war, the IOC awarded the 1920 Olympics to Antwerp, Belgium. This attempt to hasten the healing after the war led to one of the dreariest Olympics ever held, as the war-torn nation struggled to stage a successful event. Each of the following Olympiads, in succession, offered the host cities and nations an ever-growing global platform to demonstrate their national vitality and organizational capabilities. Beginning in Paris in 1924 and escalating through Amsterdam in 1928, Los Angeles in 1932, and of course Berlin in 1936, organizers in each host city strove to out-do their predecessors. Staging ever more grandiose Olympics allowed host nations to show the world not only that they had survived hardships such as war or Depression, but that they were thriving. Advancements including increasingly elaborate Olympic torch processions, Opening and Closing Ceremonies, enormous arenas and stadiums, Olympic housing and villages, and expansive improvements in infrastructure like transportation and hotels became features common to all Olympics. With rare exceptions as well, each Olympic competition featured more events, more national teams, and more athletes than the last, a growth arc leading the most recent Olympic Games to include more than 200 nations and more than 10,000 athletes (Guttmann, 2002).

At the same time, overtly political acts appeared on the Olympic stage with increasing frequency. Belgian organizers of the 1920 Antwerp Olympics, for instance, refused to invite their wartime adversaries, Germany, Hungary, and Austria, to participate. Such animosity had not dimmed much by 1924, and in fact the prospect of renewed conflict between France and Germany raised the possibility of moving the 1924 Games to Los Angeles, though this backup plan was never implemented. Paris organizers once again did not invite the Germans to send a team, and a number of events were colored by old wartime allegiances or rivalries. Simmering nationalist undertones rose to a boil by the Olympics of the 1930s, first in Los Angeles in 1932, then even more prominently in Berlin in 1936. As historian Alan Tomlinson described it, the 1932 Olympics represented "a markedly political intensification of the event" (Tomlinson, 2005, p. 60). Not only did organizers insist on carrying out the Games in the midst of economic malaise, they used them as a tool to show the world that the United States was flourishing. Thus, they enhanced the pomp and grandeur of such displays as the Opening and Closing Ceremonies, and the torch run. Perhaps for the first time, the Olympics became as much a celebration of the host city and nation as of the athletes and events (Boykoff, 2016; Guttmann, 2002).

Whatever nationalistic qualities the Los Angeles organizers contributed to the Olympics, they were only magnified and heightened by the organizers of the Berlin Olympics four years later. Personally endorsed by Adolf Hitler, and overseen by his propaganda minister Joseph Goebbels, the Olympics stood alongside such mega displays as the Nuremburg rallies to broadcast to the world the organizational and cultural supremacy of the Nazis. The "Nazi Olympics," as numerous scholars have called them, became a source of worldwide debate. Nazi repression and mistreatment of Jews permeated all levels of society, including athletic pursuit, and the question of whether the International Olympic Committee bore a responsibility to wield its influence against such atrocities sparked an international boycott debate. Ultimately, Avery Brundage and others endorsing the belief that the Olympics must remain free from politics won the day, and Hitler kept his Games. Building upon and adding to the grandeur of the L.A. 1932 Olympics, Hitler and Goebbels manipulated every aspect of the Olympics to promote Nazi Germany. From a torch run that carried the Nazi message from Greece all across Europe to Berlin, to a city draped in swastikas, to a sweeping propaganda film by celebrated film-maker Leni Riefenstahl, the 1936 Olympics represented a public relations bonanza for the Germans. Only the athletic triumphs of Jesse Owens and other minority athletes dampened the spirits of Hitler and the Nazis.[3]

If politics was becoming more evident at the Olympics in the interwar years, it was in the Cold War era that they became entrenched in the Games. Two more Olympics were cancelled due to war: the 1940 Olympics, originally awarded to Tokyo and then reassigned to Helsinki after the Japanese withdrew from participation, and the 1944 London Olympics. As it had in the aftermath of World War I, the IOC took an active part in the healing process, returning the Olympics to London in 1948 and Helsinki in 1952. It then embarked on a series of Olympiads broadening the

---

[3] The literature on the 1936 Olympics is extensive. Among books dedicated to the subject are: Guttmann, 1984; Hilton, 2006; Rippon, 2006; Hart-Davis, 1986; and Mandell, 1971.

global reach of the Games beyond its traditional European and American roots, holding Olympics in Melbourne in 1956, Rome in 1960, Tokyo in 1964, and Mexico City in 1968, before returning to Germany for the 1972 Munich Olympics. Cold War politics weighed heavily in those deliberations, as the IOC not only sought to bring the Olympics to new parts of the globe, but also to reward "neutral" nations not mired in the US-Soviet Cold War rivalry. At the same time, as the IOC itself expanded and new nations created National Olympic Committees in droves, new voting blocs formed. Voting members from the growing cohort of formerly colonized nations in Africa, Latin America, Southeast Asia, the Pacific Islands and elsewhere tended to lend their support to bids advanced by cities and nations outside the traditional European/North American nexus. Thus, the IOC's globalizing mission serendipitously coincided with a rapidly growing and diversifying voting membership (Guttmann, 2002; Boykoff, 2016; Goldblatt, 2016; Leiper, 1981).

The growing global footprint of the Olympics combined with the complexities of Cold War relations to drive politics increasingly to the forefront of the Games. In the aftermath of World War II, as the divide between East and West grew more pronounced, issues like the recognition and participation of East and West Germany, or China and Formosa, plagued the IOC. For an organization hinging its identity on the separation of sport from politics, it was impossible to deny the entry of the Soviet Union and its satellite states, despite the numerous efforts of such nations, both overt and covert, to skirt Olympic rules. So intent were IOC members on maintaining the myth of its apolitical nature that they nearly admitted even the openly and fiercely racist apartheid regime of South Africa to the Olympics, in fact doing so for a few weeks in 1968 before backtracking on the decision in the face of a massive global boycott movement (Witherspoon, 2008).

1968 and Olympic Village as Global Village

By 1968, the intersection between global politics and the Olympics was clear. The events of that year, however, brought those connections into such sharp focus that only the most grizzled defenders of the separation of sport and politics, the Avery Brundages of the world, could maintain the illusion. The selection of Mexico City as host, a process that took place in 1963, was itself steeped in global politics, as the growing prominence of recently liberated colonized nations asserted itself with the designation of a Latin American nation as host for the first time. Mexican organizers and IOC officials wrestled with issues that had become commonplace Cold War spurs: the designation, flags, and national anthems of East and West Germany; amateurism and the hypocrisy of the Eastern-bloc "state athlete"; and whether to admit South Africa. Newer concerns, such as drug testing and gender testing, were introduced in Mexico City as well (Hunt, 2009; Pieper, 2016). Not seen before, though, were heightened levels of protest and activism, both inside and outside the Olympic stadium. Far more profound on a human scale were the protests of Mexican citizens, driven primarily by tens of thousands of disenchanted students, which swelled in the streets of Mexico City and elsewhere across the nation in the summer of 1968. Motivated by an array of domestic and campus issues and spurred on by similar protest movements around the world, Mexican students forced the city to a standstill with marches numbering over 100,000 at times. As the global media began to descend on the city, and with the opening of the Olympics looming, Mexican President Gustavo Díaz Ordaz and his officials determined that the student movement must not be allowed to disrupt the Olympic Games. On October 2, ten days prior to the Opening Ceremonies, Mexican military and other security forces surrounded and opened fire upon a group of student protesters and their supporters in Tlatelolco Square. When the massacre concluded, several hundred students lay dead—the exact number remains unknown—and thousands of others languished in Mexican prisons, in some cases enduring horrible tortures for months after the attack. With the protestors silenced, the Games carried on and despite an enhanced security presence they were largely celebrated as a successful festival of peace and international harmony (Witherspoon, 2008; Witherspoon, 2016).

Still, politics entered the Olympic stadium in dramatic fashion, as the black American sprinters Tommie Smith and John Carlos both raised gloved fists on the medal stand after the 200-meter sprint. Their protest, entirely peaceful, it should be noted, was intended to draw attention to persistent issues of racism on American college campuses and inequities within the American sporting infrastructure. Their shocking breach of Olympic etiquette drew the ire of the American Olympic Committee, which swiftly banned both athletes from the Olympic Village, and created a new paradigm for athletes-as-protestors. In their moment of greatest visibility, with literally the eyes of the world upon them, Smith and Carlos chose that moment to engage in protest. Olympic organizers now had to contend with a new reality: politics in the Olympic stadium and on the medal podium.[4]

The 1968 Mexico City games, with their protests outside and inside Olympic Stadium even while being celebrated as successful (and peaceful!), reflected the collision between two 1960s global developments: the post-colonial uprising that sought to de-colonize the world through the recovery of indigenous voice and identity, and neo-liberal globalization, which articulated an imaginary of a global self-consciousness of peace, prosperity, and liberation. This collision elevated the Olympic Games, for the first time, to the level of a self-conscious global event. Post-colonial yearnings produced performative acts (violent and non-violent) of *resistance*. Neo-liberal policies sought to siphon off and re-direct such yearnings in capitalist productive/consumptive directions as the *liberation* of self-consciousness and expression. Mexico City 1968 witnessed *both*. As such these Games can be seen as the first contractions in the birth of a new age, i.e., the emerging "global village" (a term first coined by McLuhan in 1962). This neoliberal dimension to the global

---

[4] Among scholars who have discussed Smith and Carlos' protest are: Bass, 2002; Edwards, 1969; Hartmann, 2003; Henderson, 2013; Wiggins, 1992; Witherspoon, 2008.

village was further enhanced by the global media and its focus on events inside, rather than outside, the Olympic Village.[5] The 1968 Summer Olympics in Mexico City thus heralded, for the first time, the material possibility for the Olympic Games to realize the modern *mythos* on a global scale. To insure that future Olympiads would continue to grow this cosmopolitan *mythos,* Brundage would fervently declare in the year following Mexico City, "We actively combat the introduction of politics into the Olympic movement and are adamant against the use of the Olympic Games as a tool or as a weapon by any organization" (Vinokur, 1988, p. 2). The task for the IOC was clear: cultivate the burgeoning neo-liberal imaginary and not allow any more Mexico City eruptions to impede the dawning of the Olympic Age of Aquarius.

The Mexico City Olympics should thus be seen as the first in the new order of Olympiads ushered in by the combination of post-colonial identity aspirations and neo-liberal imagistic promises: the dialectical sensibility of liberation and resistance. The question facing the IOC as it pivoted to Munich in 1972 was whether Olympic neo-liberal celebration could keep the forces of post-colonial resistance at bay.

1972: The Voice of the Oppressed *will be* Heard.

In his account of the 1972 Munich Olympiad, Jørn Hansen explains that "the overriding purpose for the organizers of the 1972 Summer Munich Olympic Games was to demonstrate to the world that the post-World War II Federal Republic of Germany had become a democratic and open society" (Hansen, 2016, p. 144). The image promoted by the Organizing Committee and the Munich police force of the Games taking place in the "easygoing, transparent and open" design of the Olympic Park with the Olympic Stadium bathed in a "joyous, relaxed atmosphere" reads now as tragic irony. Citing the official language of the Organizing Committee, the intent was to avoid in any way the appearance that would cause "the Olympic Village to resemble an armed fortress" (Hansen, 2016, p. 154). Fences were lowered and without adorning barbed wire, and several main gates were always open. A new Germany, one reborn and ready to celebrate the new Age and its neo-liberal consciousness would be (fittingly) the first fully-formed instantiation of the modern *mythos*. What Mexico City (with a few uncomfortable exceptions) promised, Munich would deliver. The Munich Olympiad would be a mutually self-satisfying story of national redemption joined to global brotherhood.

But while normal and customary security safeguards to protect the "purity" of the Games were in place, what had not been prepared for was the arrival of the *extra-ordinary*. In the dark, early morning hours of September 5, 1972, eight Palestinian

---

[5] For an account of the history of radicalization in Latin American thought and action, see Krujit, et al, 2019 and especially Cedillo's chapter on Mexico (2019). For a more general account of neoliberalism and sport, see Andrews and Silk, 2012.

terrorists, wearing tracksuits and carrying gym bags, hopped the fence outside the Olympic Village and made their way to the Israeli quarters. There, they murdered two Israeli athletes and took nine more as hostages. Over the following nineteen hours, German officials attempted to negotiate with the terrorists, who demanded the release of Arab political prisoners held in Israel. In the end, a rescue attempt by the German military went awry, as a two-hour firefight on the tarmac at the Munich airport ended with five terrorists and one policeman dead, along with all nine of the Israeli hostages. Black September's arrival in Munich coincided with the "presence of the world's media [which] ensured the best possible direct news exposure" and meant that "the whole world could follow the drama in Munich" (Hansen, 2016, p. 155). News organizations from around the world interrupted regular programming to follow the unfolding drama live. Thus, millions of viewers hung on every word as ABC sports anchor Jim McKay somberly announced, "They're gone. They're all gone" (Guardian.com, 2014). The dialectic of liberation and resistance first in evidence in Mexico City had taken a violent and deadly turn.[6]

The 1972 Munich Olympics can be seen as the reverse of 1968 Mexico City: joy outside the stadium, violence within. But in this very reversal the summer Olympics of 1968 and 1972 announced the arrival of the Olympics as a site for global imaginings. The trajectory since Munich 1972 has been one in which, "in addition to the visible sport component, the Games now transcend mere sport and exist as an event in their own right as a world symbol, characterizing international understanding, friendship and peace" (Pound, 2016, p. 72). But any cosmopolitan celebration was muted by the reality that the remainders of globalization (minorities, youth, dispossessed) are always present and would use violence (symbolic or actual) to announce their identity, whether inside or outside the Neoliberal Olympic Village. Even as the modern myth of an Olympics beyond politics reached the possibility of global realization through increased national participation and increased global exposure and status, the political problem appeared even more pronounced.

The Games must go on. But after Munich, the issue could no longer be the *mythos* as achievable but, rather, the *mythos* managed. If the duelism of sports and politics could not be eliminated, then how could its worst effects be mitigated?

Managing the Cosmopolitan *Agon*

Two weeks before the slaughter of the Israeli athletes in Munich, International Olympic Committee members elected the successor to Avery Brundage. Lord Killanan, a likeable and easy-going Irishman, offered a stark contrast to the intense, sometimes tyrannical Brundage. And while Killanan shared Brundage's concerns about politics intruding upon the Olympics, he did not (indeed, he could not) embrace

---

[6] The Black September terrorist attack is recounted in many sources, including Reeve, 2011; Hansen, 2016; Goldblatt, 2016; Boykoff, 2016; Guttmann, 2002; Findling and Pelle, 2004; Guttmann, 1984.

the cause with Brundage's fervor. Killanan would have been foolish to argue that politics had no role in the Olympics while confronting issues such as: Denver backing out of hosting the 1976 Winter Olympics over financial and environmental concerns, the first time a chosen host city rejected the Olympics; the economic catastrophe that threatened the solvency of the 1976 Montreal Olympics (and, in fact, the solvency of Montreal and Canada itself); Africa's boycott of the Montreal Olympics; China's admission to the Olympic movement; and, of course, the boycott of the 1980 Moscow Olympics, spearheaded by Jimmy Carter and the United States. By the end of Killanan's presidency, politics were thoroughly embedded in the Olympic movement (Wenn and Barney, 2020).

His successor, Juan Antonio Samaranch, who served as president of the IOC for twenty-one years, was the first to openly embrace the political aspects of his position. Far more than any of his predecessors, he traveled the globe and met with political leaders, deploying the considerable power at his disposal to both assuage international differences and to influence countries to bend to the IOC's bidding. Now, the politics of the movement were out in the open. Under Samaranch, the Olympics became a visible element in world politics, as during his tenure the IOC confronted the Soviet and Eastern Bloc boycott of the 1984 Los Angeles Olympics; the return of South Africa to the Olympic movement after the end of apartheid; the end of amateurism and the introduction of professional athletes; and the advent of the Olympics as, first, a profit-making venture and, later, a financial windfall through the explosion in international television rights (Wenn and Barney, 2020). It was on his watch, as well, that the Olympic bidding process fell prey to stunning corruption, a topic beyond the scope of this chapter and well-covered by other scholars.[7]

Anyone who might have foolishly clung to the adage that the Olympics and politics did not mix would surely have abandoned that stance after the "dueling boycotts" of the 1980 and 1984 Olympics, when the grand geo-politics of the Cold War threatened the Olympic movement at its core. State leaders, U.S. President Jimmy Carter, and the Soviet Union's General Secretary Konstantin Chernenko and Foreign Minister Andrei Gromyko now wielded Olympic participation as a weapon in foreign policy, the antithesis of the original intent of the Olympic founders (Sarantakes, 2011). Carter, Chernenko and others thus confirmed the powerful claim of scholar Alex Natan, who described sport as "a propaganda weapon in world affairs" (Natan, 1969, p. 203).

With Los Angeles Olympic Chairman Peter Ueberroth, who expressed his concern that China might join the growing list of nations to boycott the 1984 L.A. Games, by bluntly acknowledging, "The Olympics are a political event" (Amdur,

---

[7] Olympic corruption and the bidding scandals are covered in many sources, including Pound, 2004; Boykoff, 2008; Barney et al, 2002; Jennings and Simson, 1992; Jennings, 1996; Jennings and Sambrook, 2000; Lenskyj, 2000; Wenn and Barney, 2020.

1983, p. V,1), we have arrived, finally, at the re-description of the modern Olympic *mythos*.

In what we might call the *post-modern mythos*, the Olympics going forward would be depicted as *too big to fail*. The success of the Olympiad becomes a signal of the imperative viability of the global community. But this requires that certain accommodations to reality must be made. And so, an idealized imaginary must now co-exist with the explicit acceptance of the political nature of the Games. The key is to *manage* the "political" so that the *mythos* (now backed by corporate sponsors, etc.) can continue with minimal disruption. So the IOC has sought not to eliminate the political *agon* but to domesticate it, whether through granting sites to illiberal yet powerful nations (China, Russia), stimulating mass consumption (merchandise), or by means of politically-correct inclusions (of non-doping Russians, of displaced refugees, etc.).[8] This development of the Games into a cosmopolitan global corporate media event now worth billions of dollars, *while at the same time* being understood as a political event, has led to what Handelman describes as the dual need for surveillance and securitization (2016). Employing the zoological metaphors of "endo" and "exoskeleton." Handelman traces out how surveillance works as the endoskeleton within the Olympic Village to preserve the "purity" of the Games, whether in terms of doping, claims of bias in judging or cheating, or in expanding program rules forbidding political statements from competitors, found mentioned only briefly in Rule 50 of the Olympic Charter.[9]

But since 1972, and becoming more imperative post-9/11, internal "purity" has been matched by the equal need for external security. As Hansen has noted, "the events in Munich were a watershed in the history of the Olympic Games. At all subsequent Games, the greatest attention was to be paid to the security of the athletes and the participants of the event" (2016, p. 156). This is the exoskeleton of the massive security apparatus outside the Olympic Village, set up to prevent the invasion of terrorist viruses or other forms of political/identity protests that could de-stabilize or threaten the Games, which still "must go on." So Handelman describes the 2012 London Olympics in which a huge security exoskeleton encompassing and enwrapping the London Olympics put the city on "a near war footing" in order to maximally ensure peace during the Games' seventeen-day run. He captures the irony:

> [W]ith the London Olympics, security and surveillance had arrived full front to put into blatant perspective the apparent contradiction between Olympic

---

[8] Throughout this final section we build upon the excellent volume edited by Vida Bajc, 2016.
[9] So the IOC has banned any overt political signaling from Olympians for the 2020 Tokyo Olympics in a 3-page official statement found here:
https://www.olympic.org/-/media/Document%20Library/OlympicOrg/News/2020/01/Rule-50-Guidelines-Tokyo-2020.pdf. For the story on this decision replete with the 1968 Smith/Carlos picture, see:
https://www.washingtonpost.com/sports/2020/01/09/ioc-athletes-no-kneeling-hand-gestures-or-any-political-messaging-tokyo-olympics/.

values of athletic competition through egalitarian coexistence and comradeship and, on the other hand, the militarization and securitization of anything and everything relating to the Games. (2016, p. 5)

By looking at this twinned development, we can better see how the dynamic of *surveillance/securitization* now serves as the necessary precondition for the Olympics as a post-modern cosmopolitan spectacle. This is now the necessary bureaucratic (IOC) and military (host nation) investment needed to keep the *mythos* truly mythical.[10]

We began this chapter on the *duelism* between politics and sports as seen in the Olympic Games by recalling that the so-called separation of *agon* from *polis* did not exist among the Greek originators of the Games. This "mythic" separation began with the modern establishment of the Games and the narrative that accompanied it. This *modern mythos* of the Games reached its most ironic expression in 1972 with Avery Brundage's claim that "the Games must go on" even as the world reeled from the televised actions of Black September and Munich security forces. But politics has always been evident in the games, both before and after 1972, and it finally culminated in Ueberroth's 1984 acceptance that "the Olympic Games are a political event." In place of the *modern mythos* has developed a *post-modern mythos* that, while accepting the political nature of the Olympics, has nevertheless sought to maintain the ideal of the Olympics as the performative site of the global village of cosmopolitan fellowship. But the price for this *post-modern mythos* is an elaborate surveillance/securitization undertaking at each and every Olympic site. Fueled by corporate and media interests the contemporary post-modern, cosmopolitan Olympics have thus magnified "into a larger and larger mega-event bursting from within itself" (Handelman, 2016, p. 17).

So, we leave with the question: Must the Games still go on?

---

[10] And of course, to keep the dollars flowing. For the rise of monied interests and the subsequent corruption of the IOC by these interests, see: Wenn and Barney, 2020; Barney et al, 2002; Llewellyn and Gleaves, 2016; Jennings, 1996; and Lenskyj, 2000 and 2020.

REFERENCES

Allen, Douglas & Lantinova, Vera. (2012). The Ancient Olympics as a Signal of City-state Strength."
 Economics of Governance, Springer, 14(1), 23-44.
Amdur, Neil. (1983, April 10). Olympic Visas Assured. *New York Times*, V, 1.
Andrews, David L. & Silk, Michael L. (Eds.). (2012) *Sport and Neoliberalism: Politics, Consumption, and
 Culture*. Temple University Press, Philadelphia.
Bajc, Vida, ed. (2016). *Surveilling and Securing the Olympics: From Tokyo 1964 to London 2012 and
 Beyond*. Palgrave Macmillan, New York.
Barnett, C. Robert. (2004). St. Louis 1904. In John E. Findling & Kimberly D. Pelle (Eds.), *Encyclopedia
 of the Olympic Movement* (pp. 33-40). Praeger, Westport, CT.
Barney, Robert K., Stephen R. Wenn, & Scott G. Martyn. (2002). *Selling the Five Rings: The International
 Olympic Committee and the Rise of Olympic Commercialism*. University of Utah Press, Salt
 Lake City.
Bass, Amy. (2002). *Not the Triumph but the Struggle: The 1968 Olympics and the Making of the Black
 Athlete*. University of Minnesota Press, Minneapolis.
Bijkerk, Anthony Th. (2004). Pierre de Coubertin. In John E. Findling & Kimberly D. Pelle (Eds.),
 Encyclopedia of the Olympic Movement (pp. 454-463). Praeger, Westport, CT.
Boykoff, Jules. (2016). *Power Games: A Political History of the Olympics*. Verso, New York.
Cedillo, Adela. (2019). Mexico's Armed Socialist Movement During the 1960s and 1970s. In Kruijt, Dirk,
 et al (Eds.). *Latin American Guerrilla Movements: Origins, Evolution, Outcomes*. Routledge,
 New York.
Edwards, Harry. (1969). *Revolt of the Black Athlete*. Free Press, New York.
Goldblatt, David. (2016). *The Games: A Global History of the Olympics*. W.W. Norton, New York.
The Guardian. (2014). *From the Archive: 6 September 1972: Munich Massacre Captured on Screen*.
 https://www.theguardian.com/theguardian/2014/sep/06/archive-1972-munich-massacre-on-
 television.
Guttmann, Allen. (2002). *The Olympics: A History of the Modern Games*. University of Illinois Press,
 Urbana.
_____. (1984). *The Games Must Go On: Avery Brundage and the Olympic Movement*. Columbia University
 Press, New York.
Handelman, Don. (2016). Prologue: Olympic Surveillance as a Prelude to Securitization. In Bajc, Vida,
 (Ed.), *Surveilling and Securing the Olympics: From Tokyo 1964 to London 2012 and Beyond*
 (pp. 3-20). Palgrave Macmillan, New York.
Hansen, Jørn. (2016). The Most Beautiful Olympic Games That Were Ever Destroyed. In Bajc, Vida, (Ed.),
 Surveilling and Securing the Olympics: From Tokyo 1964 to London 2012 and Beyond (pp. 144-
 161). Palgrave Macmillan, New York.
Hart-Davis, Duff. (1986). *Hitler's Games: the 1936 Olympics*. Harper & Row, New York.
Hartmann, Douglas. (2003). *Race, Culture, and the Revolt of the Black Athlete: The 1968 Olympic Protests
 and Their Aftermath*. University of Chicago Press, Chicago.
Henderson, Simon. (2013). *Sidelined: How American Sports Challenged the Black Freedom Struggle*.
 University Press of Kentucky, Lexington.
Hilton, Christopher. (2006). *Hitler's Olympics: the 1936 Berlin Olympic Games*. Sutton Publishing,
 Thrupp, UK.
Hunt, Thomas M. (2011). *Drug Games: The International Olympic Committee and the Politics of Doping,
 1960-2008*. University of Texas Press, Austin.
International Olympic Committee. (2020). *Who We Are?* https://www.olympic.org/about-ioc-olympic-
 movement.
Jennings, Andrew. (1996). *The New Lords of the Rings: Olympic Corruption and How to Buy Gold Medals*.
 Simon & Schuster, London.
Jennings, Andrew, & Sambrook, Clare. (2000). *The Great Olympic Swindle: When the World Wanted Its
 Games Back*. Simon & Schuster, London.
Jennings, Andrew, & Simson, Vyv. (1992). *The Lords of the Rings, Dishonored Games: Corruption,
 Money, and Greed at the Olympics*. Spi Books Trade, New York.

Kouřil, Jiří. (2019) "Olympism" and Olympic Education in Greek Antiquity". *Studia sportive, 13(1)*, 74-84. https://journals.muni.cz/studiasportiva/article/view/11537/10796.

Kruijt, Dirk, Tristán, Eduardo Rey, & Álvarez, Alberto Martin, (Eds.). (2019). *Latin American Guerrilla Movements: Origins, Evolution, Outcomes*. Routledge, New York.

Leiper, J.M. (1981). Political Problems in the Olympic Games. In Jeffrey Segrave and Donald Chu, (Eds.), *Olympism*. Human Kinetics Publishers, Champaign, IL.

Lennartz, Karl & Wassong, Stephen. (2004). Athens 1896. In John E. Findling & Kimberly D. Pelle (Eds.), *Encyclopedia of the Olympic Movement* (pp. 17-25). Praeger, Westport, CT.

Lenskyj, Helen Jefferson. (2000). *Inside the Olympic Industry*. State University of New York Press, Albany.

_____. (2020). *The Olympic Games: A Critical Approach*. Emerald Publishing: Bingley, UK.

Llewellyn, Matthew P. & Gleaves, John. (2016). *The Rise and Fall of Olympic Amateurism*. University of Illinois Press, Urbana.

Mandell, Richard. (1971). *The Nazi Olympics*. Macmillan Publishers, New York.

Natan, Alex. (1969). Sport and Politics. In J. Loy and G. Kenyon (Eds.), *Sport, Culture and Society* (pp. 203-210). MacMillan, New York.

Pieper, Lindsay. (2016). *Sex Testing: Gender Policing in Women's Sports*. University of Illinois Press, Urbana.

Pound, Richard. (2004). *Inside the Olympics: A Behind-the-Scenes Look at the Politics, the Scandals, and the Glory of the Games*. Wiley, New York.

_____. (2016). On Security and Surveillance in the Olympics: A View from Inside the Tent. In Bajc, Vida, (Ed.), *Surveilling and Securing the Olympics: From Tokyo 1964 to London 2012 and Beyond* (pp. 72-92). Palgrave Macmillan, New York.

Reeve, Simon. (2011). *One Day in September: The Full Story of the 1972 Munich Olympics Massacre and the Israeli Revenge Operation "Wrath of God."* Arcade, New York.

Rippon, Anton. (2006). *Hitler's Olympics: The Story of the 1936 Nazi Games*. Pen & Sword, South Yorkshire.

Sarantakes, Nicholas Evan. (2011). *Dropping the Torch: Jimmy Carter, The Olympic Boycott, and the Cold War*. Cambridge University Press, New York.

Tomlinson, Alan. (2005). Olympic Survivals: The Olympic Games as a Global Phenomenon. In Lincoln Allison (Ed.), *The Global Politics of Sport: The Role of Global Institutions in Sport* (pp. 46-62). Routledge, London.

Vinokur, Martin B. (1988). *More than a Game: Sports and Politics*. Greenwood Press, New York.

Wenn, Stephen R. & Barney, Robert K. (2020). *The Gold in the Rings: The People and Events that Transformed the Olympic Games*. University of Illinois Press, Urbana.

Wiggins, David. (1992, Aug.). "The Year of Awakening": Black Athletes, Racial Unrest and the Civil Rights Movement of 1968. *The International Journal of the History of Sport, 9*(2), (188-208).

Witherspoon, Kevin. (2008). *Before the Eyes of the World: Mexico and the 1968 Olympic Games*. Northern Illinois University Press, Dekalb, IL.

_____. (2016). Repression of Protest and the Image of Progress (Mexico City 1968). In Bajc, Vida, (Ed.), *Surveilling and Securing the Olympics: From Tokyo 1964 to London 2012 and Beyond* (pp. 110-125). Palgrave Macmillan, New York.

Chapter 2

Safeguarding Children When Playing Sport: An Abject Failure of Sport and Law

Steve Greenfield

Introduction

Participation in sport and recreation is viewed as a healthy desirable activity, especially for the young, and is actively promoted. Governments see sport as a vehicle to deliver a wide range of policies across a number of sectors including health (Khan *et al*, 2012), health education (Makhaya, 1998), aspects of criminal justice (Morgan *et al*, 2019), and, on a global level, development and peace (Beutler, 2008). Sport can take place within the more controlled school environment but also, as is the case in the UK, in a wide range of voluntary sports clubs (Nichols & Taylor, 2010). For a very small number of participants there is the possibility of a professional career, but for most it remains a recreational activity. Sport has a long history whereby Sports Law is a relatively new field, though law can interact with sport in numerous ways (Greenfield, 2018). One romantic view of the relationship was expressed by one of the early sport and law pioneers, Edward Grayson, who considered that: "justice in the Rule of law and Fair Play in sport are not only the twin sides of the same coin: alongside Britain's constitution they are also part of the nation's unwritten heritage" (Grayson, 1988, viii). For practitioners, such as Grayson, sport and law were both about values with the role of law being to support and uphold those principles and "protect sporting values from attacks on its integrity whether physically on the field or commercially off it" (Greenfield, 2018, 728). Undoubtedly there is an unsavoury dimension to sport whether on field violence, the use of drugs, match fixing, unlawful off field behaviour, abuse by players and/or spectators or corruption and law has a role to play in punishing such behaviour. In an unsuccessful appeal against sentence by two Pakistani cricketers convicted of "spot fixing," the Court of Appeal stressed the widespread consequences of the criminal behaviour carried out using the emotive language of "honour and betrayal." Not only was this offence contrary to law but it also offended against the values of cricket and the public interest in sport.

> The criminality was that these three cricketers betrayed their team, betrayed the country which they had the honour to represent, betrayed the sport that

had given them their distinction, and betrayed the very many followers of the game throughout the world. (*R v Amir*, 2012, para 32)

Corruption and drugs are viewed as an anathema to sporting values, and though these types of cases are relatively few in number, they have the capacity to discredit sport more widely and threaten its integrity. This is, however, professional sport with a commercial dimension and the issues are primarily the damage to the economic dimension of the game.

Safeguarding children, or rather the failure to safeguard children, involved in sport is far more serious as it attacks the very foundation of sport, the promotion of healthy enjoyment. Over the last thirty years societies have witnessed the disclosure of a huge number of victims who were abused at the hands of coaches and others connected to sport. The primary role of these adults was to instil skills and an enjoyment of games in the young or treat them for injuries. It is difficult to envisage anything more damaging to not just the image of sport, but to its inherent ideals. The sheer scale of the abuse, often with multiple victims per offender and carried out unabated over a long period, has emerged through both criminal trials and published accounts from victims. While these sexual offences may often be referred to as "historic," having taken place many years before, the impact can be lifelong and devastating. A recent example demonstrates the scale and duration associated with such offences. On July 31st, 2020 at Chester Crown Court, former football coach and football scout Barry Bennell pleaded guilty to nine sexual offences against two children that took place between 1979 and 1988. Bennell has a long history of child sexual abuse with his first *conviction* and sentence in America in 1995. In the UK he was sentenced to nine years imprisonment in 1998 with a further two years in 2015 for additional offences. In 2018 Bennell, also known as Richard Jones, was sentenced to thirty years imprisonment for fifty-two sexual offences against twelve children committed while he was working as a football coach (*R v Jones,* 2018, para 54). On his appeal against this sentence the Court of Appeal noted

> The applicant committed a vast number of sexual offences, some of them of the most serious kind. He preyed sexually on young boys in his care. His offending amounted to a gross abuse of the trust placed in him by the victims themselves, by their families and by the clubs who employed him. The consequences for the victims and their families have been appalling.
> (*R v Jones*, 2018, para 54)

Bennell illustrates a number of features that are often found in these types of cases. His respected and influential position within sport permitted him, in the words of Lady Justice Hallet, to commit a "campaign of rape on a huge scale" (*R v Jones*, 2018, para 54). This is not, though, an isolated example either in terms of the sport or the geographical location. In 2015, USA Gymnastics became embroiled in a scandal over the sexual abuse of young athletes. As the independent Investigation noted: "In all,

Nassar committed thousands of sexual assaults between the early 1990s and the summer of 2016. He abused some survivors one time, while abusing others hundreds of times over a period of many years" (McPhee & Dowden, 2018, 1). As with Bennell the sheer enormity of the abuse, both in terms of the period of time and the number of victims, by Nassar was overwhelming. Both these individual cases pointed towards a serious problem within sport that had not initially been investigated. This is a worldwide issue with reports from numerous countries (Lang & Hartill, 2015). There have been clear failures by some of those responsible for the administration of sport, which are currently subject to numerous investigations. What is less clear is how the criminal justice system has responded to this crisis, and to what extent this is a failure of not just sport but also of law.

Uncovering the 'Problem'

In the UK numerous press reports began to emerge, from November 2016, of the widespread sexual abuse of children within football, going back as far as the 1970s. As more victims came forward and had their cases reported, more ex-players felt able to unburden themselves of secrets they had held onto for so many years. The victims were generally males in their 40s and 50s who had suffered abuse as children. However, it was clear that football, and indeed sport, were part of a much wider problem throughout society. In 2014, Operation Hydrant had been established by the UK police when the scale of the investigative problem became apparent. It acts as a "coordination hub:" "to deliver the national policing response, oversight, and coordination of non-recent child sexual abuse investigations concerning persons of public prominence, or in relation to those offences which took place within institutional settings."

As Table 1 shows, this goes well beyond sport into different settings, from education to recreation, with over 3000 places identified.

Table 1: The Institutional Setting (Operation Hydrant, September 2020)

Type of Place	Number
Educational	1801
Children's homes	725
Religious institutions	508
Sport	425
Children & young people's associations & clubs	422
Other	635
Total	4516

Source:
https://www.npcc.police.uk/Hydrant/Hydrant%202020/OFFICIAL%20Op%20Hydrant%20Quarterly%20St ats%20Slides%2030%20September%202020.pdf *(last accessed 23/11/2020)*

Over 13,000 cases have been dealt with to a settled outcome, with around a third leading to a conviction. What stands out apart from the number of convictions is the high percentage of cases, almost 50%, that were not taken forward by the police

Table 2: Cases by Outcome (Operation Hydrant, September 2020)

Outcome	Number	Percentage
No Further Action by Police	6482	49%
Conviction	4395	33%
No Further action by CPS	1506	11%
Acquittal	821	6%
Caution	8	<1%
Total	13212	

Source: https://www.npcc.police.uk/NPCCBusinessAreas/OtherWorkAreas/OpHydrant/Statistics.aspx (last accessed 23/11/2020)

As Table 3 below shows, in numerous cases, the fundamental reason for not taking a case forward is the death of the suspected abuser. This is unsurprising given the period when some of the earlier offences was committed. This creates a further issue for victims to deal with, as there is no sense of justice being "achieved." In one specific instance, the seventy-five-year-old defendant, Michael 'Kit' Carson, died on the first day of his trial for sexual offences committed as a coach. His car crashed into a tree and Coroner, Simon Milburn, determined the death to be suicide.

Table 3: Reason for no further police action (Operation Hydrant, September 2020)

Reason for No Further Action by Police	Number
Suspect deceased	34%
Suspect not identified/traced	22%
Victim does not support police action	17%
Insufficient detail/evidence	9%
Other	18%

Source:https://www.npcc.police.uk/NPCCBusinessAreas/OtherWorkAreas/OpHydrant/Statistics.aspx (last accessed 23/11/2020)

In addition to the police investigation, coordinated through Operation Hydrant, there are other inquiries ongoing. Following concerns raised by MPs in February 2015, the then Home Secretary, Theresa May, announced the creation of a statutory inquiry with the following terms of reference:

> To consider the extent to which State and non-State institutions have failed in their duty of care to protect children from sexual abuse and exploitation; to

consider the extent to which those failings have since been addressed; to identify further action needed to address any failings identified; to consider the steps which it is necessary for State and non-State institutions to take in order to protect children from such abuse in future; and to publish a report with recommendations. (https://www.iicsa.org.uk/terms-reference)

This has an extremely wide brief, which is probably unmanageable given what we know of the widespread nature of the problem. Unfortunately, the Inquiry has been beset by organisational and political problems, notably with the resignations of the original chairpersons and has also lost the confidence of some of the interested parties (Laville, 2016). There is also an independent investigation organised by the Football Association itself, as well as numerous Club inquiries. As the Hydrant statistics demonstrate, although football has by far the most cases, it is the most popular sport and other sports also have cases of abuse. A fundamental issue has been the response of governing bodies and the clubs themselves and football has been in the forefront.

Governing Body and Club Responses

Sport's governing bodies are autonomous organisations, though public funding can be used to direct government policy. Eligibility for grants is a method for incorporating required policies and standards. A major problem with policy initiatives are the financial implications as resources, particularly at grass roots level, are often stretched. The conviction of swimming coach Paul Hickson in 1995 revealed the nature and scale of the safeguarding problem. (Boocock, 2002) identified three factors that prevented sport's governing bodies from investigating and addressing the problem of sexual abuse. First, denial that any problem existed within their own sport. This meant that a conviction in swimming did not necessarily impact another sport. Second, externalising or not seeing the issue as within their authority, but rather as a problem for society more generally. Given the extent of the abuse across so many different sectors of civil society, as demonstrated by the current investigations, this type of view is readily fostered. Finally, the view that it is only an issue in specific sports. The first problem for those concerned about the issue was getting governing bodies to treat it as a serious and important issue that required prioritising, both in terms of time and resources. In 2016 the Football Association, concerned by the reports of widespread abuse, set up an independent investigation led by Clive Sheldon QC. The purpose of the Review was set out as follows:

> 3. To consider the extent to which The FA was aware of any of the issues relating to non-recent child sexual abuse which have been brought to light in the press relating to the 1970's,1980s and 1990s, and [up until around 2005].

The starting point is to note the sheer enormity of the enquiry covering some thirty-five years with potentially a huge number of individuals to interview and a mass of documentation to consider.

> 4. To consider what steps The FA took to address safeguarding/child protection issues in the sport up until 2005, and to consider any failings by The FA at the time, in particular whether it failed to act appropriately to anything raised with it relating to child sexual abuse, in relation to any football club (at any level of the game including grass roots clubs) or alleged abuser that may come to light.

A key element was determining not just what the FA knew, but any actions it took from concerns raised with it from any level of the game. This was not just about the top professional clubs, but any and all clubs within the FA's widespread jurisdiction.

> 5. To consider the steps those clubs (that is any club at any level of the game including grass roots clubs) which are identified as linked to alleged sexual abusers took at the time of any incidents, and are taking to investigate what that club did or did not know and/or did or did not do in relation to child sexual abuse which have been brought to light in the press relating to the 1970s, 1980s and 1990s, and up until around 2005; in the event the Review finds such steps to be lacking the Review will look to extend its scope.

It was not just how the FA behaved that would be considered but, crucially, how individual clubs had responded to events and individuals, whether victims or offenders. Essentially, the inquiry is tasked with discovering who knew what, when and what did they do with that knowledge?

> 6. To consider what lessons can be learned by The FA and/or the clubs arising out of the investigations that are taking place/have taken place.

> 7. To make recommendations as appropriate. (Football Association, 2016)

There is of course little point in having an inquiry unless there is some measurable outcomes and change although the governing bodies would stress the historical nature of the offences and the changes that have been introduced with respect to the creation and implementation of safeguarding policies especially since 2005. The mid November 2016 revelations by Andy Woodward concerning Barry Bennell (Taylor, 2016) was a new catalyst for other victims to come forward. Amongst others Steve Walters Paul Stewart and David White all publicly accused Bennell of abuse. However, the reports were not solely about abuse by Bennell. A number of different clubs now found themselves in the spotlight, as victims publicly made accusations about their abuse at the hands of coaches, scouts and others. The key question was how to respond? A further strand emerged with reports that clubs, including a Premier League one, had made compensation payments to players coupled with strict confidentiality clauses. This was an extremely serious development as it pointed towards prior knowledge of abuse and an attempted "cover up." Within a few days, the Premier League club was named as Chelsea FC (Mendick & Rumsby, 2016). The Club responded with a statement.

> Chelsea Football Club has retained an external law firm to carry out an investigation concerning an individual employed by the club in the 1970s, who is now deceased. The club has also contacted the FA to ensure that all possible assistance is provided as part of their wider investigation. This will include providing the FA with any relevant information arising out of the club's investigation. (Chelsea FC, 2016a)

Within a week, Chelsea issued a public apology through its website to the player:

> We pay tribute to the enormous courage of the people who have spoken out about the horrific abuse which they endured, including former Chelsea player Gary Johnson. We recognise that to do so, after carrying the burden of those events for so long, must have been an extremely difficult thing to do. (Chelsea FC, 2016b)

The club also admitted that the use of the confidentiality clause was "understandable" but "inappropriate." The Independent Review that Chelsea Football Club commissioned was published in 2019 (Geekie, 2019) and it is an extremely comprehensive document, totalling some 250 pages. Other clubs also instigated investigations, as coaches and scouts may have been present at numerous clubs at different points. Eddie Heath, who was the main subject of the Chelsea investigation, had also worked at Leyton Orient and Charlton Athletic. Bennell had worked at both Manchester City and Crewe. Newcastle United, Southampton, Norwich City and then after Watford Town were among the other English clubs also linked. The Sheldon Review Report has been delayed, due to the trials of both O'Higgins and Bennell, the latter in August 2020. It is now finalising its finding, which may well make for uncomfortable reading for the game's authorities.

The Criminal Law

A fundamental question is how the criminal justice system responds to claims of abuse, particularly those that took place some considerable time in the past. Since 1986, in England and Wales, there have been two distinct elements for a reported offence. First, the investigation by the relevant police force and, secondly, a decision on prosecution by the Crown Prosecution Service (CPS). The division into investigation and independent prosecution resulted from a Royal Commission Report

(Khan, 1986; Samuels, 1986). There are a number of practical problems in pursuing the prosecution of an offence that took place a long while ago and is wholly dependent on the statement of the victim, plus any corroboration by other victims. Prosecution policy is set out by the CPS and there are different elements to consider. The starting point is *The Code for Crown Prosecutors* that sets out the general principles that inform all prosecutions. Furthermore, there is a specific policy for Child Sexual Abuse Offences (CPS, 2018) in addition to policies on Sexual Offences generally and Non-Recent Offences. There are two elements to the general principles for a prosecution the first limb is evidential: *"Is there enough evidence against the defendant?"* (CPS, 2018). There needs to be a realistic prospect of conviction based on reliable and credible evidence. The second strand is a more general point: *"Is it in the public interest for the CPS to bring the case to court?"* (CPS, 2018). There are seven aspects to consider (4.1.4 a-g) to determine the public interest dimension. A prosecution will usually take place, unless the prosecutor is sure that the public interest factors tending against prosecution outweigh those in favour. It is a balancing approach, which has not always found favour with victims. If the CPS decide not to prosecute there is the right to have this decision reviewed. This right was established in 2013 following a decision of the Court of Appeal:

> it must be for the Director to consider whether the way in which the right of a victim to seek a review cannot be made the subject of a clearer procedure and guidance with time limits. (*R v Killick*, 2012)

The right for the victim to seek a review arises in four specific circumstances. First, when the CPD decides not to initiate proceedings. Second, if it starts the process but discontinues or withdraws the charges. Third, if no evidence is then offered and, finally, if charges are left to "lie on file" (CPS, 2020). The torrent of revelations against numerous individuals has led to trials against newly identified defendants and further trials against the serial offenders, such as Bennell. The latter's convictions demonstrate the capacity for numerous trials to occur as more victims come forward, often as the result of the publicity of the last conviction.

Barry Bennell: Serial Abuser

> 1995: Convicted in Florida for an indecent assault, sentenced to 4 years imprisonment.

> 1998: Pleaded guilty to 23 charges of sexual abuse at Chester Crown Court involving 15 victims between 1978 and 1992. Sentenced to 9 years imprisonment.

> 2015: Pleaded guilty at Chester Crown Court sentenced to 2 years imprisonment.

2018: Found guilty of 43 offences sentenced to 30 years imprisonment and a year on licence. Appeal against sentence was dismissed.

2020: Pleaded guilty to 9 offences between 1979 and 1988. Sentenced to an additional 4 years imprisonment and an extra year on licence.

Both Bennell, then known as Richard Jones, and Hickson appealed against their original sentences and the judicial comments in each are revealing. Hickson was charged with seventeen counts and convicted of fifteen, of which the most serious was rape. However, "many of the counts were specimens or examples of conduct which had taken place over a substantial period of time" and there were numerous defendants. In Hickson, there was a modicum of sympathy shown by the court:

> We think that in addition to the sentence of imprisonment the court could take into account that the appellant has lost a great deal, true by his own fault. He has lost his hard-earned reputation as a coach of renown. He has lost well-paid employment and has little to hope for when he has served his sentence. (*R v Hickson*, 1997, page 10)

This view seems quite astonishing, given the serious nature of the charges and the impact on the victims. In contrast, the judges in Jones took a forthright stance that is victim centred, reflecting the contemporary changes to the criminal justice system that have stressed the rights of victims.

> The consequences for the victims and their families have been appalling. The sentence was severe, particularly where he has already served three prison sentences for similar offending; but the offences were so serious, the timescale so extended, the aggravating factors so numerous and the mitigation so limited that it would be wrong for this court to interfere with the sentence. (*R v Jones*, 2018, para 54)

It is difficult to see how any long-term serial abuser can bring forward any mitigating factors, aside from a guilty plea that at least spares the victim the trauma of the trial. Perhaps the gap between these two cases of some twenty years does demonstrate that society, and those within the criminal justice system, now have a much greater understanding of the damage that has been caused.

Compensation

A criminal trial may be very important for victims, as part of the healing process, promoting closure, and enabling them to move on with their lives. As the statistics in Table 2 and 3 above demonstrate, a large number of cases do not reach a trial, so this outcome is denied to those who have suffered abuse. This leaves the possibility of "justice" being achieved through compensation for the harm suffered at the hands of the abuser. There are two possible routes for compensation. Some clubs, notably Manchester City, (Manchester City, 2019) set out details of an internal compensation policy, while others, such as Chelsea, paid out compensation. The Manchester City scheme was launched after an internal review uncovered abuse by two individuals connected to the club, Barry Bennell and also John Broome. The scheme contained a schedule of compensation, based on a scale of the harmful activity suffered:

Table 4: Reported Excerpt from Manchester City Compensation Scheme

Eligible Scheme Claimants will be entitled to a General Damages Redress Offer for assault and any psychiatric or psychological damage caused to them by the Relevant Abuse calculated solely by reference to the most serious assault they have suffered during any period of the Relevant Abuse. as set out in the schedule below.

Nature of Assault		Single Incident	Duration of less than one year	Duration of one year or more
Indecent touching over clothes/kiss/exposure		£5,000	£7,500	£10,000
Kiss involving tongue	Tier 1	£7,500	£10,000	£12,500
Indecent touching under clothes		£12,500	£15,000	£20,000
Masturbation		£20,000	£25,000	£30,000
Anal penetration other than by penis	Tier 2	£30,000	£35,000	£40,000
Participation in oral sex		£35,000	£42,500	£50,000
Rape		£45,000	£55,000	£65,000

Source: Byrne & Stewart 2019

The proposal was criticised, with one survivor noting "This isn't close to being justice for the victims. It's been handled in the most callous way, just so they portray that it's all over and done with." (Byrne & Stewart 2019) The scheme was designed by lawyers and resembles a no fault compensation-based scheme similar to those for industrial diseases, such as asbestosis or pneumoconiosis, the difference being the lack of medical diagnosis. The essential problem is that a tariff seems stark and lacking compassion, but that is perhaps an inevitable feature of such a system. Aside from any internal compensation schemes, a victim may also seek redress against an abuser through the civil courts by claiming damages. There are, though, two significant legal hurdles aside from overcoming the psychological trauma that bringing a case may reignite. First, there is the question of time, and whether assaults that took place many years before are still actionable. The *Limitation Act* 1980 specifies the time periods under which civil legal action can be instigated and those applying to an action for personal injuries are set out in s11 (4) Except where subsection (5) below applies, the period applicable is three years from:

(a) the date on which the cause of action accrued; or

(b) the date of knowledge (if later) of the person injured.

The starting point is a period of three years to bring a legal claim for personal injuries and the time runs from either 11(4) (a) the date of the abuse or (b) when the person knew of the harm, whichever is the later. This would seem to rule out the historic claims of abuse. However, the *Limitation Act* 1980 does provide an element of discretion for the court; under s33 the court may if it considers it "equitable" to allow a claim to proceed. In reaching its conclusion, which is fundamental as if it does not disapply the time limits, the case is finished, the court must consider six factors:

(a) the length of, and the reasons for, the delay on the part of the plaintiff.

(b) the extent to which, having regard to the delay, the evidence adduced or likely to be adduced by the plaintiff or the defendant is or is likely to be less cogent than if the action had been brought within the time allowed

(c) the conduct of the defendant after the cause of action arose, including the extent (if any) to which he responded to requests reasonably made by the plaintiff for information or inspection for the purpose of ascertaining facts which were or might be relevant to the plaintiff's cause of action against the defendant.

(d) the duration of any disability of the plaintiff arising after the date of the accrual of the cause of action.

(e) the extent to which the plaintiff acted promptly and reasonably once he knew whether or not the act or omission of the defendant, to which the injury was attributable, might be capable at that time of giving rise to an action for damages.

(f) the steps, if any, taken by the plaintiff to obtain medical, legal or other expert advice and the nature of any such advice he may have received.

These cases may inevitably have little if any physical evidence but almost exclusively rely on the testimony of the victim and the accused. If there has been a relevant criminal conviction this can be introduced into a civil claim by virtue of S11 of the

Civil Evidence Act 1968 (*RSL v CM* 2018). So, in terms of limb (b) the concern is likely to be based around the reliability of oral evidence after a long passage of time and whether a fair trial can be held. A case example demonstrates the interplay between the different legal elements.

In *DSN v Blackpool Football Club* a claim was made against the football club by a then youth footballer (DSN) for a sexual assault committed by a coach in 1987. The coach/scout, Frank Roper, had been convicted of four offences of indecent assaults against young males in 1960, 1961, 1965 and 1984 and died in 2005. This case has numerous problematic elements, least not the period of time that had elapsed between the assault and the initiation of the claim, and the death of the defendant. Under the *Limitation Act*, the time period for DNS bringing a claim against Roper and or the Football Club would have expired in 1995, three years after his eighteenth birthday. Roper's death left the football club itself as the only defendant, but as Roper had not been directly employed, this also made a finding of vicarious liability more difficult. Mr Justice Griffiths clearly outlined the issues for this type of case:

    i.   Should the limitation period be extended under the discretion provided by section 33 of the Limitation Act 1980?

    ii.   Was DSN sexually abused by Roper and what was the extent of the assault?

    iii.   Is the Defendant vicariously liable?

    iv.   What is the causation and effect of DSN's psychiatric diagnoses?

    v.   What damages is DSN entitled to?

(*DSN v Blackpool Football Club, 2020 para 3*)

It might be thought that, in this case, the death of the defendant would be extremely problematic, as Roper could have denied the allegation. However, the judge perhaps surprisingly did not see this as a barrier, given the claimant's evidence and the supporting evidence of five other witnesses who described similar abuse, and that Roper was a convicted paedophile:

> I recognise that, because Roper is dead, I have not heard from him, and there is no possibility of obtaining his reaction to DSN's allegation, which might have included a denial. But I regard the evidence against Roper as cogent, indeed compelling, even bearing that in mind. Any denial by Roper would have carried very little weight given the cogency of the evidence against it. He would have had to accuse DSN of lying. Having heard DSN give evidence, and being cross examined, I am confident that such an accusation

would have had no prospect of succeeding, whatever Roper might have said. (*DSN v Blackpool FC*, 2020)

Clearly this would have been difficult to justify without the supporting testimony and the existing criminal conviction, but it says something about the strength of the claimant's testimony that the defendant's death did not defeat the limitation argument. If the integrity of the evidence was sufficient, then the question remains as to the reason for the delay in bringing proceedings. There is widespread knowledge in such cases that victims do not disclose the abuse suffered as children for a variety of reasons. A primary issue is the concern that they will not be believed, given the powerful position the adult abuser occupied but also the shame and the impact on their family. Indeed parents are secondary victims, taken in by the charm of the offender (Woodward, 2018). One concern running through a number of these cases is the victim's fear that the parent(s) will blame themselves for not protecting the child. As David Lean confessed, he hid this "secret promise made to myself that I would never disclose while she was alive" (Lean, 2018). In fact, Lean reported his abuse five days after his mother's funeral. DSN also explained his reluctance to report the abuse: "it was such a difficult thing to talk about and I did not want her to feel that it was her fault or that she had put me in a position of risk" (*DSN v Blackpool* FC 2020, para 33). There may be numerous reasons why young players fail to report the abuse until much later in their lives. Apart from anything else it means confronting a traumatic event that they may have tried to forget. Society has changed and there is a much greater understanding and acceptance of why harm is concealed for so long. The revelations of others may provide an opportunity to disclose their own abuse, as there is no longer a feeling that "it was only me" and "my fault." Given the surrounding circumstances, both individually and the societal changes of general acceptance and increased publicity surrounding child sexual abuse claims, particularly in football, the judge considered it was; "for practical purposes impossible for the Claimant to disclose the abuse before he did, or to raise a legal claim before he did" (DSN v Blackpool FC, 2020, para 42). This is a huge hurdle to overcome and it is to their great credit that the judiciary are prepared to take a realistic and empathetic view of the actual, rather than theoretical, impact of abuse.

However, even if the problems of the *Limitation Act* can be resolved in the victim's favour, there is still the question of establishing that the club is vicariously liable for the acts of the coach or scout or whichever role the offender was occupying. There are two limbs to consider. First, was the individual an employee of the club and, secondly, if so, were the acts carried out considered to be in the "course of employment." Of course, the individual offender will be liable in a civil action, aided by the *Civil Evidence Act* noted above but may not be in a financial position to satisfy any claim. The club and its insurance company are clearly a far more attractive defendant. Imposing liability on an employer has been historically justified, largely on the grounds that the employee will have been advancing the interests of the employer and that the employer will ordinarily be insured. The fist problem area that has arisen is work relationships have become more fluid and less obviously identifiable as employer/employee. The second issue is the scope of the behaviour, by the worker, for which the employer is to be held vicariously liable. The courts have moved away from the strict requirement for a contract of employment as a control test, and the extent to which the relationship is close enough to merit the imposition of liability. However, even if there is a sufficient nexus to impose liability, there is still the problem of bringing criminal acts within its scope. To hold a club liable for a coach, not directly employed, who injured a young player through carelessness is one thing, but to extend that liability for criminal acts of sexual abuse is quite another.

Mr Justice Griffiths reviewed the evidence as to the relationship between Roper and Blackpool and found it akin to one of employer/employee. This is relatively uncontroversial, given the important role that Roper played for the club. That it was unpaid was testimony to the financial position of the club rather than anything else. So, the club would be liable for any torts he committed as part of his work for the club, but the fundamental question is whether this would extend to his intentional criminal behaviour. Vicarious liability for criminal behaviour has often proved a legal conundrum, given that it can seem so far removed from the "course of employment." If a rigid view of the doctrine is adopted the only solution has been to find that the criminal behaviour in question is an unauthorised mode of carrying out the duties. However, this is clearly artificial and produces greater problems of interpretation but, as Lord Steyn noted: "Ideas divorced from reality have never held much attraction for judges steeped in the tradition that their task is to deliver principled but practical justice" (*Lister v Hesley Hall Ltd* 2002 *para 16*). In order to provide "practical justice" in this type of situations and vicarious liability, as firmly rooted in public policy, it is necessary to consider an alternative analysis that looks broadly at what the employee was tasked to do. In the case of *Lister*, this was to look after the boys in their care:

> If this approach to the nature of employment is adopted, it is not necessary to ask the simplistic question whether in the cases under consideration the acts of sexual abuse were modes of doing authorised acts. It becomes possible to consider the question of vicarious liability on the basis that the employer undertook to care for the boys through the services of the warden and that there is a very close connection between the torts of the warden and his employment. After all, they were committed in the time and on the premises of the employers while the warden was also busy caring for the children. (Lord Steyn, Lister v Hesley Hall Ltd, 2002 para 20)

Applying this type of reasoning to DSN enabled the judge to conclude:

> I am satisfied that Roper's abuse of DSN on the New Zealand tour, and the New Zealand tour itself, were so closely connected with Roper's relationship with Blackpool FC that it is just to hold Blackpool FC vicariously liable for

it. Blackpool FC, given its inadequate resources, was never going to be able to run this as an official trip, but it was as close to an official trip as made no difference. (*DSN v Blackpool Football Club*, 2020, para 175)

So, the two hurdles of whether Roper was akin to an employee when he was an unpaid volunteer, and whether his criminal acts were sufficiently linked to his role, were overcome. This left the only questions to be the harm suffered and the damages payable. What the case does demonstrate is judicial willingness to take a positive approach to addressing a serious social problem. Roper was deceased, so this was the only possible means of achieving some form of justice for the victim.

Conclusion

Undoubtedly, revelations of sexual abuse of young athletes have caused a crisis in both sport administration and public confidence. Since the earlier cases, such as *R v Hickson*, much more information has been revealed, both through court cases but also media reports, notably the work of Daniel Taylor and victim accounts (Stewart, 2017; White, 2017; Woodward, 2018). Contemporaneously, investigations by both the police and independent inquiries have added more detail. The current picture is a very disturbing one demonstrating horrific levels of abuse across decades, impacting on thousands of lives. The survivor accounts uncover the fact that while these offences may be described as "historic" the impact is lifelong and contemporary.

While this is undoubtedly a very complex problem, sport has often sadly shown itself in a poor light by taking a defensive stance towards victims. The judge in *DSN* was critical of the football club noting: "Blackpool FC's conduct since being notified of the claim, up to and including the trial itself, has made things worse than they might have been. By never accepting any responsibility and never even accepting that the abuse had taken place at all, Blackpool FC maximised the suffering caused to DSN." (*DSN v Blackpool Football Club*, 2020, Para 188) While the claim refers to an assault committed a long time in the past, when less was known about what abuse was taking place and the harm caused, the claim itself was only issued in 2017. There is no excuse for not adopting an empathetic and considered response to claims, especially given Roper's criminal history, nor for amplifying his harm. The judge also noted how the claim was dealt with:

> he was not cross examined on the basis that he was not abused, but no indication was given to DSN or any of the witnesses who bravely gave evidence to me of abuse by Roper (in a case in which they had no **personal** interest) that they would not be cross examined on that aspect until I asked for clarification myself. I was told that Blackpool FC had not responded to previous enquiries about that in correspondence, and I have been shown the correspondence. It is well known that for many witnesses the anticipation of the ordeal of having to attend court and be cross examined on painful matters

can be greater than the ordeal of cross examination itself. DSN was not spared that ordeal of anticipation. (*DSN v Blackpool Football Club*, 2020, para 188)

This is utterly shameful, given what is known about the potentially traumatic experience reliving the abuse. As David Lean explains in relation to giving evidence against Bennell: "I wanted to give evidence behind a screen. I have issues and flashbacks with my memories and didn't need to see his new current appearance to stay in my mine for the remainder of my life too" (Lean, 2018). In his evidence, the claimant from the Blackpool case, DSN, laid out his feelings:

> I am shocked by the approach taken by Blackpool Football Club. When I came forward, I expected the club to want to engage and to understand what had happened. The main reason I came forward was because it felt the right thing to do, but also, so that the football club could learn from its historical failings. I want to do this so children like my own wouldn't have to suffer in similar situations, and I have felt let down by the lack of empathy, engagement and humanity shown by Blackpool. Many people have commented on how brave I have been, but I do not feel brave in this process, just frightened, and at times like the vulnerable 12/13-year-old boy I was. (*DNS v Blackpool FC* 2020, para 188)

This case is unlikely to be an isolated example, as clubs are faced with burgeoning civil claims from numerous victims. The police and CPS have had to react to this situation and work out how to best treat and support victims; though sadly, as David Lean's case shows, it needs careful handling. The courts have now demonstrated a willingness to adopt a flexible approach to the *Limitation Act* and the concept of vicarious liability that removes the two central planks of the defence. This case makes claims more difficult to defend and will hopefully propagate a more compassionate reaction to a group of extremely brave individuals.

REFERENCES

Beutler, I. (2008) Sport serving development and peace: Achieving the goals of the United Nations through sport, *Sport in Society*, 11:4, 359-369.

Brackenridge, C. (2001) *spoilsports*, Routledge, London.

Byrne, P. & Stewart, S. (2019) Barry Bennell victim slams 'callous' compensation scheme set up by Man City, *Daily Mirror*, 28th May. https://www.mirror.co.uk/news/uk-news/barry-bennell-compensation-barry-bennell-16216562 (last accessed 23/11/2020).

Chelsea FC Board Statement December 3rd, 2016 https://www.chelseafc.com/en/news/2016/12/03/chelsea-board-statement.

Chelsea Football Club Statement (2016a) https://www.chelseafc.com/en/news/2016/11/29/club-statement (last accessed 23/11/2020).

Chelsea Football Club Statement (2016b) https://www.chelseafc.com/en/news/2016/12/03/chelsea-board-statement (last accessed 23/11/2020).

Crown Prosecution Service (2017) *Child Sexual Abuse: Guidelines on Prosecuting Cases of Child Sexual Abuse*.https://www.cps.gov.uk/legal-guidance/child-sexual-abuse-guidelines-prosecuting-cases-child-sexual-abuse.

Crown Prosecution Service (2018) *The Code for Crown Prosecutors*. https://www.cps.gov.uk/publication/code-crown-prosecutors.

Crown Prosecution Service (2018) https://www.cps.gov.uk/legal-guidance/non-recent-cases-and-nominal-penalties.

Crown Prosecution Service (2020) Victim's Right of Review https://www.cps.gov.uk/legal-guidance/victims-right-review-scheme (last accessed 23/11/2020).

Football Association (2016) Sheldon Review. https://www.sportresolutions.co.uk/images/uploads/files/Terms_of_Reference_relating_to_the_Appointment_of_Clive_Sheldon_QC_on_the_Review_in_to_Child_Sexual_Abuse_Allegations.pdf (last accessed 23/11/2020).

Geekie, C. (2019) *Review of Non-recent Child Sexual Abuse at Chelsea Football Club.* https://www.chelseafc.com/en/about-chelsea/safeguarding-review (last accessed 23/11/2020).

Grayson, E. (1988) *Sport and the Law*, Butterworths, London.

Greenfield, S. (2018) New Competitions and Contracts: Sports Entrepreneurs and Litigation from a Historical Perspective, *The International Journal of the History of Sport*. Vol 35 Issue 7-8 727-744.

Khan, K., Thompson, A., Blair, S., Sallis, J., Powell, K., Bull, F. & Bauman, A. (2012) Sport and exercise as contributors to the health of nations, *The Lancet* Vol 380, July 7, 59.

Khan, A. A. (1986). Crown prosecution service. Journal of Criminal Law, 50(3), 297-304.

Laville, S. (2016) Child abuse inquiry 'to continue' despite survivors' withdrawal, *The Guardian*, 18th November. https://www.theguardian.com/uk-news/2016/nov/18/child-abuse-survivors-group-withdraws-from-contrived-uk-inquiry (last accessed 23/11/2020).

Lean, D. (undated) *The Truth* unpublished on file with the author.

Lovett, J. Coy, M. & Kelly, L. (2018) Deflection, denial and disbelief: social and political discourses about child sexual abuse and their influence on institutional responses, Independent Inquiry into Child Sexual Abuse. https://www.iicsa.org.uk/publications/research/social-political-discourses (last accessed 23/11/2020).

Manchester City (2019) Club Statement https://www.mancity.com/news/club-news/club-news/2019/march/man-city-club-statement-review-team (last accessed 23/11/2020).

Makhaya, G (1998) Shosholoza's goal: educate men in soccer, *Agenda*, 14:39, 93-96.

McPhee, J. & Dowden, J. (2018) *Report of the Independent Investigation: The Constellation of Factors Underlying Larry Nassar's Abuse of Athletes*, Ropes and Gray. www.ropesgray.com (last accessed 23/11/2020).

McCarthy, J. (2009) *Deep Deception,* The O'Brien Press, Dublin.

Mendick, R. & Rumsby, B. (2016) Exclusive: Chelsea made secret payment to player in child sex abuse claim, *The Daily Telegraph* 30th November.

https://www.telegraph.co.uk/football/2016/11/29/chelsea-made-secret-payment-player-child-sex-abuse-claim/ (last accessed).

Morgan, H., Parker, A., Meek, R. & Cryer, J. (2019): Participation in sport as a mechanism to transform the lives of young people within the criminal justice system: an academic exploration of a theory of change, *Sport, Education and Society*, DOI: 10.1080/13573322.2019.1674274.

Nichols, G. & Taylor, P. (2010) The Balance of Benefit and Burden? The Impact of Child Protection Legislation on Volunteers in Scottish Sports Clubs, *European Sport Management Quarterly*, 10:1, 31-47.

Press Association (2016) Gary Johnson says Chelsea paid him £50,000 for silence about abuse, *The Guardian*, 2nd December. https://www.theguardian.com/sport/2016/dec/02/gary-johnson-says-chelsea-paid-him-50000-for-silence-about-abuse.

Samuels, A. (1986). Crown prosecution service. *Journal of Criminal Law*, 50(4), 432-441.

Steve Boocock (2002) The Child Protection in Sport Unit, *Journal of Sexual Aggression*, 8:2, 99-106.

Stewart, P. (2017) *Damaged: My Story*, Trinity Mirror Sport Media.

Taylor, D. (2016) https://www.theguardian.com/football/2016/nov/16/andy-woodward.

White, D. (2017) *Shades of Blue*, Michael O'Mara Books Ltd, London.

Woodward, A. (2019) *Position of Trust*, Hodder & Stoughton, London.

Cases

DSN v Blackpool Football Club Ltd, 2020 WL 01234791
GB v Stoke City Football Club Limited and Peter David Fox [2015] EWHC 2862 (QB)
Lister v Hesley Hall Ltd [2002] 1 A.C. 215
R. v Amir (Mohammad) [2012] 2 Cr. App. R. (S.) 17
R v Hickson [1997] Crim LR 494
R v Killick [2012] 1 Cr. App. R. 10 121
R v Richard Jones [2018] EWCA Crim 1499
RSL v CM 2018 WL 04854096

Statues

Civil Evidence Act 1968
Limitation Act 1980

Chapter 3

De-Anglicized: Sport and Nationhood in a Transatlantic Brazilian Perspective

Tiago J. Maranhão

Introduction

In 1948, Brazilian polymath Gilberto Freyre published the first edition of *The English in Brazil: Aspects of British Influence on the Life, Landscape and Culture of Brazil.*[1] In his work, Gilberto Freyre (2001: 66) examined how British manufacturers, ideas, and habits invaded the country to create a "gentle, velvet revolution."[2] British institutions and activities flourished in the century that followed the opening of Brazil's ports to foreign trade in 1808, particularly to Great Britain.[3]

In addition to highlighting Great Britain's fundamental role in Brazil's political and economic realms, Freyre's work sought to promote Great Britain's presence in Brazil by introducing a "new taste" of class and lifestyle *vis-à-vis* the local way, especially in cities like Belém, Recife, Rio de Janeiro, and Salvador. Intellectuals such as Freyre noted Great Britain's prominent influence in activities and institutions, such as trams, railways, gas lamps, cemeteries, hospitals, corporate buildings, industries, foundries, newspapers, schools, charities, clubs, and sporting associations. In the last quarter of the nineteenth century, sports played a crucial role in the development and maintenance of the British Empire, and were also influential in non-British colonies, especially in the transmission of cultural values.[4] The Brazilian case thus reinforces

---

[1] Gilberto Freyre was born in Recife in 1900. He began his studies at the American Baptist School Gilreath in Recife and completed his training in the United States where he attended Baylor University and Columbia University. He returned to Recife in 1923 and began his scholarly work in the field of culture and education in Brazil and abroad. His most famous book was "Casa-Grande & Senzala" (The Masters and the Slaves) published in 1933. Freyre was awarded honorary doctorates from Paris-Sorbonne University, Columbia University, University of Coimbra, University of Sussex, and University of Münster. In 1971, Queen Elizabeth II honored Freyre with the title of Sir. Gilberto Freyre died in 1987.
[2] The second edition was published in 1977, and Freyre wrote the note above in 1976. Boulevard published the English edition in 2011.
[3] See Burke & Pallares-Burke (2008); Pallares–Burke (2011).
[4] For more information about sports and the British Empire, see Hutchinson (1996) and Mangan (1998).

the claim that the British Empire had a protuberant moral dimension beyond its borders. The influence English sports had in the debates on the Brazilian national identity persisted during the twentieth century. Curiously, in the second edition of *The English in Brazil* published in the 1970s, Gilberto Freyre (2001: 66) wrote about the significant change in the physique of Brazilian soccer players resulting in their "de-anglicization." This expression fomented interest in understanding the reason why notable Brazilian intellectuals of the twentieth century, sports commentators, and the general public have contributed to cultural combat, symbolically represented by the struggle of sporting doubles. It is critical to seek the reasons for concerns about a possible "mischaracterization of the Brazilian people" and how an English sport in particular became symbolic of Brazilian national identity.

The "duelity" of the phenomena of national identity and nationhood needs to be considered in a transatlantic context. By analyzing sports and nationhood in Brazil, this chapter demonstrates how modern sports played a pivotal role in the symbolic amplification of British imperialism through the transmission of its values to non-British territories. This chapter also elucidates the term "de-anglicized" to describe the transition from British influence to a more singular "Brazilian way" of practicing modern sports, specifically soccer. The term "de-anglicized" represents a web of (re)configurations in which the "duelism" between Europeans and Brazilians was depicted through cultural ties.

The use of newspapers as primary source material is crucial in this study, given the habitually overlooked relationship between the industries of modern sports and archival press. Finally, this chapter attempts to cast further light on how this cultural "duelism"pacted the debates, in academia and in the public sphere, about Brazil's national identity throughout the twentieth century.

Origins

In *Travels to Brazil*, Henry Koster (1817) observed that the historical significance and impact of Great Britain's presence in Brazil began even before Brazil's independence in 1822. Throughout the nineteenth century, Great Britain's influence went beyond its political sway and extended to habits and customs. For example, the availability of translated texts from English, the importation of household goods, such as cutlery and tableware, clothing items, such as fabric and hats, food items, and even the most modern models of carriages were assimilated in Brazil as "English contributions."[5] In addition, Brazilian Portuguese began to adopt English vocabulary, especially terminology related to sports.

Hutchinson (1996) and Mangan (1998) noted that in the last quarter of the nineteenth century, sports were imperative in the development and governing of the

---

[5] Freyre (2001: 56-57) also credited Britons for introducing "white suits and waistcoats, tea, wheat bread, beer and whiskey, gin, rum, steak with potatoes, roast beef, lamb chop, and sleeping pajamas."

British Empire. Nonetheless, sports also played a crucial role in non-British colonies, especially through the transmission of British morals and values. British sports had a persuasive role in debates about Brazilian national identity during the twentieth century.

In Brazil, the first practitioners of modern sports came from British companies arriving at the country's shores. They conceived the modern sports ethos, the principles of 'civilization' that Brazilian elites desired and in which new bodily practices were accepted and diffused within modernist ideas. Hence, the emergence of British sports and their adoption by the Brazilian elite created a process of differentiation from the lower classes through the dissemination of modern sports in elite social clubs and institutions.[6]

The first sporting institutions in Brazil were officially founded in the mid-nineteenth century. References to the term *sportsmen* can be found not only in the documents of the 'Jockey Clubs' but also in Brazilian newspapers from the early 1850s (Diario de Pernambuco 1854: 1). The frequency of these publications demonstrates that British sporting activities gradually became part of the daily life of the elite. Decades before soccer became the most popular and valued sport in Brazil, horseracing, cricket, and rowing were the most commonly practiced sports in the second half of the nineteenth century.[7] In a country historically marked by fluvial geography, especially concerning cities such as Belém, Rio, Recife, Salvador, and even São Paulo, it is not surprise that rowing is prevalent in primary records of the nineteenth century documenting leisure activities. Rowing was ultimately incorporated into sporting competitions in Brazil.

Sporting spaces, venues, and events often emerged as a result of processes that were both local and global (Elias & Dunning 1986).[8] The practice of British sports, played by "noble men" in Brazil, also appeared in English newspapers. In 1867, for example, the *Bell's Life in London and Sporting Chronicle* and *The Sporting Life* published articles named "Cricket in the Tropics" and "Cricket at the Brazils," which described the practice of cricket in the state of Pernambuco.[9] This transatlantic connection influenced the process by which sports news and behavior manuals became instruments to control conduct and emotions. The Brazilian elite had a greater degree of access to these resources, and they consequently became a symbol of

---

[6] See Bourdieu (1991).
[7] In May 1886, hundreds of people went to the banks of the Capibaribe River in the city of Recife. They also occupied the Boa Vista Bridge and took dinghies and boats to the edge of the racetrack to watch the third nautical competition in the city. The newspaper celebrated the one-year anniversary of the foundation of the Club Regatas Pernambucano. The closing of the celebration included "the National Anthem and one big girandole of fireworks." Diário de Pernambuco (Recife, Year LXII, n.112, 18 May 1886), 4.
[8] The authors speak of "interdependency chains" to express the production of these social facts.
[9] 'Cricket in the Tropics', in Bell's Life in London and Sporting Chronicle (London, 21 December 1867), 9; or 'Cricket at the Brazils The following match was played in Pernambuco on November 1, at 120 deg. Fahrenheit,' in The Sporting Life, (London, 7 December 1867), 4.

distinction, sophistication, and progress. 10 The Brazilian elite introduced a sportsmanship code, where, to be a sportsman, it was "not enough to have a horse, [but it was] indispensable to have a spirit, to be polite, to know how to talk to the ladies, a difficult task, for which a great deal of tact and taste is required" (O Sportsman 1888: 1).

The arrival of British sports in Brazil certainly had an elitist quality, since the moral conduct of young Brazilians presented the country's future leaders as illustrious sportsmen. The young sportsmen were instructed to win the audience's 'sweet and serene look,' to inspire their courage, grace, and politeness. According to the code, behaving as an English gentleman was considered a 'difficult task' in Brazil's environment, "where foolishness cannot be saved from raising a barrier against the spirit, where brutality rules against delicacy" (O Sportsman 1888:1). Being a *sportsman* in Brazil, that is, emulating the quality of being British, was synonymous with being gentle, honest, and polite.[11]

Until about the last decade of the nineteenth century, horseracing, rowing races, and cricket were preferred among the wealthy classes in Brazil. However, at the beginning of the twentieth century, a new, urban popular culture developed in major cities, where soccer evolved to become Brazil's national sport.[12] Soccer emerged through the use of existing institutions and the creation of its own private spaces. Soccer, "the child of Britain's global economic presence," in Hobsbawm's (1996: 198) words, became inextricably linked to the social construction of dominant ideologies and policies of Brazil's national identity.

Transition

Simultaneous to the diffusion of British sports, the politics of racial segregation underwent important changes from the end of the nineteenth century to the first decades of the twentieth century (Skidmore 1974, Ribeiro 2000, Blake 2011, Carvalho 2012). The so-called "whitening process" of the Brazilian population, promoted by the aristocracy, was widely spread and defended the elimination of Afro-Brazilian and indigenous characteristics in the process of building a country that aspired to the European model of progress (Stepan 1996, Schwarcz 1999, Turda &

---

[10] "Cricket at Pernambuco Pernambuco v Excelsior." Bell's Life in London and Sporting Chronicle (London, 13 May 1865), 9. Exactly twenty-three years before the official abolition of slavery in Brazil, the English newspaper published a text written by the British expat community in the state of Pernambuco describing the game of cricket played on January 6. The announcement also informed readers in London that the practice of British leisure activities in the state of Pernambuco was introduced prior to 1865.

[11] At the turn of the century, British sports expanded, and various competitions were held across the country. A newspaper described how turf as a social practice, had become quite common among the elites from the nineteenth to the twentieth century. *Diário de Pernambuco* (Recife, 13 June 1905), 2.

[12] According to Michel de Certeau (1984), 'popular' is not itself defined by hierarchical social classes, but by its own logic to do the everyday within a social environment in which the marginalized make up the majority.

Gillette 2014). The elite's interest in athletic activities was believed to not only inspire healthy habits, but also lead to the "improvement of the race." The promotion of physical activities and sports was absolutely linked to the nationalist policy in vogue (Mangnan 1999, Alabarces 2003, Priori & Melo 2009, Pope & Nauright 2009). Building a strong body, based on the concepts of 'health,' 'strength,' and 'beauty' meant to foster a new generation of Brazilians, and thus a new and more advanced country. In this context, the public space of sports can be understood also as a space of political and racial power relations.

Within this constant cultural combat, the main impact of boosting sports among the elite was its spread over "spaces of resistance" (Lefebvre 1991), the suburban districts and communities surrounding Brazilian cities. This consequently resulted in the introduction of sports that influenced the formation of a subaltern identity that was predominantly Afro-Brazilian. At that time, a growing wave of lower-class clubs emerged in the Brazilian suburbs, most commonly as soccer teams.[13] The diffusion of soccer clubs throughout peripheral neighborhoods and suburbs is evidence of how sports were not reserved solely for the small community of English immigrants, workers of multinational companies, or elite groups. The first three decades of the twentieth century witnessed the creation of a competitive space for the progress of Brazil's modernization (Mota 2009, Carvalho 2012). It is important to note that sports proliferated across diverse groups and spaces, from athletic clubs of British heritage to youth living in peripheral spaces.

The 1930s in Brazil is a period characterized by tumultuous political and cultural transformations. A nationalist and more centralized ideological movement emerged simultaneously with the popularization of soccer. The Revolution of 1930, commanded by Getúlio Vargas, promoted industrialization, modernization, and the "reconciliation of the country." Vargas' political movement created new economic and social strategies aimed at creating a united identity for Brazil and bridging abysmal differences in Brazilian society. From political changes to academic debates on race and identity, sports served as a crucial ally in disseminating the national project of a "New State" idealized by the Brazilian *Estado Novo*.[14]

---

[13] In the state of Pernambuco, for example, clubs such as Centro Sportivo do Peres, João de Barros Foot-Bal Club (now América), Sport Club Flamengo, Santa Cruz Foot-Ball Club, and Coligação Sportiva Recifense, among others, were founded in the city of Recife. The Clube Sportivo Beberibe was founded in 22 August 1909, in the suburbs of the metropolitan area of Recife, in the city of Olinda. See Estatutos do Clube Sportivo Beberibe (Recife, Typ. a vapor J. Agostinho Bezerra, 1909). In most cases, these clubs had a short life while others, the minority, still exist today.

[14] Getúlio Dornelles Vargas was born in São Borja, Rio Grande do Sul on April 19, 1882. Vargas was the head of state of the provisional government after the 1930 Revolution. He was elected president by the Constituent Assembly on July 17, 1934 and ruled the country until the beginning of the dictatorship called the "New State" on November 10, 1937. After World War II, on October 29, 1945, Vargas was deposed. He ran for presidency under the PTB (Brazilian Labor Party) defeating the National Democratic Union (UDN) and the Social Democratic Party (PSD) and was elected President of the Republic with 3,849,000 votes. Vargas faced threats of being coerced to renounce his role or possibly being deposed and committed

Getúlio Vargas' dictatorship utilized sports to form a "new Brazil" and a "new Brazilian." Soccer was a key tool through which the state's nationalist policy was promoted and implemented. Propitious moments for this strategy were international events, a space through which Brazil could demonstrate the best qualities of the "Brazilian race" to civilized nations, especially European countries. One such arena was the 1938 World Cup in France.

The 1938 World Cup was a quintessential event, not only for the history of Brazilian sports but also for debates on scientific racism and the construction of national identity. This event shaped the ways through which soccer was articulated within Brazilian society. Soccer became a key element in understanding contemporary Brazil, and it was transformed into a national symbol and a source of pride and preservationist fervor for the "Brazilian people."

'De-Anglicized' Brazilians

During the 1938 World Cup, the figure of the Brazilian mulatto was integral to the social meaning of soccer. The mulatto, a racial category historically created, not only became the symbol of "Brazilianess" and Brazilian pride but also reinforced cultural, spatial, and visual mythologies and stereotypes. Gilberto Freyre's contribution to the field of social sciences in Brazil was instrumental in constructing notions about the Brazilian mulatto. In his article "Foot-ball mulato," published in 1938 for Brazilian newspapers, Freyre sustained that Brazil's style of soccer could be equated to a "dance," wherein the excellence of a human being could shine (Freyre 1938: 4). In contrast, Freyre portrayed European soccer, especially British soccer, as highly "mechanized." Contemporary scholars continue to engage with Freyre's ideas regarding the "Brazilian style" of soccer (DaMatta 1982, Helal, Soares & Lovisolo 2001, Bellos 2002, Wisnik 2008, Kittleson 2014).

Freyre's theoretical basis was conceived through the idea that mulattoes were the axis of a new social model destined to equip Brazil with "Brazilianness." *Mestiçagem*, or racial mixing, became the path of progress in constructing a Brazilian national identity. Freyre conceived the innovative idea of redefining the Brazil of the future by moving away from the ideology of developing a "superior white European race" to promoting a "de-anglicized," outstanding, "democratic as no other people", and original Brazil:

> In football, like in politics, Brazilian Mulattism has become known for its taste for flexion, for surprise and floridness which reminds one of dancing and capoeira steps, particularly dancing. Dionysian dance. A dance which allows improvising, diversity, individual spontaneity. While European

---

suicide in 1954. For more information about the Brazilian Estado Novo, see Burns (1993) and Bethell (2008).

football is an Apollonian expression of a scientific method and socialist sport in which personal action is mechanized and subordinated to the whole, the Brazilian football is a sort of dance, in which the person is prominent and shines.[15]

Vargas' authoritarian regime was quick to adopt this shift in ideology. Getúlio Vargas' government took advantage of Brazil's success in the 1938 World Cup. He installed loudspeakers in the streets to create greater access to the matches, and the spread of morale created a positive image of "being Brazilian." The orthodox "Apollonian" game played by Europeans became, in the imaginary of the Brazilian society, the symbolic antithesis, the "duality" of what it meant to be Brazilian: a "Dionysian" people. According to this idea, Brazil was and would always be "racially mixed," and that "original miscegenation" should not only catalyze a national sentiment but should also be both a source of pride and a demand for positive differentiation. Formerly seen as degenerative and the cause of great common evils, *mestiçagem* came to be interpreted as a positive process among Brazilians. A new tradition and a new identity were invented (Hobsbawm & Ranger 1983).

The process of this discourse provided Brazilians with a definition that is part of the imaginary mechanism of the country's contemporary society. When it is said that Brazilians needed to conciliate the [Brazilian] individualism with the [European] discipline or that "the mestizos [are] full of animal energies or irrational impulses" (Freyre 1955: 3), the ideological effect that Brazilians are undisciplined does not emerge by chance. Its specific materiality is a biological duality intertwined with a discourse of cultural combat.[16] This argument was continuously sustained by Freyre and reproduced in the note he wrote in 1977 for the second edition of *The English in Brazil*:

At first, anglicized Brazilians and the natives with some Britishness in their look and behavior; after, increasingly, the different degrees of dark-skinned individuals until their de-anglicization culminating in the amazing Pelé, after having shone in Leônidas (Freyre 2001: Preface).

"De-anglicized" soccer was essential for the emergence of a "tropicalized" style of playing soccer in Brazil, shaping a distinct "vibrantly Brazilian" manner, built in opposition to the game created in Europe (Freyre 1974: 4).[17]

---

[15] Gilberto Freyre, *Sociologia*, 1945. Excerpt taken from Coutinho (1994: 53-60).

[16] Freyre (2001: 182-184) considered Brazilian players (that is, the Brazilian people) as having a way of playing that is 'unmistakably, exclusively ours' and that the European style is "calculated, ordered, mathematical, apollonian and British." A good work on Freyre's global influence is Lehmann (2018).

[17] Gilberto Freyre worked as a contributor for several newspapers and magazines to which he fervently expressed the advantageous position of a racially mixed soccer.

This transformation created the idea that "being Brazilian is being a mulatto."

The invention of the mulatto as the national representative of Brazil was devised and defined through having its alter-referential on the other side of the Atlantic Ocean.

Widespread identification with Brazil's national soccer team, also known as "The Seleção" (The Selection), whose performances captivate the country and whose victories spawn massive celebrations, generates the image of a "united Brazilian nation" under the same colors, the same idols, and the same morale. Thus, throughout the last eight decades, a distinctive "form" of Brazilian soccer was constructed, known by media sectors as "the football-art" in which black and mulatto individuals were defined as the main creators of such style. The categorization of Brazilian soccer as 'Art' became a vehicle for Brazil's international projection. This was fueled by the national team's successive triumphs at the 1958, 1962 and 1970 World Cups. Hobsbawm (1996: 198), for example, described Brazilian soccer as an "art" form evolved from *mestiçagem* and the active participation of blacks and mulattos.

This ideology has been utilized in attempts to soften interracial conflicts in an extremely polarized society. The "mulatto escape hatch" (Degler 1971: 219) therefore functioned more as a stereotype to be exported than as an actual tool that advocated for internal pacification. Far from defending the existence of the so-called "racial democracy," what can be observed is the strong presence of this ideology for many decades as common sense in the Brazilian society, a myth instead of a transformative instrument for effective social change.[18]

Contemporary Thoughts

The construction of the "de-anglicized" Brazilian was, in essence, a search for an aesthetically genuine category of being and an "authentic" Brazilian ethos. Soccer, which is a symbolic combat between nations, was the perfect field through which the "true Brazil" could finally be celebrated.[19] At the same time, the association between the practice of soccer in Brazil, along with the passion that this sport exerts among Brazilians, and national or innate characteristics, such as enthusiasm, trickery or indiscipline, is easily noticeable.

---

[18] Marshall Eakin (2017) states that the biggest challenge faced by the State in the nineteenth century was to create the idea of Brazil. He believes that the Brazilian imagined community and Brazilian nationalism did not concretely exist before the twentieth century.

[19] Hylton (2009: 1) states that, especially in sports, human abilities are always naturalized, based on the physical and psychological characteristics of each person or social group. And the author agrees that, from these characteristics, people try to make predictions about who will win or fail in the sports arena. Hylton also notes, paradoxically, that "the racialized social structures of sport contribute to the way we construct and experience our 'identity' and that of others."

Brazilian soccer's construction as a mimesis of Brazilian society became so embedded in Brazil's public image that this public perception is still observed in the present. Italian journalist Beppe Severgnini (2014) wrote that, while "for Brazil, beauty is a dance," for Italy "and for Argentina—Italy squared, if you look at their names and faces!—beauty is breathtaking speed." To the Italian filmmaker Pier Paolo Pasolini, the Brazilian style was a "poetic soccer" in contrast to European "prose soccer."[20] In Brazil and abroad, Brazilians are believed to have a natural gift to play soccer. Brazilians are "born to play soccer," as American multinational corporation Nike stamped on Brazil's national jersey for the World Cups of 2010 and 2014, and have "Brazilianness in the blood" (UOL/FolhaPress 2018).[21] This is the powerful myth that spread throughout the twentieth century until today.

In contemporary times, soccer fans, the press, sports commentators, and Brazilians themselves have complained that, in more recent World Cups, Brazil's national team has not played like "true Brazilians," that Brazil has "lost its soul!" For example, Juca Kfouri, one of the most famous Brazilian journalists, wrote in 2017 that Brazil's national team former coach João Saldanha "a critic of the Europeanization of Brazilian soccer defending its return to a more seductive and offensive style" (Kfouri 2017).[22] On February 2019, Walter Casagrande, who played for Brazil in the 1986 World Cup and is now a commentator for Globo Group, said on live television: "the *ginga* [swinging the body from one side to the other to deceive] of Brazilian soccer is missing. The reason for our fiascos is the Europeanization of the national team!" (Sportv 2019). These dichotomous ideas about being Brazilian remain and undoubtedly influence Brazil in the new century.

The world of sports still associates the practice of soccer in Brazil to its people's innate features. In the words of Associated Press journalist Shuji Kajiyama (2014), "Brazilian kids born in favelas (shanty towns) are known for their innate talent in soccer." The athletic ability of Brazilian soccer players is seen as "innate talent" (Villanueva 2017), a genetic and racial mark that characterizes Brazilians and distinguishes them from other human beings.

In 2016, the movie *Pelé: Birth of a Legend* was released. It became available on Netflix in 2018 and received awards worldwide. The movie was financed and directed by North Americans and created an aesthetically exotic and artificial Brazil. The script confuses biology and culture by constantly establishing an intrinsic relationship between *ginga*—described in the movie as innate to black Brazilians—and the arrival

---

[20] See Wisnik (2014).

[21] For the 2018 World Cup, played in Russia, Nike named Brazil's jersey "Samba Gold."

[22] João Alves Jobim Saldanha (1917-1990) was another famous Brazilian journalist and coach of the soccer National Team right before the 1970 World Cup. Saldanha coached and qualified Brazil to the World Cup but left the team just a few days before the trip to Mexico because of a disagreement with Brazil's military dictatorship president, Emílio Médici. Mário Jorge Lobo Zagallo substituted Saldanha and became the coach who managed Brazil in its third World Cup conquest.

of African slaves, regardless of their different geographical and cultural origins. It highlights how Brazilian players, in particular Afro-Brazilians, are mocked by the Swedish coach, in a press conference before the final game of the 1958 World Cup, because of their physical traits. In reality, this press conference never occurred. The movie is full of anachronisms and inaccurate "facts," and shows how Europeans viewed Brazilians as a dazzling species because of their exoticism and their passion for being uncivilized and non-European. Politically as culturally, the construction of national identity is not only from the inside out. It is the way we see ourselves, how we introduce ourselves to the 'other,' but it is also the way through which the 'other' sees us. This mutual process forges the "imagined community" (Anderson 2016).

From the sportsmanship code and the process of whitening the country in the nineteenth century, to the characters of the movie about Pelé in 2016, a quest for Brazil's national identity permeates sports fields through political discourses. From journalists to companies like Nike, the general mentality praises the Brazilian "ginga" style. The primitivism, the sense of improvisation, and the joy of living, as pointed out by foreigners and national intellectuals, boost the same empathy that becomes a mask of prejudice. Borrowing Edward Said's (1978) idea of "Orientalism," this power/knowledge nexus within sports generalizes and misrepresents Brazil, creating a kind of "Brazilianism" perpetuated throughout our contemporary society.

The discourses produced by intellectuals, artists, the press, and popular media, reach a common conclusion: the very 'nature' and destiny of the Brazilian people is to play soccer. The perception that all Brazilians are the same, despite vast demographic differences, creates a timeless Brazil, as if the country, its people, and institutional practices do not develop, unlike "civilized" countries that constantly evolve. Brazilians are reproduced as the archetypal "other" on the international stage and Brazil is thus presented as a stagnant country. This is simply contradicted by history itself.

Conclusion

The nineteenth century witnessed the organization and codification of modern sports (Elias & Dunning 1996). The popularization of these practices had its roots in the expansion of the British Empire. In Brazil, a non-British colony, modern sports initially took place within the inner circles of the elite, who sought to emulate Europe by popularizing British sports. This chapter contributes to the understanding of the role modern sports played in integrating societies and sheds light on the construction of a "Brazilian nation." Furthermore, this work also discusses the term 'de-anglicized', which was used in Portuguese in the twentieth century to exemplify the transition from British influence to a more singular "Brazilian way' of practicing modern sports.

Brazilian identity, from a cultural perspective, was constructed from a series of symbolic exchanges, or cultural "duelisms," where the main protagonist was the Brazilian mulatto. In a short period of time, the figure of the Brazilian mulatto arose from the marginal position of Afro-Brazilians to occupy a different space in the nation's imagined popular culture, although socially and politically this position is still far from a privileged one. Examining this period of Brazil's history also creates a better understanding of how modern sports came to play a pivotal role in the symbolic amplification of British imperialism, especially through the transmission of its values to non-British territories during an era in which Britain governed its empire through moral dimensions.

Documentation illustrates the degree of agency competitive sports had in debates about Brazilian national identity. The concept of what it means to be "Brazilian" transformed and evolved throughout the twentieth century, and it continues to be contested in sporting events of the twenty-first century. The World Cup is still the most important social arena where commentators, the general public, and even academics perpetuate the discourse of "flamboyant mulattism" and the "beautiful game" performed by "de-anglicized" Brazilians.

Historically, sports have served multiple purposes that have changed and developed over time (Stoddart 1988; Perkin 2007). As shown, primary sources demonstrate that British sports were utilized as a political tool to reinforce Great Britain's global power through "civilizing" local peoples. In the particular case of Brazil, a non-British colony, the appearance of mulatto idols operated as a political distinction, insofar as their importance to modern sports. The cultural combat that defined a unique style of playing that was "truly Brazilian" instead of European is a mark of "duelism." This antithesis explains how sports, most notably soccer, can be understood in Brazil through its struggles with its concrete European double.

No process of self-identity and nation building is capable of sustaining itself without the presence of idols, "stars," or heroes, who represent the glory of the community and surpass the limits of the human condition in constant battles against an opposite "other," symbolic or not. In Brazil, the popularization of sports, notably soccer, which occurred simultaneously with organizational, structural, and political changes, accomplished the invention and construction of mulatto idols, that is, "de-anglicized" defenders and representatives of Brazilianess.

REFERENCES

Alabarces, P. (2003). *Futbologias: Futbol, Identidad y Violencia en America Latina.* Buenos Aires, Clacso.
Anderson, B. (2016). *Imagined Communities: reflections on the origin and spread of nationalism.* London: Verso.
Bell's Life in London & Sporting Chronicle (1867, December 21). *Cricket in the Tropics.* London: W.R. MacDonald.
Bellos, A. (2002). *Futebol, the Brazilian way of life.* London: Bloomsbury.
Bethell. L. (2008), *Brazil Since 1930.* Cambridge: Cambridge University Press.
Blake, S. E. (2011). *The Vigorous Core of Our Nationality: Race and Regional Identity in Northeastern Brazil.* Pittsburgh: University of Pittsburgh Press.
Bourdieu, P. (1991). *Language and Symbolic Power.* Cambridge, MA: Harvard University Press.
Burke, P. & M. L. G. Pallares-Burke (2008). *Gilberto Freyre: Social Theory in the Tropics.* Oxford: Peter Lang.
Burns, B. (1993). *A history of Brazil.* New York: Columbia University Press.
Carvalho, J. M. (2012). *The Formation of Souls: Imagery of the Republic in Brazil.* Notre Dame, Ind: University of Notre Dame Press.
Certeau, M. *The Practice of Everyday Life* (1984). Berkeley: University of California Press.
Clube Sportivo Beberibe (1909). *Estatutos do Clube Sportivo Beberibe.* Recife: Typ. a vapor J. Agostinho Bezerra.
Coutinho, E. (1994). *Gilberto Freyre.* Rio de Janeiro: Agir.
Curi, M. (2015). *Soccer in Brazil.* London and New York: Routledge.
DaMatta, R. (1982). *Universo do Futebol: esporte e sociedade Brasileira.* Rio de Janeiro: Pinakotheke.
Degler, C. N. (1971). *Neither Black nor White: Slavery and Race Relations in Brazil and the United States.* New York: The MacMillan Company.
Diário de Pernambuco (1854, February 28). *Os Netos de Lovelacio.* Recife: Year XXX, n.48.
———. (1886, May 18). *Clube de Regatas Pernambucano.* Recife: Year LXII, n.112.
———. (1905, June 13). *Esporte Prado Pernambucano.* Recife: Year 81, n.132.
Eakin, M. (2017). *Becoming Brazilians: Race and National Identity in Twentieth Century Brazil.* Cambridge and New York: Cambridge University Press.
Elias, N. & E. Dunning (1996). *The Quest for Excitement: Sport and Leisure in the civilizing process.* Oxford: Blackwell.
Filho, M. (1947). *O Negro no Futebol Brasileiro.* Rio de Janeiro: Irmãos Pongetti Editores.
Foucault, M. (1980). *Power/Knowledge: Selected Interviews and Other Writings, 1972-1977.* New York: Pantheon Books.
Freyre, G. (1938, June 17). Football mulato. *Diario de Pernambuco.*
———. (1955, June 25). Ainda a propósito de futebol brasileiro. *O Cruzeiro.*
———. (1974, June 30). Futebol desbrasileirado? *Diário de Pernambuco.*
———. (2001). *Ingleses no Brasil.* Rio de Janeiro: Topbooks, 3rd edition.
Helal, R., A. J. Soares & H. Lovisolo (2001). *A invenção do país do futebol: Mídia, Raça e Idolatria.* Rio de Janeiro: Manuad.
Hobsbawm, E. & T. Ranger (1983). *The Invention of Tradition.* Cambridge: Cambridge University Press.
———. (1996). *Age of Extremes: A History of the World, 1914-1991.* New York: Vintage Books.
Hutchinson, R. (1996). *Empire Games: The British Invention of Twentieth Century Sport.* Edinburgh: Mainstream Publishing Co.
Hylton, K. (2009) *'Race' and Sport: Critical Race Theory.* Oxon: Routledge.
Kajiyama, S. (2014, June 10). Brazilian youth show off street soccer joy as heroes await World Cup. *Global News.* Retrieved May 2, 2020 from https://globalnews.ca/news/1385974/brazilian-youth-show-off-street-soccer-joy-as-heroes-await-world-cup/.
Kfouri, J. (2017, July 2). João Saldanha foi um brasileiro raro, destemido e carismático. *Folha de São Paulo.*
Kittleson, R. A. (2014). *The Country of Football: Soccer and the Making of Modern Brazil.* Berkeley: University of California Press.
Koster, H. (1817). *Travels in Brazil.* London: Longman, Hurst, Rees, Orme, and Brown.

Lefebvre, H. (1991). *The Production of Space*. Malden, MA: Blackwell.

Lehmann, D. (2018). Gilberto Freyre: The Reassessment Continues. *Latin American Research Review,* 43.1, 208-218.

Maio, M. C. & R. V. Santos (2006). *Raça, Ciência e Sociedade*. Rio de Janeiro: Editora Fiocruz.

Mangan, J.A. (1998). *The Games Ethic and Imperialism: Aspects of the Diffusion of an Ideal*. London: Routledge.

———. (1999). *Shaping the Superman: Fascist Body as Political Icon—Aryan Fascism*. London and Portland: Frank Cass.

Melo, V. (2001). *Cidadesportiva: Primórdios do Esporte no Rio de Janeiro*. Rio de Janeiro: Relume-Dumará.

Mota, C. G. (2009). *Viagem Incompleta: A Experiência Brasileira*. São Paulo: Senac, 3rd edition.

O Sportsman (1888, April 22). *O Sportsman*. Recife: Year I, n.1.

Pallares–Burke, M. L. G. (2011). The English in Brazil: A Study in Cultural Encounters. *Portuguese Studies,* 27.1, 20-32.

Perkin, H. (2007). Teaching the nations how to play: Sport and society in the British Empire and Commonwealth. *The International Journal of the History of Sport,* 6:2, 145-155.

Pope, S. W. & J. Nauright (2009). *Routledge companion to sports history*. New York, Routledge.

Priori, M. D. & V. A. Melo (2009). *História do Esporte no Brasil do Império aos dias atuais*. São Paulo: Unesp.

Reggiani, A. (2019). *La eugenesia en América Latina*. Mexico: El Colegio de México.

Ribeiro, D. (2000). *The Brazilian People: The Formation and Meaning of Brazil*. Gainesville: University Press of Florida.

Ruberg, W. (2019). *History of the Body*. London: Red Globe Press.

Said, E. (1978). *Orientalism*. New York: Pantheon.

Schwarcz, L. M. (1999). *The Spectacle of the Races. Scientists, Institutions and the Race Question in Brazil, 1870–1930*. New York: Hill & Wang.

Severgnini, B. (2014, June 15). "Never Boring, Always Beautiful," How We Play the Game. *The New York Times*. Retrieved April 10, 2020, from https://www.nytimes.com/interactive/2014/06/15/sports/worldcup/how-we-play.html.

Skidmore, T. (1974). *Black into White Race and Nationality in Brazilian Thought*. London: Duke University Press.

Smith, A. D. (1991). *National Identity in Comparative Perspective*. Reno: University of Nevada Press.

Sportv (2019, February 5). *Casagrande diz que Seleção está europeizada: "Falta a ginga do futebol brasileiro"* [Television Broadcast]. Rio de Janeiro: Globo TV. Retrieved April 12, 2020 from https://sportv.globo.com/site/programas/bem-amigos/noticia/casagrande-diz-que-selecao-esta-europeizada-falta-a-ginga-do-futebol-brasileiro.ghtml.

Stepan, N. L. (1996). *The Hour of Eugenics: Race, Gender, and Nation in Latin America*. Ithaca and London: Cornell University Press.

Stoddart, B. (1988). Sport, cultural imperialism, and colonial response in the British Empire. *Comparative Studies in Society and History,* 30:4, 649-673.

Sussman, R. (2014). *The Myth of Race: The Troubling Persistence of an Unscientific Idea*. Cambridge: Harvard University Press.

The Sporting Life (1867, December 7). *Cricket at the Brazils*. London.

Turda, M. & A. Gillette (2014). *Latin Eugenics in Comparative Perspective*. London & New York: Bloomsbury Academic.

UOL/FolhaPress (2018, March 21). CBF e Nike divulgam o uniforme oficial da seleção brasileira para a Copa do Mundo. *Gazeta do Povo*. Retrieved May 16, 2020 from https://www.gazetadopovo.com.br/esportes/copa/2018/cbf-e-nike-divulgam-o-uniforme-oficial-da-selecao-brasileira-para-a-copa-do-mundo-e069wduq44vi6lot6vvvbkpwv/

Vigarello, G. (2005). *Histoire du corps*. Paris: Éditions du Seuil.

Villanueva, C. M. (2017, September 3). La Maquina de Tite: un equipo moderno con el 'jogo bonito' de siempre. *El Tiempo*. Retrieved May 2, 2020 from https://www.eltiempo.com/deportes/futbol-internacional/asi-juega-el-brasil-lider-de-la-eliminatoria-suramericana-que-enfrentara-a-colombia-126386.

Weinstein, B. (2015). *The Color of Modernity: São Paulo and the Making of Race and Nation in Brazil*. Durham/London: Duke University Press.

Williams, D. (2001). *Culture Wars in Brazil: The First Vargas Regime, 1930–1945*. Durham: Duke University Press.

Wisnik, J. M. (2008). *Veneno Remédio: o futebol e o Brasil*. São Paulo: Companhia das Letras.

———. (2014, June 15). "The Beautiful Game Lives Here," How We Play the Game. *The New York Times*. Retrieved April 10, 2020, from
https://www.nytimes.com/interactive/2014/06/15/sports/worldcup/how-we-play.html.

Zimbalist, J. & M. Zimbalist (Directors and writers) (2016). *Pelé: Birth of a Legend*. Beverly Hills, CA: Imagine Entertainment/Seine Pictures.

Chapter 4

That Feeling When...What? Sport, Society, and Emotions

David Scott

Sport and emotions are inextricably intertwined. Indeed, our emotional investments in sport are one of the major motivating factors that drives and sustains our engagement with it in our everyday lives. Consider those feelings we experience when participating in sport: the endless pursuit of perfection, the euphoria of victory, the self-satisfaction achieved from knowing you have given your all, the crushing emptiness of withdrawal, the bitterness of an undeserved defeat. The same can also be said for our consumption of sport from a fan's perspective: the often irrational love and heartbreak we experience supporting 'our' team, the unexpected latching-on to an unheard-of underdog and the hope that they will upset a well-established favourite, the excitement in being able to show our identification through purchasing merchandise. It might even be said that emotions are what *make* sport, that the emotions experienced within sport are the defining characteristic in explaining its prominence within our lives. Sure, these sporting competitions could be run in a purely objective manner to determine who is 'the best' in a certain discipline or game. If this were the case, then the 'entertainment' factor of sport would not be necessary anymore as they would strictly be physiological exercises for the athletes. Events could take place without fans and journalists being required, in facilities that were designed solely for athlete performance rather than spectator sightlines and comfort. Such an approach to sport would lead to an absence of the personal stories and media-driven narratives which help to popularise sport among the general public. But would these competitions really grab our attention, to the extent where they encourage us to invest so much of our time, our money, our identity, into following sport? Or to phrase these questions in a different way: what would sport be without the emotional narratives that twist and turn at unexpected junctures? What would sport be without the exalted highs and crushing lows that come through victory and defeat? What would sport be without emotion?

Despite the seemingly apparent links between sport and emotional engagement, there are still many unanswered questions that arise when sport and emotions are critically examined. While we may think that we simply enjoy the emotional rollercoaster of following sport through innocent emotional attachments, it is unquestionable that various corporate entities utilise these emotional ties in order to benefit their capitalist ventures through various means, e.g., increase sales of products, increase viewing figures, increase advertisement reach. The emotions of those actively involved in sport are also framed in a way that is distinctive from the rest of society, with athletes' emotions constantly being positioned as 'correct' or 'incorrect' in ways which would differ if they were expressed by amateur athletes or general society. This can occur both during their sporting pursuits, such as "being in the zone" and "driven to win", and when outside their sporting arena, such as automatically being held up as "role models" in wider society or media outlets chasing athlete reactions to generate content. As such, what do we actually know about emotions in sport and how they translate into everyday society? More specifically, how do we know how emotions are operationalised in sport and society, for what reasons, and from which perspectives? And more importantly, how can our understandings of the portrayal and utilisation of emotions in sport be contested with emotions in society more generally? This chapter will explore the duelistic nature of these issues by attempting to outline the varying ways in which emotions have been discussed in sporting settings and contrast them with how emotions are portrayed within society.

What are Emotions?

Before moving to discussions of emotions in sport, it is worth outlining exactly what emotions are, as they are an often misquoted and misunderstood concept. A significant reason for this is one of the premises of this chapter; that emotions can be understood differently from different disciplinary perspectives. This has led to multiple definitions being employed throughout these disciplines, with some of these understandings seeping through into common parlance and others failing to make this same leap. As such, the definition of emotions seems to have evolved into a 'common-sense' state, summarised by the moral philosopher widely credited as being the 'inventor of emotions', Thomas Brown: "every person understands what is meant by an emotion" (2010, p. 102). With this quotation, Brown referred to the universality of emotions experienced by humans throughout society; no matter a person's circumstance they understand what is being alluded to when one speaks of joy or anger, even if these feelings are relative to an individual's own life experience. However, this ambiguity has enabled emotions to be repurposed by various sources. For instance, writers from the Romantic era often glorified emotions as being intense, visceral, and aesthetically-driven, therefore positioning emotion as being 'from the heart' and rooting it in opposition to 'logical reasoning'.[1] It has also led to a common lack of distinction as to what an 'emotion' is and what a 'mood' is; typically,

---

[1] There is an even greater charge often levelled at writers associated (both directly and indirectly) with the Romantic era, most famously by C. S. Lewis (2013), that romantic love is a culturally-specific emotion 'invented' by European writers in the 12th Century.

emotions are mostly episodic reactions which last a matter of seconds, whereas moods "last much longer [they] are background states that raise or lower our susceptibility to emotional stimuli" (Evans, 2019, p. 42). As such, these characteristics enable us to have a better understanding of what emotions *are* by displaying what emotions are *not*.

While Brown's quotation is perhaps the best attempt there is at providing a concise consensus, there are many different facets of emotions that still require consideration. For instance, it is notable that there is a biological, physiological, and neurological origin from which emotions stem within our bodies as an internalised neural response to an external stimulus (e.g., Oosterwijk et al., 2012). This might be considered from an evolutionary standpoint, as emotions have been vital to mankind's survival, for instance, the 'fight or flight' responses to a dramatic increase in adrenaline (e.g., Liu et al., 2020). Research from medical, nursing, and psychology studies has also shown that what can be termed 'basic' emotions, such as happiness, sadness, fear, and anger, are in fact innate, as opposed to socially learned behaviours developed over time by mimicking parents or adults, meaning that emotions are inherently human (e.g., Roch-Levecq, 2006). While there are many other viewpoints that might be included when considering emotions, such as moral philosophy, education, and anthropology among others, it is perhaps the work within psychology that requires the most attention. This is due to the continuing attempts to encapsulate emotions through various classifications, lists, and measurements, with numerous attempts to provide definitive lists as to what emotions are (e.g., Kleinginna Jr. & Kleinginna, 1981). Such an approach has proved influential, with psychological understandings of emotions arguably being the most prominent perspective to date in the investigation of emotions within sporting contexts.

Current Conceptions of Emotions in Sport

While the overriding influence of psychological conceptions of emotions within sport is not in itself problematic, this somewhat limited focus has led to a reiteration and reproduction of what emotions are, how they can be researched, and how they are utilised within a sporting context. The main appeal of psychological conceptions of emotions are that they claim to be able to definitively identify and list emotions, as well as position emotions as being individually appraised and expressed, thus making individual, and individuals', emotions measurable through various objective scales.[2] This practice is particularly prevalent within the 'cognitive' and 'behavioural' paradigms of psychology which contest that emotions follow a linear mechanistic pattern (Reilly, 2000). This cognitive-behavioural perspective, while an umbrella term for a variety of interrelated approaches, is also the predominant theoretical and

---

[2] A very small range of examples of such scales include the "Differential Emotions Scale" (Izard, 1991), the "Discrete Emotions Questionnaire" (Harmon-Jones et al., 2016), and the "Multidimensional Emotion Questionnaire" (Klonsky et al., 2019), to name but a few.

practical paradigmatic framework utilised within sport psychology (Turner et al., 2020). As a result, this association may have led the potential effects of society and culture on emotion to be largely overlooked, and at best reduced, in an attempt to perceive emotions as something that can be identified, controlled, and nullified in order to increase performance. Emotions are reduced to individual or intrapersonal sensations, rather than allowing for social, interpersonal, and intersubjective explanations to be included too (Tamminen & Bennett, 2017). This cognitive-behavioural view from sport psychology might help to explain why emotions in sport are more widely viewed through such an individualistic lens.

To elaborate on this argument further, it is worth drawing from wider bodies of literature within sport to fully understand the way in which emotion tends to be discussed, before it then crosses into the lexicon of sporting culture more broadly. For instance, there are numerous studies within coaching research that discuss the need to control emotions in order to excel and achieve results, with a prime example being the desire to reduce the typical pre-game anxiety and nerves which most people experience by making the 'butterflies fly in formation' (Hanton & Jones, 1999). This is just one instance where emotions are portrayed as something to be overcome or battled against, as if they are a barrier to victory. Such an understanding of emotion feeds into the wider conception of training the athlete to become a 'docile body' (Chase, 2006), so that they can be trained and manipulated into a pure performance machine by their coach. The message being expressed here appears to be that experiencing, and sometimes even acknowledging, emotions is 'bad'; that an athlete's role is not to *think* or *feel*, but just to *do*. These messages about emotion within an elite performance context are picked up on and reported by a key, if not *the* key, influencer of sporting culture: the media. This chapter is far too short to discuss the ever-increasingly symbiotic relationship between sport and the media in an increasingly globalised world.[3] However it is increasingly clear that the media has a significant influence on the presentation and language of various conceptions within sport to wider society. Emotions appear to have been susceptible to this influence, as their portrayal in the sporting media seem to receive a unique form of attention in contrast to emotions in everyday society.

An example of this comes from discussing athletes as 'being in the zone': a state where their full attention is dedicated to their sporting task to the exclusion of all else in the world. There are endless examples of media quips from athletes trying to explain this sensation, with one famous example being from the former Formula 1 driver, Ayrton Senna, describing his feelings while driving at the 1988 Monaco Grand Prix:

> I was no longer driving the car consciously. I was driving it by instinct, only I was in a different dimension. I was way over the limit but still able to find

---

[3] However, for those who wish to read more, a salient starting point is Hutchins, Li, & Rowe (2019)

even more. It frightened me because I realised I was well beyond my conscious understanding. (Kapadia, 2010)

While Senna here is discussing, either directly or indirectly, depending on your definition, the emotional sensations he felt, various commentators have used this quotation to support their own particular point of view. For instance, this quotation is often used by sport media and fans to demonstrate the 'otherworldliness' of Senna, thereby positioning the athlete and their emotions as different or 'othered' to those experienced by us plebeian mortals. This is perhaps key to understanding *why* emotions in sport are portrayed so differently as to how they are in society: *they* are different to *us*. Taking a more philosophical or sociological approach to understanding emotions, the focus expands beyond just the individual to also consider social, cultural, and interpersonal associations too. Taking the above example, the emotional connection Senna espouses may be related to several associated factors, such as the fact he was driving on a circuit that he could literally see from where he lived, therefore enabling geographical and cultural connections to the experience. It is also pertinent that, at this time, Senna was in the midst of a fierce battle for his first world title with his more illustrious teammate, Alain Prost; both drivers were in the dominant car on the grid and thus were duelling for power and preference within the team. Could it be that what Senna experienced was more widely influenced by the varying interpersonal relationships ongoing within and between his teammates, as well as other situational and cultural aspects?

It is important to note that 'being in the zone' has been explored more widely within a psychological domain, most voraciously by Csikszentmihalyi (2020), which has resulted in these expressions being applied within fields such as art, surgery, and education. While this may appear to somewhat mitigate the initial argument posed here, it does provide a starting point to discuss how emotions in sport are 'othered' from those experienced in wider society, and how broadening out from the individualistic psychological understandings prevalent in sporting contexts might enable for greater discussions that incorporate society and culture.

Sociological Theories of Emotion

Some of the original foundations of sociological emotional theory are posed by philosophers such as Adam Smith and Thomas Brown. Their initial ideas, regarding emotions being integral to understanding social life and society more widely, have been developed by a wide range of disciplines over the last century to enable emotions to be understood as embodied, relational, and culturally-specific. Therefore, what follows is a somewhat whistle-stop tour of more modern, key sociological and emotional theory development, although any exclusions are purely for the purposes of brevity and not a reflection of their importance. Perhaps the best place to start is with Arlie Hochschild's hugely influential work (1979; 1983), which considered how emotions can be viewed as being socially embedded and 'performed' by an individual, due to a conscious or unconscious desire to adhere to the cultural norms inherent within a specific context. This was termed as individuals interpreting how to present their emotions in relation to the 'feeling rules' of a given situation. Essentially, 'feeling rules' imbibe the background cultural milieu of any social setting, which might influence someone as to how they should act; for example, one is *expected* to feel happy at a celebration, or sad during remembrance services. How an individual *expects* to feel, or how they *should* feel, which are not always the same thing, is also influenced by an individual's interpretative and ideological framework that is founded on their past experiences, meaning they can alter over time. Hochschild argued that there are numerous social situations where an individual is forced to act incongruously to how they feel, with these occasions typically taking place in public arenas. The effort required in suppressing certain emotions and displaying the 'correct' emotions is labelled by Hochschild as 'emotion work' and 'emotional management'. This performative aspect of emotions varies between 'deep acting', which can involve the individual making a vested effort to *feel* the emotions they wish to portray, or 'surface acting', which involves greater superficiality within the individual's emotional performance and can lead to a less believable performance. How an individual responds to these socially-defined and contextually-dependent 'feeling rules', and whether 'deep' or 'surface acting' takes place, provides a potential avenue into how individuals view both their self and how they are seen by others.

There have been subsequent developments of these initial theorisations of emotion, with one of the most prominent being the work of Sara Ahmed (2004; 2010). Ahmed furthers understanding of how emotions are expressed by individuals within a socio-cultural context by positioning emotions as intentional, meaning that they are always 'about' or 'directed towards' something. Therefore, emotions are argued to be about a person's movement, attachments, and connections within their lived world. How individuals understand their emotions is inherently related to their social and cultural context, which impinges upon their association between language and emotions. This is best described by Ahmed herself when she argues, "even when we feel we have the same feeling, we don't necessarily have the same relationship to the feeling" (2004, p. 10). More modern developments within the sociology of emotion have been captured within Debra Hopkins and colleagues' (2009) book, and Randall Collins' (2019) explication of 'emotional energy' in relation to his 'interaction ritual' theory.

While much of the discussion so far has been around the lack of such sociologically-informed emotional theory within the world of sport, there is actually a solid corpus of work in this area that arose in the 1970s. Elias and Dunning (1970) were some of the first researchers within sociology to cogitate how emotions are interlaced within how we experience 'leisure spectacles', including live sport. This figurational approach was developed by Maguire (2011), who argued that a socio-cultural perspective on emotions within society and leisure must consider each element interdependently, therefore enabling not just social but also psychological, historical, and biological understandings when considering emotions in sport. More recently there has been a growing movement towards 'sensory' research within sport[4] that explicitly positions an individual's body as not only a site of physical activity, but also as a means of perception during bodily experiences (Groth and Krahn, 2017), which hints at a potential avenue for more embodied accounts of emotion in sport.

There are numerous sensorial qualities within sport, exercise, and physical activity that are inseparable from the emotions we experience when we use our body; for instance, the excitement, or sometimes dread, of pulling on gym clothes, the sensations of exertion, and sometimes exhaustion, throughout the different stages of an exercise session, the proprioception involved in controlling, or lack thereof, that we feel in using our limbs and body (Scott, 2020). All these elements help to create the sensorial, intersubjective, and situated dimensions of individuals' emotional experiences of sport and exercise (Tamminen & Bennett, 2017). There have been some isolated attempts at including sociological understandings of emotions within a performance sport setting, although usually as a secondary point of focus, such as Thing's (2001) discussion of the embodied and affective experiences of Danish top-level female athletes, and Lilleaas' (2007) explorations of masculinities during interviews about emotions with professional handball players. However, these examples are largely exceptions to the majority rule of there being a dearth of research within this area, meaning that the sociological understanding of emotions within sport is still largely a lacuna. Such a relative absence of sociological understandings of emotions within sport therefore renders duelistic tensions inevitable, as the emotional links between, throughout, and within sport and society have been left underexplored and undervalued.

Emotions in Sport

While the history of sociological emotion theory is clearly rich and varied, there is a very prominent gap in the application of such theory within the context of sport. Instead, the overreliance on cognitive-behaviouralist notions of emotions within sport has led to the proliferation of related language throughout the context, particularly regarding how emotions are to be experienced 'correctly' and 'incorrectly', into the common language used by those associated with sport such as athletes, fans, coaches, officials, the media, among others. To query why this has occurred and highlight how this continues to happen in sport, I will use three examples to explore the duelistic tendencies of how emotion is portrayed and understood differently within sport than it is in comparison to everyday societal life, as well as indicate areas that could prove ripe for greater sociological research and critique.

---

[4] See Allen-Collinson & Owton (2015) for an overview

Celebrations

This may seem like a somewhat obvious place to start, given the voracity of celebrations we are so often used to seeing in sport. After all, isn't the pursuit of victory, and as such earning the *right* to celebrate, one of the main drivers behind sport's very existence? As an active participant in sport, whether athlete, fan, coach, we are always searching for the next moment within which we are able to celebrate, whether it is in the final result of the contest or down to the celebration of a successful pass, tackle, or visible exertion of effort. One of the great appeals of sport is that it enables us to escape from the everyday, where visceral and passionate celebrations rarely play a frequent role, into this other world where the potential for an emotional release through physical or vicarious achievement often becomes addictive.

However, celebrations might not be quite as straightforward as they first seem. At the elite performance level of sport, do celebrations really operate in this pure, cathartic, instinctive manner that is described above? Think about your favourite athlete; do you associate them with a particular celebration? Over the last 20-30 years, coincidently during the rise of neoliberalist economics and societies in the Western World, athletes have been increasingly encouraged to have a 'signature' celebration; think of LeBron James' "silencer", Deion Sanders' "prime time", Cristiano Ronaldo's "sí". These are all premeditated, concocted, specifically planned celebrations that enable each athlete to add this association to their personal brand recognition, thus adding greater marketing and advertising potential to their portfolio. Similar cynical links can also be made to the choreographed team celebrations we often see, which provide crucial content for the numerous social media channels each club now curates, alongside the potential for heightened team cohesion and spirit. Then there are the ways in which athletes are increasingly encouraged to celebrate winning trophies in a sanitised manner, the 'trophy presentation ceremony' acting as a set script as to when and how athletes *should* perform certain emotions and actions. So although we might be drawn to sport in part for the emotional release, which can come through participating within celebrations, it is important to note the distinct gap in the ways in which celebrations, and the emotional investments within these actions, take place between those from everyday society, i.e. sports fans, and the athletes themselves.

These celebration routines are not the main link I wish to deliberate on here though. Instead, there is a particular incident that prompted me to consider the nature of celebrations in sport and how they demonstrate a fissure from society. Back in August 2017 I watched the Manchester City versus Bournemouth English Premier League soccer match, which was delicately poised at 1-1 heading into the 7th minute of added time. Just as it looked as though the game was going to finish as a draw, Raheem Sterling's speculative effort from outside of the penalty took a deflection and went into the goal, sparking wild celebrations. Sterling sprinted towards the fans and flung himself into their open embraces, wanting to share his elation and joy with them. However, once he had made his way back onto the pitch the referee showed him a yellow card, which was his second of the game and led to him being sent-off. His manager, Josep Guardiola Sala:

> "I do not understand the decision, winning in the last minute is always special, if you cannot celebrate without fans, tell me the reason why. Maybe we should not play with fans"[5] (Firstpost, 2017).

While this is by no means an isolated incident, with numerous examples available from a wide range of sports, herein lies the crux of the issue: that celebrations, or more pertinently over-celebrations, are controlled, regulated, and punished by the governing bodies of various sports. As such, these rules are effectively determining *how* athletes are able to feel and express their emotions, which is at odds with how emotions are actually experienced, as immediate, intersubjective, explosions of physical and emotional sensations. The opposite might also be explored, from examples where athletes are accused of 'under-celebration', leading fans and the media to speculate *why* an athlete does not celebrate *in the right way* after scoring or claiming victory. In both circumstances, it is clear that there is a significant amount of emotional regulation involved within sporting celebrations which has not been explored before.

While this emotional regulation might rightfully be compared to Hochschild's 'emotion work' and 'emotion management', due to the existence of both explicit and implicit social rules imbibed within the particular sporting context, I instead would like to draw upon the arguments I outlined earlier regarding the prevalence of cognitive-behavioural notions of emotion within sport. In this sense, the emotions expressed through celebrations are more in alignment with the desire to control and reduce emotions due to the apparent 'danger' they represent through celebrations, both physically, i.e., crushing within crowds of spectators when celebrating with the fans, and more representationally, i.e., with athletes being positioned as 'role models' whom children will mimic. Knowing how to celebrate might be understood as an extension of the athlete being trained to be a 'docile body', with their unquestioning obeyance of the laws of the context extending to their emotional reactions while performing. Again, these cognitive-behaviouralist tendencies can be seen within the language used by the media when depicting such emotional displays, with instances of over-celebration typically being 'senseless' or 'violating the rules', and under-celebration arousing suspicion and drawing questions about passion and commitment to the cause; in each case, the emotions at play were *wrong*. However, this goes against the grain of how we would expect celebrations to look like within sport from a societal understanding of emotions. By drawing upon Hochschild's 'emotion work'

---

[5] This was a somewhat prescient comment considering how soccer, and most elite sport globally, is having to be played at the time of writing during the COVID-19 pandemic.

and 'emotion management' we would expect victory to be widely welcomed as a situation where 'surface acting' is not necessary in the refinement of our emotions. Perhaps an alternative sociological understanding of these instances of celebration-suppression might be considered through the work of Michel Foucault (1988), in particular his conception of the 'panopticon' and 'technologies of the self'; in essence, those within the 'panopticon' are encouraged to modify and self-regulate their behaviour, as it is impossible to know when, or if, they are being observed by an authority figure. Through this understanding we might be able to explore the decision makers themselves and the reasons why they wish to control athletes' emotions and celebrations in such ways, as well as athletes' desires to comply via a 'technology of self'.

Death

I would now like to shift the focus from one emotional extreme to the other, and from one of the major appeals of sport to one of the areas that has perhaps not been considered too much before: death in sport. Or to be more precise, the death of athletes and how this is experienced within the context of sport, and how this differs from how death is contended with in everyday society. From a cultural perspective, the way in which the death of an athlete is greeted seems to be so different to how we encounter death at a more personal level. Of course, death in society is mostly associated with a great deal of sadness and sorrow, with the extent of our emotional mourning more or less proportionate to the emotional attachment we had to the individual in question; the greater we knew someone and the stronger the bond we had with them, the more upset we generally are. However, when it comes to the death of well-known sporting figures the emotions we feel, and that we are *expected* to feel, appear to take on their own set of rules. There is typically a great sense of tragedy, of wistful nostalgia for the talent that has been lost, and a great veneration of their achievements and successes, no matter the emotional connection made during their lifetime as either an athlete or a person. This is particularly evident when an athlete has died seemingly prematurely, which strengthens the rituals experienced in the immediate aftermath and exacerbates this phenomenon.

There are two examples I will use to help exemplify this: the deaths of Kobe Bryant and Vichai Srivaddhanaprabha. While both had different roles in sport, each of these incidents help to highlight different aspects of how the death of those associated with sport is treated differently within society. Kobe Bryant, widely considered to be one of the all-time great basketball players of the NBA for the Los Angeles Lakers during a 20-year career, was killed in a helicopter crash at the age of 41 on 26th January 2020. Coincidentally, Vichai Srivaddhanaprabha was also killed in a helicopter crash, at the age of 60 on 27th October 2018. Rather than being an athlete, Srivaddhanaprabha was a businessman who founded the King Power duty free empire and was chairman of Leicester City Football Club, overseeing the remarkable success of Leicester City winning the English Premier League as 1000-1 outsiders in 2016.

Following each respective accident, the general reactions were very similar: shock and disbelief at the untimely passing of a prominent figure within sport. What followed were many rituals we might commonly associate with deaths within sport: a gathering of fans at memorial services, tributes at games for a certain period of time afterwards, the renaming of awards and places. However, why should we simply accept these as the 'right' things to do following a death in sport? More importantly, *who decides* what is the 'right' way to react in these situations? The reason for including the Srivaddhanaprabha example is because it struck me as to how frequently commentators, both in the traditional media and on social media, claimed that all the tributes were done in 'the right way'.

Similar claims were also made about the tributes and decisions following Bryant's death, many of which were televised before and during the Los Angeles Lakers' first game after his death, which drew the second highest ever viewing figures for ESPN. In both cases, this was despite each individual having significant controversy concerning their past behaviours: Srivaddhanaprabha having been accused of tax evasion and monopolisation, Bryant being accused of sexual assault and homophobia. But why were these indiscretions mostly overlooked when mourning these characters? How has this knowledge as to what is 'right', what should be done to 'honour' these figures, and even why such public recognition is needed, been cultivated within sport?

Looking more closely at the language used during these periods of mourning, there are clear consistencies with the way emotions are discussed within a cognitive-behavioural framework. The media persistently report narratives around these being times of reflection on individuals' contributions, how loved they were, and transmit tributes from fellow sporting figures. This would suggest that these emotions are not only being 'permitted' within this time frame, but are actively being encouraged, as though only when mourning the death of somebody from sport is it the appropriate time to feel a sense of sadness and loss. It would seem that, from a mediatised perspective at least, the expression of emotions is interlaced with public relations, with the need for figures in the public eye to *look* as though they are mourning in the 'right' way resulting in the overlooking of past indiscretions in lieu of respect for past achievements.

How else might we come to understand these experiences of death within a sporting context then? A somewhat sensible parallel might be drawn between these portrayals of emotion and death with the literature concerning celebrity deaths. Indeed, there are even some papers that combine the two worlds of sport and celebrity together, with Radford and Bloch (2012) discussing the death of NASCAR driver Dale Earnhardt, Sr. in the context of remembrance via merchandise consumption. This literature discusses how the relationship between celebrities and society can be explained as being 'parasocial', in that the illusion of intimacy is constructed between fans and celebrities (Rojek, 2007). Related literature has identified the patterns of rituals observed during the time of a celebrity death (Burgess *et al*, 2019), and how these practices are policed by other fans through the increasing incorporation of social media platforms within everyday life (Gach *et al.,* 2017). While these theorisations provide a certain level of understanding as to how death in sport is treated differently than death in society, they are overlooking the cultural specificities of sport and the unique emotional ties entwined within it. Again, the influential work of Hochschild's 'emotion work' (1979) might be drawn upon more strongly to help understand these experiences to an extent, with the implicit and explicit 'emotion rules' concerning the subject of death itself leading to an explicit expectation of valorising those whom society place on such a questionably high pedestal.

A more cultural understanding of emotions and death within sport might also prove fruitful, with a deeper interrogation of the specific cultural framework of sport and the varying roles emotions have within this context. This is to say that culturally-specific emotions are not necessarily innate, rather that they emerge through the prevalence of certain conditions that encourage and reproduce them over time (Evans, 2019). Given this, viewing emotions in sport as being culturally-specific enables us to invert the gaze and begin to understand the reasons *why* certain emotions and actions are attached to the death of sporting figures; could it be simple veneration of those who have contributed to developing and sustaining the context, or might there be more cynical underlying reasons, such as sustaining the public image of sport, a push for increased consumption through memorabilia, or a distraction to avoid questions being asked about sport's possible contribution to their demise? [6] Without applying these more social and cultural lenses of emotion to sport we will not be able to fully understand how emotions are operationalised during times of death in ways that differ from everyday society.

Confidence

Confidence is an unavoidable term, due to its prevalence at every juncture of sport. Athletes continuously ascribe their relative performances due to a feeling of, or lack of, confidence. For example, Carl Lewis once famously said "if you don't have confidence, you'll always find a way not to win"; more recently, Sloane Stephens stated "when you have confidence, you can do anything". Coaches also tend to place such great importance on confidence, as typified by the Tom Landry quotation, "I didn't believe in team motivation, I believed in getting a team prepared so it knows it will have the necessary confidence when it steps on the field". The media consistently chronicle issues of confidence throughout sporting contexts, while fans cannot help but speculate on the confidence level of their favourite athletes based on their performance, body language, and even the 'look in their eyes'. The links between how confidence is oversimplified in this manner and the dominant cognitive-behavioural is fairly apparent and can be summarised using a simple formula: increased confidence

---

[6] For an example, see how long it has taken American Football to Soccer to take any interest in their potential contribution to diseases such as chronic traumatic encephalopathy and dementia.

= good, decreased confidence = bad. However, such an oversaturation of this term has led us to become desensitized as to what it actually means. What *is* confidence, and what does it *feel* like? What are its purposes and roles within our lives, both within and beyond sport?

Firstly, it is important to clarify that confidence can actually be classified as an emotion, which some scholars from particular disciplinary backgrounds might contest. It is perhaps notable that confidence as an emotion gains the most support from sociologists, who tend to explain it as a social and relational emotion, and therefore at odds to the traditionally individualistic focus on emotions from psychologists. One of the forerunners in theorizing confidence as an emotion, within a sociological perspective, is Jack Barbalet (1993; 1996), who posits that confidence is a necessary emotion within individual action and human agency. His arguments are rooted in the economic sense of what confidence entails, more specifically in how investments are decided upon within the stock market, but explicates these arguments to wider society. He contends that confidence influences how a person feels able to bring "the future into the present by providing a sense of certainty to what is essentially unknowable" (Barbalet, 1996: 81). In other words, it would be impossible to be future-oriented without confidence, as it is needed to enable us to act within society. Without confidence we would not be able to make decisions about our actions in the immediate future, meaning that our actions are as much about confidence and emotions as they are rationality, reason, and reflection. As noted by Barbalet, individuals "do not choose their emotions, [but] they can choose to act on them or not" (1996: 87). This discussion is in a similar vein to how the prominent philosopher Adam Smith also discussed the role emotions play in society; that it was in fact rational to be emotional and no science of the mind would be complete without considering the emotional element (2010). This argument by these two scholars is an important one to clarify: that emotion should not be positioned as an enemy of logic or reason, but that sensible decision making requires both emotion *and* rationality.

Confidence is therefore no less crucial than has been claimed by athletes, coaches, and the media; however, by drawing from more sociological and philosophical understandings of it, we might now be able to discuss it in a more emotional sense. The implications of confidence pertaining to clarity in individuals' decision making are that it is not so much something that can be 'increased' or 'decreased' simply through inspirational talks. Rather, confidence is bound up within our societal and cultural ties, and therefore lies within a liminal space throughout sport and society. While in elite sport this conception of confidence has not yet been explored from a research perspective, it has been investigated in areas where sport is actively used to 'increase' confidence, such as sport-for-development courses (Scott, 2020) and women's sport and leisure advertisements (Gill & Orgad, 2015). It is noticeable that these papers both highlight the contested nature of 'body confidence' in particular and attempt to deconstruct the social, cultural, and individual influences that confer on understandings of confidence. This is similar to Ahmed's (2010) theorisations on the 'promise of happiness', which discusses how the constant push to fit in with the narrative of 'happiness' can lead individuals towards or away from specific experiences due to social pressures. The absence of such discussions within performance sport is therefore conspicuous by its absence, which again owes much to the predominance of cognitive-behavioural mechanisms of confidence being employed at large. As such, this discussion of confidence hopefully demonstrates the potential that more sociological understandings of emotions have in exploring the duelistic elements of emotions within sport and society.

How Can We Give Sport 'All the Feels'?

The three examples outlined above are not intended to provide a comprehensive overview of how emotions can be conceived in relation to the duelism between sport and society; instead, they are suggested as a starting point to enable a discussion which has yet to be fully engaged with: why are emotions in sport perceived so differently than those pertaining to other areas of society? There are many other avenues that might be considered in attempting to address this question; for example, the influence of societal factors such as gender, race, ethnicity, age, disability, class, and the intersectionalities that are experienced within and between these categorisations. For instance, why is it that the actions of athletes such as Serena Williams and Lewis Hamilton, both athletes of colour from working class backgrounds, are framed in a seemingly more emotional manner than their peers, even when their actions are equivalent? There is not enough space here to discuss the colonial and bourgeois overtones embedded within narratives connected with these and similar athletes, but it is my hope that others are able to dissect these occurrences by utilising more of an emotional perspective.

This chapter has argued that emotions in sport are far more complex than they are currently portrayed within wider society. Our understandings of them can be enhanced by broadening the scope of language used beyond what is currently entwined within cognitive-behavioural understandings of emotions. For instance, there is evidence that context-specific emotion rules (Hochschild, 1979) apply within sport, which suggests that there is some overlap in how emotions can be understood in line with other areas of society. However, this chapter has outlined how there are also many points of departure that showcase the unique societal arena cultivated by sport, in terms of emotion. By using perspectives of emotion which utilise theories from sociology as well as psychology, biology, and/or neurology, there is potential to question and query this duelistic component of sport and society even further. Such investigations might enhance understandings of sport in relation to numerous areas, including sport and identity, fandom, consumption, intersectionalities, active/passive participation, relationships, celebrity. Most importantly though, it will allow those involved in sport to critically question their own emotional practices and investments within this realm of their lives.

REFERENCES

Ahmed, S. (2004) *The cultural politics of emotion*. Edinburgh University Press.

Ahmed, S. (2010) *The promise of happiness*. Duke University Press.

Allen-Collinson, J., & Owton, H. (2015) Intense embodiment: sense of heat in women's running and boxing. *Body and Society, 21*(2), 245-268.

Brown, T. (2010). *Thomas Brown: Selected philosophical writings* (Dixon, T. Ed.). Imprint Academic (Original work published 1820).

Burgess, J., Mitchell, P., & Münch, F. V. (2019) Social media rituals: the uses of celebrity death in digital culture. In Z. Papacharissi (Ed.) *A Networked Self: Birth, Life, Death*. Routledge, pp. 224-239.

Chase, L. F. (2006) (Un)disciplined bodies: a Foucauldian analysis of women's rugby. *Sociology of Sport Journal, 23*(3), 229-247.

Collins, R. (2019) Emotional micro bases of social inequality: emotional energy, emotional domination and charismatic solidarity. *Emotions and Society, 1*(1), 45-50.

Csikszentmihalyi, M. (2020) *Finding flow: the psychology of engagement with everyday life*. Basic Books.

Elias, N., & Dunning, E. (1970) The quest for excitement in unexciting societies. In G. Lüschen (Ed.) *The cross-cultural analysis of sport and games*, Sipes.

Evans, D. (2019) *Emotion: a very short introduction* (2nd Edition). Oxford University Press.

Firstpost (2017) *Premier League: Manchester City boss Pep Guardiola questions Raheem Sterling red card for goal celebration*. Available at: https://www.firstpost.com/sports/premier-league-manchester-city-boss-pep-guardiola-questions-raheem-sterling-red-card-for-goal-celebration-3977663.html (first accessed 19/05/20).

Foucault, M. (1988) *Technologies of the Self: A Seminar with Michel Foucault*, Tavistock.

Gach, K. Z., Fiesler, C., & Brubaker, J. R. (2017) "Control your emotions, Potter": an analysis of grief policing on Facebook in response to celebrity death. *Proceedings of the ACM on Human-Computer Interaction, 1* (CSCW), 1-18.

Gill, R., & Orgad, S. (2015) The confidence cult(ure). *Australian Feminist Studies, 30*(86), 324-344.

Groth, S., & Krahn, Y. (2017) Sensing athletes: sensory dimensions of recreational endurance sports. *Journal of Ethnology and Folkloristics, 11*(2), 3-23.

Hanton, S., & Jones, G. (1999) The acquisition and development of cognitive skills and strategies: I. Making the butterflies fly in formation. *The Sport Psychologist, 13*(1), 1-21.

Harmon-Jones, C., Bastian, B., & Harmon-Jones, E. (2016) The discrete emotions questionnaire: a new tool for measuring state self-reported emotions. *PLoS One, 11*(8), doi: 10.1371/journal.pone.0159915.

Hochschild, A. R. (1979) Emotion work, feeling rules, and social structure. *The American Journal of Sociology, 85*(3), 551-575.

Hochschild, A. R. (1983) *The managed heart: commercialization of human feeling*. University of California Press.

Hopkins, D., Flam, H., Kuzmics, J., & Kleres, J. (2009) *Theorizing emotions: sociological explorations and applications*. Campus Verlag.

Hutchins, B., Li, B., & Rowe, D. (2019) Over-the-top sport: live streaming services, changing coverage rights markets and the growth of media sport portals. *Media, Culture & Society, 41*(7), 975-994

Izard, C. E. (1991) *The Psychology of emotions*. Plenum Press.

Kapadia, A. (Director). (2010) *Senna* [DVD] Universal Pictures

Kleinginna Junior, P. R., & Kleinginna, A. M. (1981) A categorized list of emotion definitions, with suggestions for a consensual definition. *Motivation and Emotion, 5*, 345-379.

Klonsky, E. D., Victor, S. E., Hibbert, A. S., & Hajcak, G. (2019) The multidimensional emotion questionnaire (MEQ): rationale and initial psychometric properties. *Journal of Psychopathology and Behavioural Assessment, 41*(3), 409-424.

Lewis, C. S. (2013) *The allegory of love: a study in medieval traditions*. Cambridge University Press (Original work published 1936).

Lilleaas, U-B. (2007) Masculinities, sport, and emotions. *Men and Masculinities, 10*(1), 39-53.

Liu, G., Papa, A., Katchman, A. N., Zakharov, S. I., Roybal, D., Hennesset, J. A., Kushner, J., Yang, L., Chen, B-X., Kushnir, A., Dangas, K., Gygi, S. P., Pitt, G. S., Colecraft, H. M., Ben-Johny, M.,

Kalocsay, M., & Marx, S. O. (2020) Mechanism of adrenergic Ca,1.2 stimulation revealed by proximity proteomics. *Nature, 577*, 695-700.

Maguire, J. (2011) Welcome to the pleasure dome? emotions, leisure and society. *Sport in Society, 14*(7-8), 913-926.

Oosterwijk, S., Lindquist, K. A., Anderson, E., Dautoff, R., Moriguchi, Y., & Barrett, L. F. (2012) States of mind: emotions, body feelings, and thoughts share distributed neural networks. *NeuroImage, 62*(3), 2110-2128.

Radford, S. K., & Bloch, P. H (2012) Grief, commiseration, and consumption following the death of a celebrity. *Journal of Consumer Culture, 12*(2), 137-155.

Reilly, C. E. (2000) The role of emotion in cognitive therapy, cognitive therapists, and supervision. *Cognitive and Behavioural Practice, 7,* 343-345.

Roch-Levecq, A-C. (2006) Production of basic emotions by children with congenital blindness: evidence for the embodiment of theory of mind. *British Journal of Developmental Psychology, 24*(3), 507-528.

Rojek, C. (2007) Celebrity and religion. In S. Redmond & S. Holmes (Eds.) *Stardom and Celebrity: A Reader.* Sage, pp. 171-180.

Scott, D. S. (2020) The confidence delusion: a sociological exploration of participants' confidence in sport-for-development. *International Review for the Sociology of Sport, 55*(4), 383-398.

Smith, A. (2010) *The Theory of Modern Sentiments,* Digireads.com (Original work published 1759)

Tamminen, K. A., & Bennett, E. V. (2017) No emotion is an island: an overview of theoretical perspectives and narrative research on emotions in sport and physical activity. *Qualitative Research in Sport, Exercise and Health, 9*(2), 183-199.

Turner, M. J., Aspin, G., Didymus, F. F., Mack, R., Olusoga, P., Wood, A. G., & Bennett, R. (2020) One case, four approaches: the application of psychotherapeutic approaches in sport psychology. *The Sport Psychologist, 34*(1), 71-83.

Chapter 5

Shuffling Sideways: The Arrested Development of (Girl) Goaltenders in Hockey Films

Jamie Ryan

> Goalies are different….the differences between 'players' and 'goalies' are
> manifest and real, transcending as they do even culture and sport.
> —Ken Dryden, *The Game*

In hockey culture, the goaltender position[1] is often thought of as unnatural because purposely putting yourself in front of high velocity objects rather than dodging them, or better yet not putting yourself into such a position to begin with, is not considered natural. Yet, sports are highly unnatural. Sports do not naturally arise from the land or the human spirit, despite their various creation myths[2] and while the human penchant for play (see Huizinga) may be natural, sports are constructed and regulated through rules and governing bodies that decidedly mark them as more "invented traditions" (see Hobsbawn) and closer to culture than nature. The unnaturalness of sport is perhaps most apparent in a game such as hockey, as there is nothing natural about strapping sharp blades to your feet and fighting over a small black disc; but more than this, sports also work against human biology. Sports sociologist Bissonnette Anderson (2010) notes "much of the violence and risk-taking associated with sport is *unnatural*" since "sport teaches athletes to undo their naturally protective instincts" (p. 38, p. 49). So, while goaltenders may represent the most overt example of athletes working against their "naturally protective instincts" most players engage in similarly unnatural behaviour. Questions arise like, why are goalies considered different?[3] Why does the mark of unnaturalness only stick to goaltenders? And why is there a seemingly easy slide between the unnaturalness of the goaltender position on the ice

---

[1] It should be noted that I am a hockey goaltender.
[2] In the case of hockey, the sport is not a natural reaction or battle against winter.
[3] A contributing factor to the weirdness of the hockey goaltender is that they are (visually) other on the ice. Goalies spend the game in and around their net separate from the rest of the team, and they also look different from players because of their larger equipment.

to the unnaturalness or weirdness[4] of a person who plays goal off the ice? The hockey film genre is partially responsible for the promotion and maintenance of the supposed connection between a weird player position on the ice and a weird person off it. In *The Cinema of Hockey*, Iri Cermak (2017) writes, "Films frequently mobilize the goalie role to meet the cinema's need for eccentric or picturesque types because the player's image in popular culture is that of an odd duck" (p. 249). Weird goalies are a staple in the hockey film genre[5] and while their behaviour usually marks them as different in films directed for adult audiences, a quick and easy visual signifier to mark goalies as different in children's films is through sex. The girl goaltender, on a boys' team, is a common trope in children's hockey films, and it is her sex, rather than her behaviour, that marks her as different. Girl goaltenders in film actually work against the genre convention of the goaltender-as-comic-relief since girl goaltenders tend to be quite serious and not a source of humour, which creates the troubling calculus of women in hockey as out of place or unnatural.

My chapter focuses on girl goaltenders Julie Morneau in *Les Pee-Wee 3D: L'hiver qui a changé ma vie* (2012),[6] and Julie 'The Cat' Gaffney in *The Mighty Ducks* (1992-1996), and comparatively draws from their respective goalie partners, Bissonnette and Greg Goldberg.[7] Hockey goaltenders, in film, exist in the liminal space of being on the team but not fully belonging to the team or, put another way, players are taken as the norm and goalies are treated as deviations from this norm. The tenuous relationship of goaltender to players/team is often made visual through girl goaltenders, and in *Les Pee-Wee 3D* and *The Mighty Ducks* trilogy the goaltender battle, for the starting position, between a female and male goalie helps elucidate who can belong on the team. Goaltenders in the hockey film genre are treated as sites of arrested development; they are portrayed as more feminine than forwards and defencemen, and in the sports film genre femininity tends to be denigrated and treated as regressive. However, in *Les Pee-Wee 3D* and *The Mighty Ducks* trilogy the male goaltenders are able to grow out of their arrested development by the end of the film while the girl goaltenders remain stuck in their gender and sex. The main storyline for both Bissonnette (*Les Pee-Wee 3D*) and Goldberg (*The Mighty Ducks*) is about them overcoming their fear of being hit/hurt by the puck and their movement from

---

[4] I use 'weird' and 'unnatural' largely interchangeably throughout my paper since hockey films, especially comedies, tend to equate the unnatural position of the goaltender with a person who is weird or not quite right, or put another way not quite natural and thus, in a sense, unnatural.

[5] Some of the more well-known examples are Denis Lemieux in Hill, G. R. (Director). (1977). *Slap Shot* [Film]. Universal Pictures, Greg Goldberg in *The Mighty Ducks* trilogy, Marco 'Belchie' Belchoir in the Dowse, M. (Director). (2011). *Goon* [Film]. Alliance Films, and Jacques 'Le Coq' Grande in Schnabel, M. (Director). (2008). *The Love Guru* [Film]. Paramount Pictures.

[6] *Les Pee Wee 3D* is a French language film and so the quotes I include are translated into English.

[7] *Les Pee-Wee 3D* is heavily inspired by *The Mighty Ducks*, not in terms of plot but rather genre tropes (especially concerning the goalie), so the name Julie Morneau is likely an homage to the girls from the Ducks trilogy: 'Julie' referencing the Ducks' girl goaltender and 'Morneau' is extremely similar to the last name of the other female Duck, Connie Moreau.

femininity to a goaltender masculinity. In other words, to grow up in these films means to grow into masculinity. The association of growth with masculinity, and thereby femininity with a lack of growth or regression, is obviously a troubling formula, but it is even more troubling considering that sex equals gender in children's sports films, and so girls are prevented from growing into masculinity because they are already read as feminine despite not embodying or performing femininity, i.e., Morneau and Gaffney are both tomboys. Compounding on this gendered problematic, the sports genre is quite pedagogic and teams need to learn a lesson and grow from the start to the end of the film if they are to earn the climatic win. So if girls cannot grow, they cannot win. Sex and gender are sites of arrested development for Morneau and Gaffney in their films, which is embodied in how Bissonette and Goldberg win the climatic game while Morneau and Gaffney do not.[8] My paper is divided into two sections: my first section focuses on the feminine male goalies, Bissonette and Goldberg, while my second section focuses on the female goalies, Morneau and Gaffney. In section one, I argue that the goaltender is constructed as a feminine position in the hyper masculine game of hockey, and show how Bissonette and Goldberg learn a masculinity that is not available to Morneau and Gaffney because they are women. My second section argues that these films portray hockey as a site of "cruel optimism" for girls, a term queer theorist Lauren Berlant (2011) coins to describe "an enabling object that is also disabling" (p. 25). In these films, the girl goaltenders fail the central themes of their respective movies, while the rest of the team fulfills them, and so these films suggest neither Morneau nor Gaffney can properly grow or have a future in hockey; they are stuck in their sex, which in sports films is so often a site of arrested development. Since sports films tend to be extremely (hetero)normative and pedagogic, in my conclusion I ask what these films teach us about being a girl goalie in hockey. In this chapter, I argue that these films focus on bringing goalies in-line with the rest of the team by promoting a conformity to player normality. Boys are able to overcome their femininity by (l)earning masculinity and thereby being brought closer to the team/norm; however, Morneau and Gaffney are not able to overcome their femaleness and so remain as deviations from the line. The difference between femininity and femaleness in these films, is the difference between fulfilling or failing the theme of the movie and the future happiness that the big climatic win so often implies. I ultimately posit that in the calculus of gender in children's hockey films, it seems that girls can only ever lose, even if they win.

---

[8] Gaffney is in net for the final win and I explain later in the chapter how Gaffney still loses when the Ducks win.

The Feminine Goaltender

A hockey goaltender's performance is based on traits traditionally framed as feminine, and in film what makes the goaltender weird or different from the rest of their team is often their comparative femininity, as shown through the effeminate figures of Goldberg and Bissonette and then more obviously through the female characters of Gaffney and Morneau. To clarify, I am not arguing that goaltenders as people are feminine, but rather that the role of the goaltender itself is implicitly feminine; the position, regardless of who is in net, embodies an assemblage of attributes that are culturally constructed as feminine.9 In *The Male Body*, Susan Bordo (1999) notes that "[i]nviting, receiving, responding" are understood as feminine while masculinity is "that which takes, invades, aggresses" and that "[t]hese hierarches date back to the ancient Greeks, who believed that passivity, receptivity, penetrability were marks of inferior feminine being" (p. 190). When the qualities Bordo identifies as masculine and feminine are applied to hockey, forwards and defencemen occupy a more aggressive masculine position, since they fight the other team for the puck and try to "invade" the opponent's end and net; whereas, the goaltender inhabits a more feminine position, since they are receptive subjects who respond to the opponent's attacks. Moreover, goalies are also usually penetrated by the puck several times a game as the puck goes past or through them and enters the net, which in restrictive (hetero)normative understandings of gender further marks goaltenders as feminine, since to be "'penetrated' or 'invaded' by others" is to be "a feminised body" (Ahmed 2015, p. 2). Thus, goalies are the invaded or penetrated [10] while players are the invaders or penetrators, so in the restrictive calculus of hockey gender, forwards and defencemen occupy more masculine positions, while the goaltenders occupy more feminine ones.

Additionally, even though hockey is a hypermasculine game, the goaltender does not fulfill the ideals that mark hockey as masculine. Sports sociologist Brian Pronger (1999b) writes, "The most masculine competitive sports are those that are the most explicitly spatially dominating" (p. 382). In fact, "[i]t is precisely this capacity to dominate that is at the core of many men's traditional ideals of masculinity" (Gruneau and Whitson, 1993, p. 196). However, goalies cannot truly spatially dominate their opponents because their role is to protect the net and stop the puck. The rules also

---

[9] It is worth mentioning that goalies should be coded as masculine based on their size. In her book on masculinity in sport, Varda Burstyn (1999) notes that "bigness itself has become crucial to the signification of masculinity in relation to femininity" (p. 149). Similarly, William Arens (1974) argues that football equipment is an amplification of masculinity (p. 79) and Jason Blake (2010) makes a similar point about hockey player equipment (p. 86-87). Goaltenders have the biggest equipment in hockey but not the same masculine aura. The fact that the perceived gender performance of a goaltender overrides the size/masculine formulation thereby points to the potency of the goalie's feminine subjecthood.

[10] Goalies can score goals, but they are exceptionally rare in high level hockey and only seven goalies have scored, rather than been credited with, goals on an empty net in the NHL.

restrict goalies' movements and thus their ability to "dominate." The *National Hockey League Official Rules 2019-2020* states that goalies are not allowed to play the puck past the center ice line (2019, Rule 27.7) and cannot play the puck outside of the trapezoid behind their net (2019, Rule 27.8). [11] Goalies cannot dominate their opponents spatially nor can they do so physically; goalies rarely leave their crease to check other players and players are forbidden from checking goaltenders, even if the goalie is outside of their crease (2019, Rule 69.4). [12] Moreover, "goalies traditionally do not fight" (Hughes-Fuller, 2002, p. 190). This further marks goalies as the dominated rather than the dominating, [13] which in the calculus of normative understandings of gender ties goaltenders to more restrictive and traditional notions of femininity. Furthermore, sports sociology Mary Louise Adams (2013) writes, "In the world of sport, contact is one thing that segregates male and female athletes and that often distinguishes 'masculine' and 'feminine' sports" (p. 520). Therefore, in a sport about dominating an opponent physically, spatially, and on the scoreboard, hockey goalies are unable to dominate their opponents and thus unable to participate in the culturally constructed notions of masculinity; this along with the goaltender's "passivity, receptivity, penetrability," and their tendency to react rather than act all congeal inside the goaltender's body to decidedly mark them as feminine subjects in a hypermasculine game. In other words, goaltenders are playing a feminine game inside a masculine sport.

Moreover, I take the goaltender's shuffle [14] as representative of their inability to fulfill the culturally constructed ideas of what makes a man/player masculine (i.e. scoring, hitting, dominating, aggression). Or put another way, the goaltender's shuffle, with its side to side movements, is a tool to understand the goaltender as a site of arrested development in the arena of hockey, which is most explicit in their feminine portrayal in the hockey film genre. On the ice, goaltenders tend to shuffle, or move side to side, more than they tend to skate forward. So while hockey is a more vertical game for players, it is a more horizontal game for goalies, which is reflected in the dimensions of the rink, goal net, and goal crease, all of which are wider than they are long or tall. [15]

---

[11] Goalies are the only players whose movement is truly restricted. Players can enter the goalie's crease they just cannot interfere with the goalie (2019, Rule 69.1).

[12] There are also several unspoken rules in high-level hockey, sometimes referred to as "The Code," about not hitting the opponent's goalie and if you do to expect retaliation.

[13] Hockey goaltender Dominik Hašek's nickname was "The Dominator" but it was because he was hard to score on not because he was an aggressive goalie.

[14] Retired goaltender, Corey Hirsch (2007) describes the shuffle as when the goalie "stay[s] in their stance moving sideways they do this by sliding their outside skate along the ice while pushing the opposite foot" (para. 5).

[15] The official rink size listed in the *National Hockey League Official Rules 2019-2020* is two hundred feet long and eighty-five feet wide (2019, Rule 1.2) while the official size of the goaltender's net is four feet high and six feet wide (2019, Rule 2.1) and the official size of the goal crease is eight feet wide and six feet long at the highest point of the semi-circle's radius (2019, Rule 1.7).

The goaltender's horizontal movements on the ice help signal their inability to move forward or become a "proper" masculine man in hockey films. Cermak (2017) notes the goaltender is characterized "as a peculiar sort whose antics resemble the benevolent trickerism of the child" (p. 249). However, to push this further, in hockey films goaltenders not only resemble the "trickerism of the child" but simply resemble the immaturity of the child. In hockey films, the goaltender's weirdness and effeminacy is a way to show they are not proper, meaning masculine, men, and to show goaltenders are stuck in a regressive femininity. Pronger (1999a) writes, "In our culture, gender is a kind of prison" (186), which is amplified in such a gendered and restrictive arena as sport. But to paraphrase Pronger, for goaltenders in hockey films, gender is a kind of crease: goalies are stuck in a feminine position on the ice that marks them as weird, childish, or victims of arrested development, and goalies can skate side to side in this crease, but they cannot properly and fully grow out of it until they embrace a masculinity that is only ever afforded to hockey forwards and defencemen; as such the goaltender position in film, particularly for girl goalies, is a site of Berlant's cruel optimism, which I will return to in the second section of this paper.

Shuffling sideways characterizes the arrested development of the goaltender in hockey media. Gender and cultural theorist Elspeth Probyn (1996) considers "desire as movement" as desire moves us and propels us to move towards that which we desire (p. 41). Yet, goaltenders are confined in and around their crease on the ice, which in the taxonomy of hockey films aligns them more with stagnation than growth. Shuffling sideways is the term I use to signal the arrested development of the goaltender in hockey films, and the cruel optimism in the belief that they will grow, and borrows its idea of "sideways growth" from Kathryn Bond Stockton's *The Queer Child*. Stockton (2009) notes how "[c]hildren grow sideways as well as up—or so I will say—in part because they cannot, according to our concepts, advance to adulthood until we say it's time" (6). Similarly, in film, hockey goaltenders do grow but their growth is rarely read as growth because it is outside the framework of acceptable hockey masculinity. The goalie is already significantly deviant from definitions of proper hockey masculinity, and so when goalies grow they do not grow up but rather grow closer to the line of hockey player masculinity. In Canada, hockey has "a traditional role as a training ground for masculinity" (Gruneau and Whitson, 1993, p. 195), just as sport more broadly is "a 'school for masculinity" (Burtstyn, 1999, p. 5). Stockton (2009) envisions the child "grow[ing] to the side of cultural ideals" (p. 13), or a movement *out* and away from the imagined line of growth, while I envision growth in hockey goaltenders as a movement *in* and towards the imagined line of growth, which in hockey is masculinity. So just as a goalie shuffles sideways, a goalie also grows sideways. In other words, hockey goaltenders' growth is rarely read as growth unless it is about goalies learning how to properly perform a goaltender's lessened version of masculinity; such is the case with Goldberg and Bissonette as their growth, or even their personhood as males, is not readable until it is in masculine terms. Moreover, these players grow but they do not grow up; goalies grow closer to the imagined line of proper masculinity, but their achievement of embodying masculinity is always belated. However, while Goldberg and Bissonette can and do grow up, and thereby win the big concluding game in their films, Morneau and Gaffney do not because sex for girls is treated as a site of arrested development and cruel optimism. In the calculus of these films, Morneau and Gaffney are destined to shuffle sideways. They may grow but it is never read as growth; they may dream of belonging and winning but these dreams are continually delayed.

The alignment of unnaturalness with femininity inside the goaltender's body is a troubling taxonomy that suggests femininity is unnatural in hockey, and therefore females are unnatural in hockey. And in *Les Pee-Wee 3D* and *The Mighty Ducks* trilogy, femininity is something that the male goalies must overcome. At the start of *Les Pee-Wee 3D* and *The Mighty Ducks*, Bissonette and Goldberg are afraid of the puck and they recoil from shots to avoid getting hit. For instance, in *The Mighty Ducks*, Coach Bombay ties Goldberg, in full goalie equipment, to a hockey net and has the Ducks fire pucks at Goldberg to show him that getting hit does not hurt. As Bombay is tying Goldberg to the net, he says, "This is your Bar Mitzvah, Goldberg. Today you will become a man," to which Goldberg responds, "Coach, I think you got the ceremonies mixed up. It's more like a circumcision" (Herek, 1992). However, it is not Coach Bombay but Goldberg who has his ceremonies mixed up because in hockey the only way to become a man is by performing manhood on the ice; Goldberg emerges from the initiation ceremony as a man before he experiences his Bar Mitzvah, which suggests that hockey identity/masculinity supersedes and displaces religious or cultural identity. Both Bissonette and Goldberg are marked as feminine and therefore poor goalies who must (l)earn masculinity in order to become better goalies; but then where does the intertwinement of masculinity with growth, and femininity with stagnation, leave Morneau and Gaffney? Neither Morneau nor Gaffney are feminine and both are presented as tomboys, so if Morneau and Gaffney are already masculine, how do they become better goalies? Well, the films seem to suggest that they do not. Femininity is a site of arrested development that boys must overcome, but femaleness is a site of arrested development within which girls are stuck. In these films, girl goalies are stuck in the normative crease of gender that forbids them from being read as anything other than female or feminine even when performing masculinity. Thus, the goaltender position in hockey films becomes a site of cruel optimism and arrested development, or what I term shuffling sideways: male goalies shuffle sideways toward an identity/masculinity that they will never fully embody because of the feminine subject position of the goaltender position, while female goalies, because of their sex and player position, are even further from the normative line that they are shuffling sideways towards but will never reach. These films posit that being a girl goaltender is at odds with having a future in the sport, thereby rendering hockey as a site of cruel optimism for these girls as the sport will never return the investment, or more simply the love, they have put into it.

The Cruel Optimism of Girl Goaltenders

This section focuses more on *Les Pee-Wee 3D*, but the ideas for this paper originally occurred to me while re-watching *D3: The Mighty Ducks*. *D3* features Gaffney and Goldberg competing for the starting goaltender position on a new team at a new school and with a new coach. Gaffney wins the starting goaltender position and Goldberg tries to recapture it before the coach moves him to defence. The Ducks win the big climatic game with Gaffney getting a shutout in net, and Goldberg scoring the game winning goal in the dying seconds of the game. So while Goldberg's game winning goal supplants Gaffney's performance, perhaps even suggesting that Goldberg wins the goaltender battle while not even being a goaltender, what renders Gaffney as a site of cruel optimism is that she is excluded from the theme of the movie while Goldberg, along with the film's protagonist Charlie Conway, becomes the very embodiment of the theme. The theme of the third *Mighty Ducks* film is about being open to change and learning from it; this is repeatedly said to the Ducks in various ways from the Dean of the school's welcoming address, to a history teacher's lesson, to a conversation between Conway and Hans, the mentor figure of the first and third *Mighty Ducks* films. Conway complains about his new coach and says, "He doesn't exactly seem open to new learning experiences" to which Hans replies, "Well the question is, are you?" (Lieberman 1996). The Ducks learn to change throughout the latter half of the film as they move from an offensive to defensive team. Moreover, the two characters who exhibit the biggest change are Conway and Goldberg: Conway learns to be less selfish by passing the puck more and by playing more defensively and Goldberg moves from goaltender to defence. In her book on Hollywood sports films, Deborah V. Tudor (1997) writes, "The classical narrative pattern builds toward the final confrontation of the 'big game' which will be won by a heroic gesture" (p. 184). Conway and Goldberg embody the lesson of the movie during the emotional climax when Conway passes the puck to Goldberg, rather than shooting it himself, and Goldberg scores the game winning goal. However, Gaffney is left outside the theme of the movie as she does not change; the other Ducks change by learning to play defensively, but this does not apply to Gaffney since she was never an aggressive goaltender and her style of play does not change. Gaffney is not able to embody the theme of the film and therefore grow. Gaffney is left in the arrested position of being a great goalie, but also a goalie who cannot grow or become better, so she will be left behind. Thus, even when the girl goalie wins, she loses.

In both *Les Pee-Wee 3D* and *The Mighty Ducks* trilogy, the female goalie wins the goaltending battle on the ice, but each girl goalie ends up losing thematically and so hockey becomes a site of cruel optimism for these girls. Berlant (2011) writes, "[C]ruel optimism exists when something you desire is actually an obstacle to your flourishing" (p. 1). Goaltenders are sites of arrested development, girl goalies even more so, and in children's hockey films, hockey is a cruel attachment for girl goalies since hockey is an obstacle to their flourishing; they are excluded from the emotional core of their films and from the thematic lesson that players must learn and enact, and so their growth is forever belated and something they continually shuffle sideways towards without ever achieving.

In *D3: The Mighty Ducks* Gaffney is left outside the film's theme, but in *Les Pee-Wee 3D* Morneau's goal in the film, her storyline, is overtaken by the film's protagonist, Janeau Trudel. In other words, in *D3*, Gaffney is excluded from the film's theme while in *Les Pee-Wee 3D*, Morneau's personal motivation is overtaken as the theme of the movie for Janeau and the rest of the team. *Les Pee-Wee 3D* follows young Janeau after he moves to a new town and tries to deal with the grief of losing his mother. His new neighbour, Morneau, sees Janeau is a talented player and pushes him to try out for the local hockey team, the St-Hilaire Lynx, to bolster their chances of winning the Quebec International Pee-Wee Hockey Tournament. Morneau is the starting goaltender and the backup, Bissonette, is afraid of the puck and so there should not be a goalie battle, but in a qualifying game for the tournament Morneau gets checked while playing the puck and gets a concussion, which forces her to miss the tournament she always "dreamed" of winning (Tessier, 2012). Morneau is by far the better goalie and is one of the stars of the team. However, Morneau helps teach Bissonette to not be afraid of the puck and he becomes a better goaltender, though not as good as Morneau, and the Lynx go on to win to the tournament with Bissonette in net and Morneau watching from the bench.

Despite *Les Pee-Wee 3D* coming out sixteen years after *D3: The Mighty Ducks*, *Les Pee-Wee 3D* is more regressive in its treatment of sex and its cruel optimism is more apparent. Morneau's injury can be read as her sex's fault, rather than the boy who hit her. When Morneau collides with the player she gets knocked flat on the ice while the boy stays on his feet; he also says that he did not hit and hurt her "on purpose," which could imply it was Morneau's "female frailty"[16] that resulted in her injury (Tessier, 2012). So, when the Lynx win the final game, Morneau is left out on the bench and feels like she did not truly win, as she was not the one in net. In other words, again, even when the team wins the girl goaltender loses. However, the less obvious, but more devastating, loss is Morneau's loss of her "dream" and its transference to Janeau.[17] When Janeau first meets Morneau, one of the first thing she says to him is, "I'll be the first girl goalkeeper in the world to win the Pee-Wee tournament. Listen, I'm going to tell you to your face: it's my dream" (Tessier, 2012). Such a direct address is also an address to the audience to set up Julie's motivation in the film. However, winning the tournament is not Janeau's goal at the beginning of the film; he did not know about the tournament and does not seem to care about winning until later in the film. Instead, Janeau's plotline is about dealing with the grief of losing his mother, reconnecting with a father with whom he is not especially

---

[16] This plays into the pervasive myth that women are frail, which Colette Dowling highlights in her book, *The Frailty Myth*, and how the myth of female frailty persists in sports.

[17] In fact, the hockey plot is transferred from Morneau to Janeau. At the beginning of the film, Janeau is not interested in playing hockey for the Lynx, but Morneau pushes him to try out and motivates him to be a better player.

close, and finding his place in a new town and school, all of which he struggles with throughout the film. The transference of the "dream" plotline to Janeau happens an hour and a half into a two-hour movie, when Janeau's father, who Julie and her mother literally deliver by driving him to the tournament, takes Janeau aside before the championship game and says, "I just want to tell you one thing...you have to dream. Because when you win, you win your dreams... But you have to dream, son. You have to dream" (Tessier, 2012). Janeau's father's direct address mirrors Morneau's earlier address to Janeau. Therefore, since Morneau cannot play hockey, her "dream" plotline is implicitly taken over by Janeau, which then becomes explicit a few scenes later. While the Lynx are sitting in the dressing room during the second intermission in a game they are losing 6-1, Morneau says to the team, "It's my dream to win this tournament, you all know that...Listen, guys, I'm here, I'm here with you. *But this is your game.* It's your game, Éric. It's your tournament" (Tessier, 2012, emphasis mine). Thus, Morneau's dream is given, or taken over, by the boys; while "*this is your game*" refers to the championship game it also reads, and implies, that hockey is not a game for girls. It is also important to note that Morneau's dream was to "be the first girl goalkeeper in the world to win the Pee-Wee tournament," but being the first girl goaltender to win the tournament is parsed down into simply winning the tournament; thus, any trangressiveness of a girl making history is forgotten in lieu of winning a hockey game. The fact that Morneau does not get to fulfil her plotline is not itself problematic, but it is the compiling of other main characters getting to fulfill their plotlines, the ambiguous attribution of her injury to her sex rather than the boy who unfairly hit her, and the overtaking of the dream plotline by Janeau and the rest the boys' team that make this transference problematic. Hockey becomes a site of cruel optimism for Morneau. Berlant (2011) writes, "These kinds of optimistic relations are not inherently cruel. They become cruel only when the object that draws your attachment actively impedes the aim that brought you to it initially" (p. 1). Morneau's love for hockey is not inherently cruel, it is only when she invests her dreams into hockey that it becomes a site of cruel optimism because the movie, and the hockey film genre in general, suggest that hockey is no place for girls and thus Morneau's dreams will never be fulfilled. Even more so, Morneau is not even afforded the role of the motivator who gets to deliver the big rousing speech that inspires the players to come back and win the game. Morneau delivers her speech, and then Janeau delivers his speech and this is the speech that fires up the team and leads them to charge out of the dressing room and onto the ice, leaving Morneau behind, alone and crying. Thus, Morneau becomes less a person and more a motivator for Janeau; she tells him about her dream and the tournament, pushes him to join the team, pushes him to be a better player, then delivers a speech that motivates him to seemingly deliver a more inspiring speech. Morneau becomes a site of liberal inclusion, but this inclusion only reaches so far and it seems it only reaches as far as the bench, as Morneau's is left watching the climatic game from there. Despite, Morneau loving hockey and seemingly investing all her time into the sport, since most of her screen time away from the rink is spent either talking about hockey or practicing, hockey does not love her back and she is not given a future in the sport. In the more serious, adult-oriented sequel *Junior Majeur*, Morneau no longer plays hockey and instead is a student journalist who writes on hockey and is Janeau's love interest, which again points to the shuffle sideways of females in these films:[18] they are always beside the hockey team and no matter how much they try to become a part of the team they never will; hockey acceptance or conformity remains an always belated goal for these female goaltenders.

Hockey becomes an impasse for Morneau because in hockey films, sex is an impasse; Morneau cannot overcome her sex and so she cannot become a man or more masculine, like Bissonette or Goldberg, and win. Berlant (2011) writes, "[I]mpasses in zones of intimacy that hold out the often-cruel promise of reciprocity and belonging to the people who seek them" (p. 21). Hockey is such a zone of intimacy. In both films, hockey is a cruel promise that is imagined to reciprocate the investment of the girl goalies, but instead thematically lets the girls down. Morneau is more a site of liberal inclusion than a character herself and is not even afforded the correct name when the Lynx get new jerseys with nameplates. Julie's last name is Morneau but her nameplate says "Menard,"[19] because Morneau's sex is what matters; sex is proof of the film's liberal inclusivity and not her individuality. Morneau and Gaffney's team win the final games but Morneau and Gaffney do not, and by excluding these two characters from the themes, or dreams, of their movies it is cruel optimism for either Julie to think that hockey will return the emotional investment they have put into it and it is a cruel optimism to think that either player has a future in the sport they love so much.

Conclusion

In hockey films, sex is a site of both arrested development and cruel optimism for girls, particularly for the girl goaltenders on boys' teams. However, it is important to

---

[18] Her shuffle sideways only seems to widen at the end of the sequel. Morneau spends the film wanting to be a hockey journalist, but then at the end of the film tells Janeau she is going to university in France for journalism; the film never addresses why someone so focused on becoming a hockey journalist would study in a country where hockey is not popular. Ultimately, the emotional (and spatial) distance of Morneau from hockey seems to only grow further in the future.

[19] Most of the Lynx players are not introduced or given names, so the last names on the jerseys come from the last names of people who worked on *Les Pee-Wee 3D*: the director Éric Tessier (number 19), writer Emmanuel Joly (7), writer Jean-Sébastien Poirier (45), co-writer Martin Bouchard (16), producer Christian Larouche (55), first assistant director Bissonette Parenteau (44), cinematographer Bernard Couture (43), art director David Pelletier (18), production manager Marie-Ginette Landry (17), and executive producer Valérie Bissonnette (31). Some of these are common French last names and so one or two names may be coincidence, but overall, the last names of the players are clearly drawn from those who worked on the film. However, Morneau is the only character whose name is replaced. Robert Ménard is an executive producer of the film and "Menard" is the name on the back of Julie's jersey. Morneau loses her identity in the final game perhaps because she is on the bench and not playing so she is forgettable, and her name/identity no longer matter.

note that this shuffling sideways is antithetical to the reality of the sport, as most high-level female hockey goalies played boys hockey growing up.[20] So then the question arises, why is there such a disparity between the reality of girl goalies and their representations in film? Or if, as Rick Altman (1999) notes, "film genres are *functional* for their society" (p. 26) then what is the function of the hockey film genre, and its treatment of gender? Carly Adams and Jason Laurendeau (2018) write, "Hockey was—and remains—a social location for the indoctrination of young boys into the codes of masculine behaviour" (p. 113). However, Adams and Laurendeau's calculus can also be applied to sports films. Hockey, and sports, films are similarly such a social location, but their pedagogy is usually more implicit. A central theme of the hockey film genre is masculinity. This is why so many popular hockey films focus on fighters rather than skill players, which is also apparent in the films I discuss, particularly in Bissonette and Goldberg's storylines. Hockey films are a vehicle for the promotion of hockey masculinity; this excludes goaltender masculinity and women, regardless of gender performance. Children's hockey films implicitly promote the idea that women do not belong in hockey, or, like goaltenders themselves, are unnatural. Thus, the girl goaltender is a problematic assemblage of femininity, unnaturalness, femaleness, and weirdness, which thereby somewhat equates, or at the very least associates, these ideas with one another. In Deborah V. Tudor's *Hollywood's Vision of Team Sports* (1997), she writes, "Part of the ideological work of sports films is to provide a space for resolution of family and gender problems sports as a structure which recreates, restores and reaffirms the familial and gender organization of Western culture" (p. 79). So, while these films do include girls, their inclusivity only goes so far, and they ultimately reaffirm hockey as a masculine game for boys to become men. Or put another way, the arrested development of girl goaltenders is tied to their gender: in hockey they can only move up so far, or they can only shuffle sideways for so long and so close. According to these films, no matter how good a female goalie is they are destined to fail; they are stuck in the arrested development and cruel optimism of shuffling sideways toward a love, or return, they will seemingly never receive. *Les Pee-Wee 3D* and *The Mighty Ducks* trilogy offer an implicit didactic lesson: to be a woman in a man's game is to lose, no matter how good you are, and while there may be some room for girls among boys on the ice, there is no room for women among men.

---

[20] For instance, at the most recent Olympics all the goaltenders for the American (Alex Rigsby, Maddie Rooney, Alex Hensley) and Canadian teams (Genevieve Lacasse, Ann-Renée Desbien, Shannon Szabados) played boys hockey at various levels growing up. Additionally, most of the women who have played professional men's hockey have been goalies, such as: Danielle Dube, Kelly Dyer, Viona Harrer, Claudia van Leeuwen, Meeri Räisänen, Noora Räty, Florence Schelling, Shannon Szabados, Erin Whitten, and most famously Manon Rhéaume. Similarly, many goalies in the National Women's Hockey League, and the Professional Women's Hockey Players Association played boys' hockey at some point growing up.

REFERENCES

Adams, C., & Laurendeau, J. (2018). 'Here they come! Look them over!': Youth, Citizenship, and the Emergence of Minor Hockey in Canada. In J. Ellison & J. Anderson (Eds.), *Hockey: Challenging Canada's Game/Au-delà du sport national*, (pp. 111-124). Canadian Museum of History/University of Ottawa Press.

Adams, M. L. (2013). No Taste for Rough-and-Tumble Play: Sport Discourses, the DSM, and the Regulation of Effeminacy. *GLQ: A Journal of Lesbian and Gay Studies: The Athletic Issue, 19*(4), 515–544.

Ahmed, S. (2015). *The Cultural Politics of Emotion* (2nd ed.). University of Edinburgh Press.

Altman, R. (1999). *Film/Genre*. BFI Publishing.

Anderson, E. (2010). *Sport, Theory and Social Problems: A Critical Introduction*. Routledge.

Arens, W. (1975). The Great American Football Ritual. *Natural History, 84*, 72–80.

Berlant, L. (2011). *Cruel Optimism*. Duke University Press.

Blake, J. (2010). *Canadian Hockey Literature: A Thematic Study*. University of Toronto Press.

Bordo, S. (1999) *The Male Body: A New Look at Men in Public and in Private*. Farrar, Straus and Giroux.

Burstyn, V. (1999) *The Rites of Men: Manhood, Politics, and the Culture of Sports*. University of Toronto Press.

Cermak, I. (2017). *The Cinema of Hockey: Four Decades of the Game on Screen*. McFarland & Company.

Dowling, C. (2001). *The Frailty Myth: Redefining the Physical Potential of Women and Girls*. Random House.

Dowse, M. (Director). (2011). *Goon* [Film]. Alliance Films.

Dryden, K. (2013). *The Game: 30th Anniversary Edition*. Harper Collins.

Hughes-Fuller, H. P. (2002). *The Good Old Game: Hockey, Nostalgia, Identity*. (Doctoral Dissertation). Retrieved from ProQuest Dissertations & Theses Global. NQ81202.

Gruneau, R., & Whitson, D. (1993) *Hockey Night in Canada: Sport, Identities, and Cultural Politics*. Garamond Press.

Herek, S. (Director). (1992). *The Mighty Ducks* [Film]. Walt Disney Pictures.

Hill, G. R. (Director). (1977). *Slap Shot* [Film]. Universal Pictures.

Hirsch, C. (2007, October 15). *Teaching a Beginner Goaltender*. Hockey Canada. https://www.hockeycanada.ca/en-ca/news/2007-gn-066-en.

Hobsbawn, E. (2016). Introduction: Inventing Traditions. In Bissonnette Hobsbawn & Terrence Ranger (Eds.), *The Invention of Tradition*, (pp. 1-14). Cambridge University Press. (Original work published 1983).

Huizinga, J. (1955) *Homo Ludens: A Study of the Play-Element of Culture*. Beacon Press. (Original work published 1938).

Lieberman, R. (Director). (1996). *D3: The Mighty Ducks* [Film]. Walt Disney Pictures.

National Hockey League. (2019). *National Hockey League Official Rules 2019-2020*. https://nhl.bamcontent.com/images/assets/binary/308893668/binary-file/file.pdf

Probyn, E. (1996). *Outside Belongings*. Routledge.

Pronger, B. (1999a). Fear and Trembling: Homophobia in Men's Sport. In P. White & K. Young (Eds.), *Sport and Gender in Canada*, (pp. 182–196). Oxford University Press. 1999.

Pronger, B. (1999b). Outta My Endzone: Sport and the Territorial Anus. *Journal of Sport & Social Issues, 23*(4), 373–389.

Schnabel, M. (Director). (2008). *The Love Guru* [Film]. Paramount Pictures.

Stockton, K. B. (2009). *The Queer Child or Growing Sideways in the Twentieth Century*. Duke University Press.

Tessier, É. (Director). (2017). *Junior Majeur* [Film]. Christal Films.

Tessier, É. (Director). (2012). *Les Pee-Wee 3D: L'hiver qui a changé ma vie* [Film]. Christal Films.

Tudor, D. V. (1997). *Hollywood's Vision of Team Sports: Heroes, Race, and Gender*. Garland Publishing.

Weisman, S. (Director). (1994). *D2: The Mighty Ducks* [Film]. Walt Disney Pictures.

Chapter 6

Jocks and Nerds: The Role of Sport in the North American Education System

Tom Fabian

> Body, shape, extension, movement and place are chimeras. So, what remains
> true? Perhaps just the one fact that nothing is certain.
> —Descartes, 1641/2017, p. 20; §24

The symbolism and symbiosis of duality is a fundamental dynamic of human society. According to Rintala (1991), "Western civilization has a philosophical tradition based upon dualisms and dichotomies" (p. 260). Examples include self-other, us-them, good-evil, left-right, male-female, true-false, fight-flight, part-whole, subject-object, and the list can go on. One such influential dichotomy was posited by seventeenth-century French philosopher René Descartes, the concept of mind-body dualism. Also known as substance dualism, the Cartesian position is that mind (brain) and matter (body) are two distinct and separable substances. This dialectic is often assumed within pedagogical theories of physical education, the education of both mind and body. More broadly, mind-body duality is observed through the social institutions of sport and education. Sport acts as a conduit for bodily expression, while education is the curator of the mind. Thus, physical education, along with the popularly held notion that sport is an educational tool and the popularization of the varsity sport industry, encompass the bridge between the sportive and educational establishments. However, within this sport-education complex, a "duelity" exists, a cultural opposition, between the body and mind.

The crux of the matter is epitomized in the juxtaposition of the educational missions of schools, colleges, and universities and the increasing significance of North American varsity athletic programs. In the mission statement of my institution, St. Francis Xavier University (n.d.), for instance, nowhere does it state that sport is an integral part of the educational process: "To provide quality education and research opportunities that prepare students to explore the world while inspiring them to become passionate about our disciplines, and to conduct research and provide services that are relevant and meaningful for the academic community and society." The mission statements of most universities are written in similar terms. Although, even with a rich sporting history, a small, liberal arts college in Maritime Canada, such as St. Francis Xavier, pales in comparison to the 'Power Five' conferences in the United States.[1] These university athletic conferences, with an onus on successful football programs, are the apex of the commercial behemoth that is the National Collegiate Athletic Association (NCAA) (Frazier, 2016). Examples that illustrate the opulence of this system include NCAA revenues of over $1 billion for the 2016-17 academic year (Rovell, 2018), a 24-hour ESPN network dedicated to broadcasting University of Texas Longhorns sports worth $11 million per year until 2031 (Fetchke et al., 2016), or the lavish $28 million locker room of the Louisiana State University football team, replete with individual sleeping pods, a mini-theatre, and pool (Licata, 2019). Although not all American, and almost no Canadian, varsity programs are guilty of this level of extravagance, it begs the question: What is the purpose of sport in higher education? As will be argued throughout this chapter, sport and education represent a duality that is difficult to rationalise.

The dynamic relationship, or duality, between sport and education is what I term the sport-education complex. Similar, in concept, to the sports-media complex (Jhally, 1984), wherein the internal organization of higher education has been fundamentally altered by its affiliation with sport, the sport-education complex can be considered an important symbiotic partnership in North American society. Three key aspects of this complex will be elaborated on in this study to highlight the indelible nexus between sport and education. First, there are many proponents of the social and educational benefits of sport participation, which require further scrutiny and dissection. Second, since the onset and proliferation of physical education, those inside academia have criticized it by using Descartes' theory of mind-body dualism. Third, an examination of the prominent position held by varsity athletics within institutions of higher learning points to a dissonance in academic priorities. As I will argue, the sport-education complex is a clash of cultures, in which sport is lauded as an educational tool, physical education is derided as an afront to academia, and varsity athletics undermine the educational mission of the institution.

Sport Participation Motives: Survival, Socialization, Education

Although Guttmann's model (1978) for the characteristics of modern sport tells us much about the development of sport as a practice, it tells us less about the motivations to participate.[2] At the risk of oversimplifying the history of participatory motivations, ancient sport was linked to survival and warfare, medieval sport revolved around socialization, and the purpose of modern sport was meant to impart values and

---

[1] The 'Power Five' comprise the Atlantic Coast (ACC), Big 10, Big 12, Pac-12, and Southeastern (SEC) Conferences.
[2] Allen Guttmann's oft-quoted seven characteristics of modern sport are: secularism, equality, bureaucratization, specialization, rationalization, quantification, and the pursuit of records.

virtues upon the participants. Contemporary sport participation motives, in turn, are twofold: (1) Economic advancement via the conduit of professional sport, and (2) the development of physical, social, and life skills through youth sport programs. The latter motivation encompasses the educational aspects of sport participation, especially among youth athletes, and espouses the belief that 'sport builds character.' Although there are many positive outcomes of youth sport participation in the twenty-first century, the onus on overcomformity has led some scholars to imply that there is an inherent "positive deviance" in the youth sport system (Hughes & Coakley, 1991).[3] As such, even within the innocent educational moments praised as the foundation of this system, a conflict arises questioning what, in fact, young people are actually 'taking away' and internalizing from their involvement in youth sport programs. For instance, young boys are often praised for learning new skills, such as catching a ball or effectively communicating, but praise is also imparted for a 'good' body check, a gloating celebration, or justified violence for the honour of one's teammate. In youth sport, there is a fine line between learning bodily movements and overconformity to a deviant system.

The history of sport participation has evolved, over thousands of years, from a necessity of subsistence to a means of social control. Much of what we would consider today as sport was once a skill needed for survival. For instance, among the Inuit and Dene Indigenous communities of Northern Canada, "most traditional northern games and contests developed not so much as sport and entertainment, but as preparation for life and survival on both physical and psychic levels" (Jones, 1989, p. 62).[4] Other early sporting activities, such as Indigenous snowshoeing and canoeing, Mongol archery and wrestling, or the ancient Olympic Games can all be categorized as survival, or martial, skills. Later, during the Middle Ages and Renaissance in Europe, motivation to participate in sport shifted to socialization with members of one's own class (Huggins, 2008). For example, upper classes partook in hunting, while lower classes engaged in folk football. Then, within the context of the Industrial Revolution, sport was modernized in the British public school system and, among educators, there was "substantial subscription to the belief in the value of games in education" (Mangan, 2010, p. 242). Within this brief history, it can be gleaned that sport participation has served a number of motivations, such as survival skill development, socialization with peers, and molder of virtuous men, and the notion of sport as an educational tool resonates to this day.

By the end of the nineteenth century, as modern sport was developing into a global phenomenon, sport administrators, notably, Modern Olympic Games founder,

---

[3] Often observed in organized sport, overconformity is a deviant behaviour referring to an uncritical acceptance of norms without question or qualification, and often leading to mental health, family life, chronic pain, and socialization issues. Examples including hazing (initiation) rituals, 'playing through the pain,' or fighting in hockey.
[4] The Arctic Winter Games, founded in 1969, still pay homage to these traditional games every two years.

Pierre de Coubertin, were "motivated to improve the education and personal development of young people through sport participation" (Gould & Carson, 2008a, p. 287). As such, today, many sport psychologists attribute sport with the ability to develop life skills (Bredemeier & Shields, 1986; Brunelle et al., 2007; Danish et al., 1993; Danish, 2002; Danish et al., 2004; Danish et al., 2005; Fraser-Thomas et al., 2005; Gould et al., 2006; Gould & Carson, 2008a, 2008b; McCallister et al., 2000; Papacharisis et al., 2005; Petitpas et al., 2004). Life skills are defined as skills that enable individuals to thrive in education, the workforce, and their lived environments, and are categorized by Theokas et al. (2008) as "behavioral (taking turns) or cognitive (making good decisions), interpersonal (communicating effectively) or intrapersonal (setting goals)" (p. 72). Some of the life skills that can be learned through sport include teamwork, fair play, leadership, respect for rules and authority, time management, communication, decisive action, managing conflict, dealing with failure, and developing networks (Whitehead et al., 2013). Even in relatively unorganized contexts, such as on the playground, Sutherland and Gosteva (2019) conclude that "apparently simple play activities may offer multiple opportunities for exploration of diverse social behaviours, including co-operation, competition, conflict and aggression" (p. 35). Albeit, simply participating in sport does little to impart life skills; rather it is the intention of the sport facilitators or organizations that can bear fruit in terms of educational outcomes. As Ewing et al. (2002) ask: "How many youth sports programs are designed to teach physical, social, moral, and educational benefits so often attributed to sport participation" (p. 43)? The widespread intentionality of such programs, however, is more likely catered to enjoyment and sportive outcomes, instead of educational ones. As a result, some scholars, such as Doty (2006), for instance, adamantly oppose the notion that sport builds character, in and of itself, pointing to a negative relationship between participation in sports and character development. Others compromise, arguing that "competitive sport may be 'naturally suited' for teaching initiative, teamwork and social skills, but less well suited for teaching exploration and identity work, emotional self-regulation, peer relationships and knowledge, and developing connections to an adult network and acquiring social capital" (Holt & Sehn, 2008, p. 28). This line of thinking, which weakens the previously-held view of sport as an educational tool, is based in conflict theory (Oglesby, 1974; Eitzen, 1988; Crone 1999), and adheres to the notion that sport actually promotes, rather than supresses, deviant behaviours stemming from the psychological ramifications of parental pressures, early specialization, and overconformity.[5]

The first counterargument to the 'sport as educational tool' rhetoric is the often-exploited parent-child relationship in youth sport, a supposed bastion of educational

---

[5] Conflict theory assumes that there are inequalities between groups within a society. Based on Karl Marx's notions of capitalism and class conflict, conflict theory holds that power and economic domination maintain the social order.

opportunities. A large proportion of volunteer coaches in the youth sport system are often parents of children on the team and, therefore, the system itself is based on the whims and motivations of parents, not necessarily the youth themselves. However, many parents are inadequately prepared to appropriately bridge the dual roles of both parent and coach, often blurring the line and causing feelings of anxiety for their child-athlete. Although parents may appear to have a keen understanding of the motivations for youth sport participation, Marsh et al. (2015) conclude that parents are often unclear about how to effectively become involved in their children's sporting life. Nevertheless, parental involvement is often influenced by the "parents' past experiences in sport and as a sport parent; their beliefs, goals, and values; the youth sport context; and concerns regarding other parents, coaches, and their own behavior on their involvement in their children's sport" (Knight et al., 2016, p. 176). This conflict between not knowing how to be involved and becoming involved based on parent-centric motives leads to a contentious parent-child relationship with numerous adverse effects. For instance, in a seminal study on this relationship, Weiss and Fretwell (2005) observed "incidences of pressure, high expectations, conflict, criticism, lack of empathy, negative feelings, rebellious behaviour, and preferential treatment," which supported previous theories about the negative influence of parent-coaches on "youth's feelings of anxiety, doubts about competence, and reduced enjoyment of and motivation to participate in the activity" (p. 300). As a result, these negative consequences of parental involvement in youth sport can often undermine the potential for the development of non-sport skills, notably, social, psychological, and life skills. Therefore, parental involvement in youth sport, albeit a necessity, can disrupt the educational potential of sport participation.

The second hindrance to sport as an educational tool is the negative psychological effects of early sport specialization. Within the characteristics of Guttmann's aforementioned model (1994), specialization is a key aspect of modern sport, an expertise that many youth athletes are consciously striving towards. As explained by Malina (2010), contributing factors to early specialization in the North American youth sporting system include: (1) Perceptions of such behaviour in former Communist bloc sport programs, (2) parental pressures, (3) the 'child prodigy' label, (4) targeting college athletic scholarships, (5) the financial benefits of a potential professional career, (6) sporting goods industry marketing and advertisement efforts, and (7) academic research on the development of sporting excellence, often conducted by sport psychologists. The opportunity to capitalize on a robust professional sports market, through the early specialization of athletic skills, with the potential to develop an exceptional talent, exemplifies the indelible capitalist ethos of the contemporary sports industry. However, in recent years, there have been a multitude of studies highlighting the psychological detriments of early sport specialization Baker, 2003; Baker et al., 2009; Brenner, 2016; Gould, 2010; Hecimovich, 2004, Hill & Hansen, 1988; Horn, 2015; Jayanthi et al., 2013; Malina, 2010; McFadden et al., 2016; Myer et al., 2015; Normand et al., 2017; Padaki et al., 2017; Russell & Symonds, 2015; Russell et al., 2017; Smith, 2015; Waldron et al., 2020; Wiersma, 2000. Some of the more notable psychosocial outcomes of early specialization include burnout, intrinsic amotivation, high sport stress, decreased resilience, and low perceived social support (Waldron et al., 2020). Similar to the psychosocial consequences of parental involvement, early specialization, a hallmark of the North American youth sporting system, significantly deters the positive educational outcomes promoted as the prime motivator for youth sport participation.

The third, and last, afront to the belief of sport as an educational tool is the pervasiveness of deviance in contemporary sporting culture. Sefiha (2012) postulates that "deviant behavior emerges from the organization and dynamics endemic to sports cultures and the meanings athletes assign to their participation in this arena" (p. 950). The aspect of deviance that most challenges the sport-education complex is the notion of overconformity, whereby athletes adhere to subcultural norms inherent in the 'sport ethic,' such as "willing to pay the price, strive for distinction, accept risks, and exceed limits" (Hughes & Coakley, 1991, p. 322). With the aforementioned motivations for participation in youth sport, and the propensity for early sport specialization in North America, the risks of overconformity are heightened. As argued by pioneering sport sociologist Stanley Eitzen (1988), sport is a microcosm of society, where the powerful coerce dissenters to conform or face punishment (p. 194). Overconforming behaviours that limit athlete autonomy (e.g., hazing rituals) or moral agency (e.g., playing through pain), and are often associated with team subcultures, diminish the opportunities for the development of ethical perspectives, which are affiliated with the sport-education complex.

The dynamic interplay between sport and education in society starts with the role that sport can play as an educational tool. Modern, organized sport, as we know it today, was incubated in nineteenth-century educational institutions, such as British public schools, laden with values and lessons thought to mold virtuous leaders of tomorrow. Further promulgated by international sport leaders at the onset of the globalizing twentieth century, sport participation was upheld as an educational tool. Life skills, such as teamwork, discipline, and communication, are still considered pillars of the youth sporting system. However, endemic to these character-building traits are subtle deviant behaviours, such as parental pressure, early specialization, and overconformity, that undermine the core educational principles of sport. In this first aspect of the sport-education complex, a duelity exists between youth sport stakeholders, who promote the virtues of sport participation, and conflict theorists, like Stanley Eitzen, who understand the power plays, capitalist underpinnings, and deviant nature of the contemporary sports industry. As such, a more theoretical, pedagogical, and systematic approach is required to reconcile the social institutions of education and sports. In effect, the field of physical education was developed for exactly such a function.

The Scholar-Athlete: A Jock Among Nerds?

Physical education is so much more than mere 'gym class.' Although often derided as an 'easy grade' for 'jockular' types, a stressor for the 'bookish,' and a break from the academic rigours of deskwork, physical education reformers have been attempting to position the discipline as an alternative way of learning. By the 1940s, physical educationists were shifting the discourse from bodily exercise to learning through exercise. For instance, in a speech to physical educators, Sven Korning declared that it was "not physical education, but an education by physical means" (Gidney, 2015, p. 165), while Canadian intercollegiate sport administrator Maurice Van Vliet wrote that "university students should not be forced to educate the physical but should be educated through the physical" (Lamont, 1988, p. 29). Around the same time, Earle Zeigler began a prolific career as a founding scholar in the field of sport studies in North America. [6] Defining physical education as the "art and science of human movement applied to sport, dance, play, and exercise" (p. 14), Zeigler (1973) proposed three specialized curricula for the study of physical education at the university level: (1) human motor performance, (2) teaching, coaching, or administering human motor performance, and (3) the arts and social science focus of the field. Even today, many university faculties of Physical Education or Kinesiology are subdivided into the bio-sciences (motor performance), sport psychology, sport management (sport business, coaching, and leadership), and sociocultural studies (history, sociology, philosophy, and anthropology), making it one of the most diverse fields in the academy. At the primary and secondary school levels, Daryl Siedentop's (1994) "sport education" curriculum model has gained a foothold by aiming to develop competent, literate, and enthusiastic sportspersons. Essentially, the contemporary aims of physical education curricula at all academic levels is twofold: To teach physical competency and physical literacy. In the first half of the twentieth century, a mind-body duality existed in academia, whereby educators strived to develop a sound mind in a sound body (*mens sana in corpore sanum*) to "ward off elements of decay and degeneracy endemic to modern civilization" (Gidney, 2015, p. 4). Whereas, in recent decades, the field of physical education has been in decline, facing strong opposition from those that do not consider it a 'serious' academic discipline. Drawing on Cartesian theory, these developments point to a mind-body 'duelity' in the physical education discipline. From its European roots to its contemporary crisis, the history and philosophy of physical education provide the foundation and fissure in the sport-education complex.

The earliest physical educators were the ancient Greeks. Philosophical predecessors to Descartes, such as Plato, speculated that the whole being was made up

---

[6] Zeigler spent much of his academic career at the University of Western Ontario (1949-1956, 1971-1989) and was a pivotal figure in the development of the fields of both sport management and sport humanities, particularly history and philosophy.

of body and mind/soul, both of which required proper training. However, it was not until the Enlightenment writings of John Locke (1693/1889) and Jean-Jacques Rousseau (1762/2010), about the need for physical activity among children, that the floodgates were finally opened for the widespread acceptance of the physical education movement. These vanguard philosophers influenced the first generations of physical educationists, including Johann Friedrich GutsMuths and his protégé Friedrich Ludwig Jahn (and his devotees Charles Folien, Charles Beck, and Francis Lieber) in Germany, Per Henrik Ling in Sweden, Franz Nachtegal in Denmark, Americans Joseph Cogswell, George Bancroft, Catharine Beecher, and Mary Lyon, and the aforementioned Pierre de Coubertin in France (Krüger & Hofmann, 2015). The 'muscular Christian' principles of developing a healthy body, mind, and spirit, as promoted through the Young Men's Christian Association (YMCA), was also born of this confluence of ideas (Putney, 2001). Although, throughout the "long nineteenth century" (Hobsbawm, 1987), much of the impetus to promote physical education stemmed from a jingoistic military zeal and preparing men for war. Examples of nationalist physical education movements include Jahn's development of *turnen* (gymnastics) in reaction to the Napoleonic Wars (1803-1815) (Eisenberg, 1996), the influence of the Franco-Prussian War (1870-1871) on Coubertin's Olympic Movement (Loland, 1995), "the shocking revelation of the rejection of over 30 percent of the men drafted for the U.S. armed services during World War I" (Flowers, 2009b, p. 585), or military drill training during the interwar period in Canadian public schools (Morrow, 1977). Finally, after the Second World War, with the development of physical education programs in universities the objectives of physical education pedagogies in North America shifted in focus from 'bodies for the nation' to bodily knowledge (Gidney, 2006).

Contemporary physical education curricula propose to deliver the following two outcomes: physical competency and physical literacy (Tompsett et al., 2014). The former objective focuses on learning new motor skills (e.g., sport forms), safe movement strategies, and general motor control. The latter promotes the buzz-term 'healthy active lifestyle' by introducing students to fitness programs, health education, and purposeful lifelong physical pursuits. Building on the theories of sport physiologist Arthur Steinhaus, Zeigler (1994) proposed thirteen principles of physical education, including: reversibility, overload, flexibility, bone density, gravity, relaxation, aesthetics, integration, integrity, priority of the person, live-life-to-its-fullest, fun and pleasure, and longevity.[7] Almost two decades later, Zeigler (2011)

---

[7] To provide some explanations of these principles: (1) Reversibility refers to the need for maintenance of the body or initial effects will reverse; (2) muscles must be overloaded (pushed beyond capacity) to develop; (3) stretching/flexibility and (6) resting/relaxation are essential elements of physical activity; (4) physical fitness preserves bone density, (5) counters the effects of gravity on the body, and (13) can add to longevity of life; (7) body image (aesthetics) plays a role in physical activity; (8) physical activities provide opportunities for social integration; (9) integrity and honesty are virtues learned through fair play; and (10), (11), and (12) are rather self-explanatory.

added a fourteenth principle, academic achievement, based on a series of studies that found a positive correlation between physical fitness levels and academic success (Ahmed et al., 2007; Hillman et al., 2008; Chomitz et al., 2009). Although most physical educationists tend to agree on Ziegler's principles, it is Siedentop's (1994) 'sport education' approach to instruction that has sparked academic debate. Although sport education promotes fitness and sport participation (physical competencies), scholars question goal attainability (Kirk, 2006) and whether the "pedagogical framework [is] capable of enhancing physical education's ability to provide all pupils with experiences that have lifelong meaning and value" (Penney et al., 2002, p. 56). Unfortunately, these types of pedagogical disagreements are a detriment to the credibility of an already-fractured academic discipline.

The field of physical education has been in decline in higher education, almost since its inception (Zeigler, 2003). Additionally, an inferiority complex, stemming from the mind-body debate in academia, has resulted in further divides between physical education reformers and university administration. The first half of the twentieth century marked great progress in the field, culminating in the 1940s and 1950s, when physical educators sought to bring credibility to their discipline by establishing degree-granting programs, founding scientific research groups (precursor to the field of kinesiology), and professionalizing the job of physical educator. However, as noted by Gidney (2015), "the specialization of the field and educators' attempt to establish a footing within the research university resulted in the sidelining of the practical side of the program" (p. 141). A 'crisis' ensued for the latter half of the twentieth century, in which the field of physical education was "seen to be struggling to find direction and purpose within the context of significant changes in the purpose, and practice of education in contemporary societies" (Light & Fawns, 2001, p. 69). Much of the misdirection and inferiority can be attributed to the Cartesian conundrum of separating the development of mind and body; of upholding the mind as superior to the body, and those that train the body to be inferior to those who train the mind. Descartes' widely-accepted metaphysical theory has profoundly reverberated throughout the contemporary physical education establishment.

Numerous seventeenth-century philosophers contemplated the juxtaposition of the material, tangible, physical substance of the body and the psychological, spiritual, intangible construct of the mind. Thomas Hobbes' theory of materialism, for instance, reduced the mind to a physical process; Baruch Spinoza suggested that the mind and body were a single entity; and Gottfried Liebnitz posited that the mind and body were mutually exclusive forms of reality (Henning et al., 2018). Another of their contemporaries, René Descartes, however, believed that the mind and body were distinct substances with their own properties: thought and movement, respectively. This distinction has been the crux of physical education pedagogies and, indeed, the sport-education complex. Educational philosopher Steven Stolz (2014), outlines the inherent duality of the field:

The very nature and meaning of physical education seems problematic because the term 'physical' seems to indirectly refer to the body, its nature and functioning, whereas the term 'education' typically implies the mind and its development (Reid, 1996b). This influence is significant for physical education because it would appear to be based on dubious philosophical foundations and also the inability to reconcile the dualism of the mind and body that underlies Western culture and its philosophies of education. (p. 5)

This superiority of the body over the mind is, perhaps, most evident in educational institutions. Educational content requiring 'thinking' trumps that which is learned through bodily movement, highlighting an obvious condescension from scholars to athletes and a hierarchy of knowledge, positioning physical education at the "bottom of the educational food chain" (Johnson, 2012, p. 188). As a result, in lieu of the practical, physical education reformers have sought to progress the scientific and the theoretical, in order to gain status and credibility as a conventional academic subject. Whereas, what is actually needed is a reconciliation of the two 'substances.' The more that "activists' work with embodied pedagogies disrupts the debilitating mind/body dualism that privileges and values the mind while objectifying the body as something controlled, manipulated, and 'looked at'," (Oliver & Kirk, 2017, p. 311), the more the field of physical education can prosper in its intended objectives: "reconciling mind-body dualism through theoretical aspects of movement sciences; and focusing the curriculum on individual and community health" (Hay, 2016, p. 319). As such, Cartesian dualism has the potential to uphold the physical competency and literacy aims of physical education curricula. It would seem, then, that the discipline's only obstacle, in relation to wider academia, is the inferiority complex of its adherents.

As an academic discipline, the heyday of physical education was in the first half of the twentieth century, when "bodily health was a visible marker of an individual's mental strength and moral fortitude, as well as an indicator of the future stability, and virility, of the nation" (Gidney, 2015, p. 4). Since then, in the academy, an age-old duel between 'jocks' and 'nerds', founded on the principles of Cartesian dualism, has undercut the philosophy of physical education. The ability to reconcile the education of both mind and body is put forth in the tandem goals of contemporary physical education curricula. Physical competency exploits the virtues of the body, through movement, motor control, and aesthetics, while physical literacy relies on the mental capacity to rationalize the benefits of a healthy active lifestyle. Although dualism portrays physical educators as "nonintellectual, nonacademic, nonessential, and nonartistic" (Kretchmar, 2005, p. 81), the academy is at fault for this derision, not the intention of the discipline itself. A core tenet of the sport-education complex, trainsing *both* the mind and body, is at the roots of Western philosophy. In effect, it is higher education that needs to be righted. In North America, at least, it seems that this foundational mind-body premise has been forgotten in universities in favour of a more carnal enterprise: varsity athletics.

Be True to Your School: The Varsity Conundrum

Hall-of-Fame surf-rock band the Beach Boys released the song *Be True to Your School* in 1963 as a tribute to their high school. The song's, and their high school fight song's, melody, however, is borrowed from the century-old varsity fight song of the University of Wisconsin (Price, 2009). The song extolls the virtues of loyalty to one's alma mater through the cultural signals encompassing varsity sport. An increasingly polarizing subject, more so in the United States than in Canada, intercollegiate athletics has long been a commercial entertainment aspect of higher education that, oftentimes, seems at odds with the institution's ultimate mission. From mascot identity to NCAA hegemony, school sport is a unique phenomenon in North America. In 1929, the Carnegie Foundation, which researches educational policy change, published a scathing report of the state of college athletics. In its preface, the president of the foundation, Henry Pritchett (1929), snidely asked the question, through the voice of a visiting European scholar at a varsity football game: "What relation has this astonishing athletic display to the work of an intellectual agency like a university"(p. vi)? Indeed, many scholars have answered this question in the subsequent ninety years, with little reform resulting from their efforts. One educational activist, John Gerdy (2006), simply laments that "American education's experiment with elite athletics has been a failure" (p. 14). As a last, and culminating, facet of the sport-education complex, the history and controversies of varsity sport in North America highlight the cultural clash, or duelity, between sport and education.

The North American 'college experience,' the professor-student relationship, the campus green, and varsity sport, to name a few features, is based off the template set by the British, specifically Oxbridge, system. Initially, student-run, *intra*scholastic sport was used as a character-building exercise, but also as a welcome distraction for rebellious students seeking extracurricular outlets. By the middle of the nineteenth century, however, sport, in this case intramural sport, "came to dominate the extracurriculum while challenging the curriculum for importance on the college campus" (Smith, 1988, p. 13). The first *inter*collegiate competitions were rowing races; the famed Oxford-Cambridge boat race began in 1829 and was mimicked in 1852 by Harvard and Yale. These nascent contests produced a renewed zeal for institutional loyalty within the student body and increased public attention that university administrators were not soon to dismiss. As noted by preeminent sport historian Guy Lewis (1970), "in many ways, sport contributed to the destruction of the isolated academic world and helped make the nation more conscious of its colleges" (p. 222). So, when the American football boom erupted in the 1890s, it was a foregone conclusion that varsity sport was to be a lucrative commercial entity for the thousands of competing institutions of higher education throughout the United

States and Canada for years to come (Fabian, 2016).[8] The bureaucratization of intercollegiate competition unfolded with the co-option of student sport clubs, first entrusted to the supervision of academics, then the hiring of professional coaches, and eventually the creation of salaried athletic directors in the first decades of the twentieth-century. Originally housed under the auspices of the Physical Education department or faculty, so as to maintain the academic integrity of the intercollegiate program, the eventual creation of independent, or arm's-length, athletic departments ultimately furthered the commercial motives of varsity stakeholders. The contemporary opulence and flagship status of varsity programming has been scrutinized *ad nauseum* by many critical academics (Chu, 1989; Sperber, 1990a, 1998, 2011; Thelin, 1996; Gerdy, 2000, 2006; Zimbalist, 2001; Duderstadt, 2003; Flowers, 2009a; Clotfelter, 2011; Hacker & Dreifus, 2011; Smith, 2011; Nixon, 2014; Gurney et al., 2017; Bennett, 2019), calling for reform within the hegemonic NCAA. Key among the dissenters was American studies scholar Murray Sperber (1990b), who illustrates the commercialization of the college sports industry quite poignantly:

Intercollegiate athletics, especially the big-time version, has become College Sports Inc., a huge commercial entertainment conglomerate, with operating methods and objectives totally separate from, and often opposed to, the educational aims of the schools that house its franchises. Moreover, because of its massive hypocrisy and fiscal irresponsibility, College Sports Inc. places many colleges and universities under constant threat of scandal and other sports-induced maladies. (pp. K1-K2)

In effect, the appropriation and commercialization of a student-led activity has been the bane of higher education for the past century. The aforementioned Carnegie Foundation report on *American College Athletics* (1929) blamed "commercialism, and the negligent attitude toward the educational opportunities for which the college exists" (Savage et al., p. 306) for the crisis in varsity sport. Major capital projects to build 70,000+ football stadiums, low student-athlete graduation rates, and the heightened influence of boosters all marked the early twentieth-century collegiate sports scene. As noted glumly by Hacker and Dreifus (2011), although "college athletics originally came into the campus as an innocent form of recreation and diversion over the years the athletics incubus has overtaken academic pursuits, compromised the moral authority of educators, and gobbled up resources that should have gone to their basic missions" (p. 2). Over sixty years later, a report produced by the Knight Commission (1993), a multidisciplinary panel of collegiate sport reformers, yielded similar results, citing the commercial motives of varsity athletics as being in direct conflict with the values imbued by higher education. In the intervening years, little had been remedied in the exploitative relationship between higher education and elite-level sport. Major scandals over the past fifty years, including sexual violence (Jacoby, 2019), academic fraud (Lyall, 2014), and match-fixing

---

[8] To note, I am referring to universities *competing* for student applications, at this point, not on the playing field.

(Leonhardt, 2006), to name just a few, have marked the contemporary zeitgeist of college athletics as morally corrupt. Stanley Eitzen, with coauthor George Sage (1982), also bemoaned the corruption of academic ideals endemic to universities with major sports programs. With the arms race to recruit the top scholarship athletes, the concomitant entitlement of said student-athletes, and the new regulations allowing the marketization of star athletes (Witz, 2020), there seems to be no end in sight for the commercial interests of college sport. What remains to be asked, then, is how do institutions of higher education justify this clash of cultures?

Other than the institutional branding on the backs of jerseys and the *student*-athletes themselves, the exuberance of big-time college athletics has little to do with the academic mission of the institutions. Historian of higher education John Thelin (1996), elaborated on this point in his seminal *Games Colleges Play*:

> Intercollegiate athletics are American higher education's 'peculiar institution.' Their presence is pervasive, yet their proper balance with academics remains puzzling. A check of institutional accreditation self-studies, mission statements, and annual reports suggest that an American university seldom discusses intercollegiate athletics as part of its primary purposes of teaching, research, and service. The irony of this silence is that, for many universities, big-time athletics stand out as a central activity, a program likely to be protected and promoted. (p. 1)

Whether it is termed an irony, a quandary, or a duelity, sport in higher education is difficult to justify. In a project reviewing the educational value of college sports, Shulman and Bowen (2000) narrowed down university mission statements to two themes: Knowledge for its own sake or for preparing flexible minds, and education for leadership or success in life. As the authors note, the former has little to do with varsity sport, but the latter theme hints at the leadership values developed through sport. Elucidated in the first aspect of the sport-education complex above, there is a strong belief, including among athletic directors and university administrators, that sport is an ideal educational tool. Clotfelter (2011) posits that education, money, visibility, and school spirit are the core reasons institutions use to justify varsity sport. Similarly, Chu (1989) highlights the functions of varsity sports as a contribution to a sense of campus community, an opportunity for student engagement, and the feeling of athletic success for the institution, and, of course, the participants. While, Carsonie (1991) delves into the educational values of varsity sports, in which he includes character-building, upward socioeconomic mobility, sport as an artistic discipline, and self-awareness. As can be understood from these various scholars' research and interpretations, institutions of higher education justify varsity athletics via many excuses, most of which can be quite easily discounted, since none of them support the purpose of the institutions themselves. In 1909, former President of the United States Woodrow Wilson, then president of Princeton University, best summarized the upended relationship between the university and varsity sport when he was quoted as saying: "The side shows are so numerous, so diverting... that they have swallowed up the circus" (Geiger, 2015, p. 414n).

Widely popular and accepted as commonplace, intercollegiate sport has become a focal point of the public gaze and an economic driver of university affairs. Not mentioned in mission statements, in fact, sometimes even contradicting them, varsity sport in North America is problematic and in need of reform. Therefore, as a conclusion of sorts, I propose four hypothetical solutions to the dilemma. First, a 'separation of church and state.' Varsity sports teams have become immensely popular for small, university-town communities, but the teams themselves need not be under the financial and legal auspices of the university itself. As with the Université Laval (Quebec City) model, perhaps business conglomerates could franchise out the school branding, and recruit university-aged players, but the operation remains completely separate from the academic institution (Bratt, 2016). Second, I propose restructuring the athletics department to report directly to the Dean of Physical Education (or Human Movement, Kinesiology, etc.), so as to regain an element of academic integrity within the decision-making process. A Canadian version of the Carnegie Report, written by A. W. Matthews (1974), whose recommendations were reiterated by Zeigler (1975), advocated for this type of change in the mid-1970s. A third idea is to eliminate varsity sport altogether and facilitate intercollegiate intramural competition, led by students and amateur in every aspect. Although this idea harkens back to a simpler time, when students organized extracurricular sporting activities, perhaps it is time that universities return to the halcyon days of sport *for* students. Fourth, and last, I offer a progressive approach whereby universities only field varsity teams of sports that are popular among the student population. Frankly, this would eliminate the most resource-heavy sport of football, as this is not generally played recreationally, but would open the door to competitive Frisbee, esports, and Quidditch.9 If universities perceive themselves as progressive institutions, serving the educational and developmental needs of their student bodies, then perhaps this sport-by-committee approach may provide an innovative solution. In summary, university sport requires reform. Some hypothetical options, proposed here, include detaching varsity teams from the university, relocating to the Physical Education department, only offering student-led intramural sport, or developing a sport-by-committee approach. Thinking differently about sport offerings, for whom sports are offered, and how sports are offered may provide a critical new lens through which to reimagine this broken and crucial element of the sport-education complex.

---

9 Quidditch is a fictitious game, conceived by British author J. K. Rowling for her fantastical *Harry Potter* universe, which has gained momentum on university campuses as an inclusive and inventive pastime. Its popularity has grown to such proportions that the Intercollegiate Quidditch Association was founded in 2007.

Conclusion

The dynamic interplay between the important social institutions of sport and education can be thought of as a sport-education complex. The two overlap in three key areas. First, in the oft-referenced notion of sport as an educational tool, sport is deemed an ideal conduit for the development of life skills and other educational values. Second, based on the philosophy of mind-body dualism, the field of physical education is an attempt, by academia, to enact the education of the whole person. Third, the significant place that varsity athletics holds within academic institutions represents the commercialization of the sport-education complex. Although, as has been argued throughout this chapter, these three facets of the sport-education complex represent the intrinsic duality and cultural loggerheads between the two entities. Sport teaches both life skills and deviance, physical education is a derided discipline, and varsity sport is exploiting the academic mission of institutions of higher learning. The culture clash between the 'jockular' and nerd-like is ingrained in Western educational philosophy, sporting practices, and gender norms. Often linked conceptually, but dissociated practically, sport and education are pillars of our society, and like other social pillars, such as—politics, economics, family, etc.—they often imperfectly overlap. The sport-education complex is not an indictment of either sport or education, rather a commentary on two incompatible cultures forced to coexist in the ever-expanding North American sports industry.

REFERENCES

Ahmed, Y., MacDonald, H, Reed, K., Naylor, P, Liu-Ambrose, T., & McKay, H. (2007). School-based physical activity does not compromise children's academic performance. *Medicine & Science in Sports Exercise, 39*, 371-376.

Baker, J. (2003). Early specialization in youth sport: A requirement for adult expertise? *High Ability Studies, 14*(1), 85–94.

Baker, J., Cobley, S., & Fraser-Thomas, J. (2009). What do we know about early sport specialization? Not much! *High Ability Studies, 20*(1), 77–89.

Bennett, J. T. (2019). *Intercollegiate Athletics, Inc.: How big-time college sports cheat students, taxpayers, and academics*. Routledge.

Bratt, D. (2016). A Comparison of Canadian and American University Sports. In D. Taras, & C. Waddell (Eds.), *How Canadians Communicate V: Sports* (pp. 95-116). AU Press.

Bredemeier, B. J., & Shields, D. L. (1986). Moral growth among athletes and non-athletes: a comparative analysis. *Journal of Genetic Psychology, 147*(1), 7-18.

Brenner, J. S. (2016). Sports specialization and intensive training in young athletes. *Pediatrics, 138* (3), 1–8.

Brunelle, J., Danish, S. J., & Forneris, T. (2007). The impact of a sport-based life skill program on adolescent prosocial values. *Applied Developmental Science, 11*(1), 43-55.

Carsonie, F. W. (1991). Education value: A necessity for reform of big-time intercollegiate athletics. *Capital University Law Review, 20*(3), 661-690.

Clotfelter, C. T. (2011). *Big-time sports in American universities*. Cambridge University Press.

Chu, D. (1989). *The character of American higher education and intercollegiate sport*. State University of New York Press.

Coakley, J. (2002). Using sports to control deviance and violence among youths: Let's be critical and cautious. In M. Gatz, M. A. Messner, & S. J. Ball-Rokeach (Eds.), *Paradoxes of youth Sport* (pp. 13-30). State University of New York Press.

Chomitz, V. R., Slining, M. M., McGowan, R. J., Mitchell, S. E., Dawson, G. F., & Hacker, K. A. (2009). Is there a relationship between physical fitness and academic achievement? Positive results from public school children in the Northeastern United States. *Journal of School Health, 79,* 30-37

Crone, J. (1999). Toward a theory of sport. *Journal of Sport Behaviour, 22*(3), 1-9.

Danish, S. J. (2002). Teaching life skills through sport. In M. J. Gatz, M. A. Messner & S. J. Ball-Rokeach (Eds.), *Paradoxes of youth and sport* (pp. 49-60). State University of New York Press.

Danish, S., Forneris, T., Hodge, K, & Heke, I. (2004). Enhancing youth development through sport. *World Leisure Journal, 46*(3), 38-49.

Danish, S. J., Forneris, T., & Wallace, I. (2005). Sport-based life skills programming in the schools. *Journal of Applied School Psychology, 21*(2), 41-62.

Danish, S. J., Petitpas, A. J., & Hale, B. D. (1993). Life development intervention for athletes: Life skills through sport. *The Counseling Psychologist, 21*(3), 352-385.

Descartes, R. (2017). *Meditations on First Philosophy* (J. Cottingham, Trans.). Cambridge University Press. (Original work published 1641).

Doty, J. (2006). Sports build character?! *Journal of College and Character, 7*(3), 1-9.

Duderstadt, J. J. (2003). *Intercollegiate athletics and the American university: A university president's perspective*. University of Michigan Press.

Eisenberg, C. (1996). Charismatic nationalist leader: *Turnvater* Jahn. *The International Journal of the History of Sport, 13*(1), 14-27.

Eitzen, D. S. (1988). Conflict theory and deviance in sport. *International Review for the Sociology of Sport, 23*(3), 193-204.

Ewing, M. A., Gano-Overway, L. A., Branta, C. F., & Seefeldt, V. D. (2002). The role of sports in youth development. In M. Gatz, M. A. Messner, & S. J. Ball-Rokeach (Eds.), *Paradoxes of youth sport* (pp. 31-47). State University of New York Press.

Fabian, T. (2016). *Alma mater wrapped in pigskin: The role of varsity football in Canadian universities* [Unpublished master's thesis]. De Montfort University.

Fetchke, M. J., Roy D. P., & Clow K. E. (2016). *Sports marketing*. Routledge.

Flowers, R. D. (2009a). Institutionalized hypocrisy: The myth of intercollegiate athletics. *American Educational History Journal, 36*(2), 343-360.

Flowers, R. D. (2009b). Physical education, history of. In E. F. Provenzo, Jr., J. P. Renaud, & A. B. Provenzo (Eds.), *Encyclopedia of the social and cultural foundations of education* (pp. 583-585). SAGE Publications.

Fraser-Thomas, J. L., Côté, J., & Deakin, J. (2005). Youth sport programs: an avenue to foster positive youth development. *Physical Education and Sport Pedagogy, 10*(1), 19-40.

Frazier, J. (2016). Existence of economies of scale within athletic departments at Power Five Conferences colleges and universities. *International Journal of Business & Economics Perspectives, 11*(1), 38-50.

Geiger, R. L. (2015). *The history of American higher education: Learning and culture from the founding to World War II.* Princeton University Press.

Gerdy, J. R. (2000). College athletics as good business? In J. R. Gerdy (Ed.), *Sports in school: The future of an institution* (pp. 42-54). Teachers College Press.

Gerdy, J. R. (2006). *Air ball: American education's failed experiment with elite athletics.* University Press of Mississippi.

Gibbons, S. L., Ebbeck, V., & Weiss, M. R. (1995). Fair play for kids: effects on the moral development of children in physical education. *Research Quarterly for Exercise and Sport, 66*(3), 247-255.

Gidney, C. (2006). The athletics–physical education dichotomy revisited: The case of the University of Toronto, 1900–1940. *Sport History Review 37*, 130-149.

Gidney, C. (2015). *Tending the student body: Youth, health, and the modern university.* University of Toronto Press.

Gould, D. (2010). Early sport specialization: A psychological perspective. *Journal of Physical Education, Recreation, & Dance, 81*(8), 33–37.

Gould, D., & Carson, S. (2008a). Personal development through sport. In H. Hebestreit & O. Bar-Or (Eds.), *The young athlete* (pp. 287-301). Blackwell Publishing.

Gould, D., & Carson, S. (2008b). Life skills development through sport: Current status and future directions. *International Review of Sport and Exercise Psychology, 1*(1), 58-78.

Gould, D., Collins, K., Lauer, L., & Chung, Y. (2006). Coaching life skills: a working model. *Sport and Exercise Psychology Review, 2*(1), 10-18.

Gurney, G., Lopiano, D., & Zimbalist, A. (2017). *Unwinding madness: What went wrong with college sports and how to fix it.* Brookings Institution Press.

Guttmann, A. (1978). *From ritual to record: The nature of modern sports.* Columbia University Press.

Hacker, A., & Dreifus, C. (2011). *The athletics incubus: How college sports undermine college education.* Times Books.

Hay, P. J. (2006). Assessment for learning in physical education. In D. Kirk, D. MacDonald, & M. O'Sullivan (Eds.), *The handbook of physical education* (pp. 312-325). SAGE Publications.

Hecimovich, M. (2004). Sport specialization in youth: A literature review. *Journal of the American Chiropractic Association, 41*(4), 32–41.

Henning, M. A., Lyndon, M., Hawken, S. J., & Webster, C. S. (2018). Mind-body processes. In M. A. Henning, C. U. Krägeloh, R. Dryer, F. Moir, R. Billington, & A. G. Hill (Eds.), *Wellbeing in higher education: Cultivating a healthy lifestyle among faculty and students* (pp. 7-19). Routledge.

Hill, G. M., & Hansen, G. F. (1988). Specialization in high school sports: The pros and cons. *Journal of Physical Education, Recreation, & Dance, 59*(5), 76–79.

Hillman, C. H., Pontifex, M. B., Raine, L. B., Castelli, D. M., Hall, E. E., & Kramer, A. F. (2009). The effect of acute treadmill walking on cognitive control and academic achievement in pre-adolescent. *Neuroscience, 159*, 1044-1054.

Hobsbawm, E. (1987). *The Age of Empire 1875–1914.* Weidenfeld & Nicolson.

Holt, N. L., & Sehn, Z. L. (2008). Processes associated with positive youth development and participation in competitive youth sport. In N. L. Holt (Ed.), *Positive youth development through sport* (pp. 24-33). Routledge.

Horn, T. S. (2015). Social psychological and developmental perspectives on early sport specialization. *Kinesiology Review, 4*(3), 248–266.

Huggins, M. (2008). Sport and the British upper classes c.1500–2000: A historiographic overview. *Sport in History, 28*(3), 364-388.

Hughes, R., & Coakley, J. (1991). Positive deviance among athletes: The implications of overconformity to the sport ethic. *Sociology of Sport Journal, 8*(4), 307-325.

Jacoby, K. (2019, December 16). Predator Pipeline. *USA Today.* https://www.usatoday.com/in-depth/news/investigations/2019/12/12/ncaa-looks-other-way-athletes-punished-sex-offenses-play/4360460002/.

Jayanthi, N. A., Pinkham, C., Dugas, L. R., Patrick, B., & LaBella, C. (2013). Sports specialization in young athletes: Evidence-based recommendations. *Sports Health, 5*(3), 251–257.

Jhally, S. (1984). The spectacle of accumulation: Material and cultural factors in the evolution of the sports/media complex. *Insurgent Sociologist, 12*(3), 41-57.

Johnson, T. G. (2012). The significance of physical education content: "Sending the message" in physical education teacher education. *Quest, 64*(3), 187-196.

Jones, R. A. (1989). Arctic Winter Games Untapped potential. *Journal of Physical Education, Recreation & Dance, 60*(8), 62-64.

Jozsa Jr., F. P. (2013). *College Sports Inc.: How commercialism influences intercollegiate athletics.* Springer.

Kirk, D. (2006). Sport education, critical pedagogy, and learning theory: Toward an intrinsic justification for physical education and youth sport. *Quest, 58*(2), 255-264.

Knight, C. J., Dorsch, T. E., Osai, K. V., Haderlie, K. L., & Sellars, P. A. (2016). Influences on parental involvement in youth sport. *Sport, Exercise, and Performance Psychology, 5*(2), 161-178.

Knight Foundation. (1991, 1992, 1993). *Reports of the Knight Commission on intercollegiate athletics.* https://www.knightcommission.org/wp-content/uploads/2008/10/1991-93_kcia_report.pdf.

Kretchmar, R. S. (2005). *Practical philosophy of sport and physical activity.* Human Kinetics.

Krüger, M., & Hofmann, A. R. (2015). The development of physical-education institutions in Europe: A short introduction. *The International Journal of the History of Sport, 32*(6), 737-739.

Lamont, K. (1988). *"We can achieve": A history of women in sport at the University of Alberta.* Academic Printing & Publishing.

Leonhardt, D. (2006, March 8). Sad suspicions about scores in basketball. *The New York Times.* https://www.nytimes.com/2006/03/08/business/08leonhardt.html.

Lewis, G. (1970). The beginning of organized collegiate sport. *American Quarterly, 22*(2), 222-229.

Licatta, A. (2019, July 23). *LSU football unveiled its state-of-the-art $28 million locker room, complete with luxury sleep pods.* Business Insider. https://www.businessinsider.com/lsu-football-new-locker-room-college-football-2019-7.

Light, R., & Fawns, R. (2001). The thinking body: Constructivist approaches to games teaching in physical education. *Critical Studies in Education, 42*(2), 69-87.

Locke, J. (1889). *Some thoughts concerning education.* Cambridge University Press. (Original work published in 1693).

Loland, S. (1995). Coubertin's ideology of Olympism from the perspective of the history of ideas. *OLYMPIKA: The International Journal of Olympic Studies, 4*, 49-78.

Lyall, S. (2014, October 22). U.N.C. investigation reveals athletes took fake classes. *New York Times.* https://www.nytimes.com/2014/10/23/sports/university-of-north-carolina-investigation-reveals-shadow-curriculum-to-help-athletes.html.

Malina, R. M. (2010). Early sport specialization: Roots, effectiveness, risks. *Current Sports Medicine Reports, 9*(6), 364–371.

Mangan, J. A. (2010). Imitating their betters and disassociating from their inferiors: Grammar schools and the games ethic in the late nineteenth and early twentieth centuries. *The International Journal of the History of Sport, 27*(1-2), 228-261.

Marsh, A., Zavilla, S., Acuna, K., & Poczwardowski, A. (2015). Perception of purpose and parental involvement in competitive youth sport. *Health Psychology Report, 3*(1), 13-23.

Matthews, A.W. (1974). *Athletics in Canadian Universities.* Association of Universities and Colleges in Canada.

McCallister, S. G., Blinde, E. M., & Weiss, W. M. (2000). Teaching values and implementing philosophies: dilemmas of the youth sport coach. *The Physical Educator, 57*(1), 35-45.

McFadden, T., Bean, C., Fortier, M., & Post, C. (2016). Investigating the influence of youth hockey specialization on psychological needs (dis)satisfaction, mental health, and mental illness. *Cogent Psychology, 3*(1), 7–16.

Morrow D. (1977) The Strathcona Trust in Ontario, 1911-1939. *Canadian Journal of History of Sport and Physical Education, 8*(1), 72-90.

Myer, G. D., Jayanthi, N., Difiori, J. P., Faigenbaum, A. D., Kiefer, A. W., Logerstedt, D., & Micheli, L. J. (2015). Sport specialization, part I: Does early sports specialization increase negative outcomes and reduce the opportunity for success in young athletes? *Sports Health, 7*(5), 437–442.

Nixon II, H. L. (2014). *The athletic trap: How college sports corrupted the academy.* Johns Hopkins University Press.

Normand, J. M., Wolfe, A., & Peak, K. (2017). A review of early sport specialization in relation to the development of a young athlete. *International Journal of Kinesiology & Sports Science, 5*(2), 37–42.

Oglesby, C. (1999). Social conflict theory and sport organization systems. *Quest, 22*(1), 63-73.

Oliver, K. L., & Kirk, D. (2017). Transformative pedagogies for challenging body culture in physical education. In C. D. Ennis (Ed.), *Routledge handbook of physical education pedagogies* (pp. 307-318). Routledge.

Padaki, A. S., Popkin, C. A., Hodgins, J. L., Kovacevic, D., Lynch, T. S., & Ahmad, C. S. (2017). Factors that drive youth specialization. *Sports Health, 9*(6), 532–536.

Papacharisis, V., Goudas, M., Danish, S. J., & Thedorakis, Y. (2005). The effectiveness of teaching a life skills program in a sport context. *Journal of Applied Sport Psychology, 17*(3), 247-254.

Penney, D., Clarke, G., & Kinchin, G. (2002). Developing physical education as a 'connective specialism': Is sport education the answer? *Sport, Education and Society, 7*(1), 55-64.

Petitpas, A. J., Van Raalte, J. L., Cornelius, A. E., & Presbrey, J. (2004). A life skills development program for high school student athletes. *The Journal of Primary Prevention, 24*(3), 325-334.

Price, J. (2009, Winter). Fight on for her fame. *on Wisconsin, 110*(4), 13.

Pritchett, H. S. (1929). Preface. In H. J. Savage, H. W. Bentley, J. T. McGovern, & D. F. Smiley (Eds.), *American college athletics* (pp. vi-xxii). The Carnegie Foundation for the Advancement of Teaching.

Putney, C. (2001). *Muscular Christianity: Manhood and sports in Protestant America, 1880-1920.* Harvard University Press.

Rintala, J. (1991). The mind-body revisited. *Quest, 43*(3), 260-279.

Rousseau, J-J., (2010). *Emile, or, on education* (C. Kelly & A. Bloom, Trans.). Dartmouth College Press. (Original work published in 1762).

Rovell, D. (2018, March 7). *NCAA tops $1 billion in revenue during 2016-17 school year.* ESPN. https://www.espn.com/college-sports/story/_/id/22678988/ncaa-tops-1-billion-revenue-first.

Russell, W., Dodd, R., & Lee, M. (2017). Youth athletes' sport motivation and physical activity enjoyment across specialization status. *Journal of Contemporary Athletics, 11*(2), 83–95.

Russell, W., & Symonds, M. (2015). A retrospective examination of youth athletes' sport motivation and motivational climate across specialization status. *Athletic Insight, 7*(1), 33–46.

Savage, H. J., Bentley, H. W., McGovern, J. T., & Smiley, D. F. (1929). *American college athletics.* The Carnegie Foundation for the Advancement of Teaching.

Sefiha, O. (2012). Bad sports: Explaining sport related deviance. *Sociology Compass, 6*(12), 949-961.

Shulman, J. L., & Bowen, W. G. (2000). *The game of life: College sports and educational values.* Princeton University Press.

Siedentop, D. (1994). *Sport education: Quality PE through positive sport experiences.* Human Kinetics.

Smith, M. M. (2015). Early sport specialization: A historical perspective. *Kinesiology Review, 4*(3), 220–229.

Smith, R. A. (1988). *Sports and freedom: The rise of big-time college athletics.* Oxford University Press.

Smith, R. A. (2011). *Pay for play: A history of big-time college athletic reform.* University of Illinois Press.

Sperber, M. (1990a). *College Sports Inc.: The athletic department vs. the university.* Henry Holt and Company.

Sperber, M. (1990b). College Sports Inc.: The athletic department vs. the university. *The Phi Delta Kappan, 72*(2), K1-K12.

Sperber, M. (1998). *Onward to victory: The creation of modern college sports*. Henry Holt and Company.

Sperber, M. (2011). *Beer and circuses: How big-time college sports is crippling undergraduate education*. Henry Holt and Company.

St. Francis Xavier University. (n.d.). *Our mission statement*. http://www2.mystfx.ca/mscs/our-mission-statement.

Stolz, S. A. (2014). *The philosophy of physical education: A new perspective*. Routledge.

Sutherland D., & Gosteva, A. (2019). Playgrounds for learning, communicating and playing. In L. Couper & D. Sutherland (Eds.), *Learning and connecting in school playgrounds: Using the playground as a curriculum resource* (pp. 30-45). Routledge.

Theokas, C., Danish, S., Hodge, K., Heke, I., & Forneris, T. (2008). Enhancing life skills through sport for children and youth. In N. L. Holt (Ed.), *Positive youth development through sport* (pp. 71-82). Routledge.

Thelin, J. R. (1996). *Games colleges play: Scandal and reform in intercollegiate athletics*. Johns Hopkins University Press.

Tompsett, C., Burkett, B., & McKean, M. R. (2014). Development of physical literacy and movement competency: A literature review. *Journal of Fitness Research, 3*(2), 53-74.

Waldron, S., DeFreese, J. D., Register-Mihalik, J., Pietrosimone, B., & Barczak, N. (2020). The costs and benefits of early sport specialization: A critical review of literature. *Quest, 72*(1), 1-18.

Weiss, M. R., & Fretwell, S. D. (2005). The parent-coach/child-athlete relationship in youth sport: Cordial, contentious, or conundrum? *Research Quarterly for Exercise and Sport, 76*(3), 286-305.

Witz, B. (2020, April 29). N.C.A.A. outlines plan to let athletes make endorsement deals. *New York Times*. https://www.nytimes.com/2020/04/29/sports/ncaabasketball/ncaa-athlete-endorsements.html.

Whitehead, J., Telfer, H., & Lambert, J. (Eds.). (2013). *Values in youth sport and physical education*. Routledge.

Wiersma, L. D. (2000). Risks and benefits of youth sport specialization: Perspectives and recommendations. *Pediatric Exercise Science, 12*(1), 13–22.

Ziegler, E. F. (1973). Discipline definition should precede curriculum development. *Physical Educator 30*(1), 14.

Zeigler, E. F. (1975). Advantages of a totally unified organizational structure for physical education and sports in a university setting. *Physical Educator 32*(4), 186-187.

Zeigler, E. F. (1994), Physical education's 13 principal principles. *Journal of Physical Education, Recreation & Dance, 65*(7), 4-5.

Zeigler, E. F. (2003). Guiding professional students to literacy in physical activity education. *Quest, 55*(4), 285-305.

Zeigler, E. F. (2011). A new "Principal Principle" (#14) of physical activity education is emerging. *The Physical Educator, 68*(3), 115-117.

Zimbalist, A. (2011). *Unpaid professionals: Commercialism and conflict in big-time college sports*. Princeton University Press.

Chapter 7

Messi and Maradona: The Best Player in Football History as the Doppelgänger?

Lukasz Muniowski

In this chapter I attempt to explain why, even though Lionel Messi may be the superior football player to Diego Maradona in terms of statistics and individual achievements, he is not always regarded as highly as the latter. Like any other player wearing the number ten shirt for Argentina that came after Maradona, Messi was cast in the position of his follower, yet he shares more similarities with his compatriot than any other Argentinian footballer to the present. While being a great dribbler and passer are skills normally associated with a typical attacking midfielder/second striker in South American football, Messi is also left-footed, short, boyish and plays for Barcelona, a club Maradona represented for two seasons. Messi's newest contract with the Catalan club, signed in 2017, includes a buyout clause of $835 million, which, when activated, would make him the most expensive football player in history. Maradona earned that distinction twice: in 1982, when he was traded from Boca Juniors to Barcelona for $9.2 million, and in 1984, when he left Catalonia for S.S.C. Napoli for $10.48 million.

To contextualize my argument, it currently appears that neither Messi, nor any other modern football player, will ever enjoy the same special status as Maradona in Argentinian sporting culture. From one perspective, it is a case of oversaturation, as there is presently an excess of football games available for consumption. The modern spectator can watch league games, numerous cup games and international competitions, and also friendlies. Furthermore, one can follow superstars on social media and play as them in sports video games. In the process, through constant mediation and easy accessibility, one gets accustomed to the image of superstars, causing them to become familiar and lose their aura of intangibility. Furthermore, the number of games has correspondingly increased the risk of injuries due to shorter recovery times and underlined the need for rotation, which furthers the division between more and less important games (Dupont and Nedelec et al.). These present circumstances were not the case for Maradona and other superstars from the late-twentieth century, who were special because the televised games they played in were considered rare, and therefore special, events. Most people around the world only had the chance to see Maradona in sports highlights, select European cup games, Copa America, and the World Cup. They saw his goals or moments of pure brilliance, while many of his on-pitch exploits were only passed on by word of mouth, creating an aura of mystery and elusiveness. Because he was so distant, and watching him was a rare pleasure, Maradona was considered more than human; football fans turned him into a cultural legend, a mythical hero. Some, like the believers of *Iglesia Maradoniana*, the Church of Maradona, even consider him to be a god.

My objective is to critically interrogate the validity of comparisons between Lionel Messi and Diego Maradona, as well as Maradona's superior cultural position to that of Messi. To do so, I will use two archetypal figures: the double and the *pibe*. Calling Messi a doppelgänger in this context should in no way be regarded as an insult to his incredible football abilities. The power of the legend of Maradona is simply so strong that it was inevitable for the next great Argentinian footballer to be thrust into his shadow. In the conclusion to his article about the similarities between the two players, Bartłomiej Brach writes that:

> Even Diego Maradona said that he wants Messi to become the greatest in history to put an end to the dispute whether Maradona or Pelé is the best. According to El Grafico (2010) El pibe de oro said: 'All of them. Brazilians, Germans, Spaniards will have to accept the fact that the greatest was born in our country. He is now the best in the world; plays at an inaccessible level. He plays football with Jesus.' (2011, p. 424)

As Brach attests, there is no conflict between the two players and Maradona even taught Messi how to get better at shooting free kicks when he was the coach of the Argentina national football team in the years 2008 to 2010. Both athletes speak about each other with the utmost respect. Messi even distanced himself from the comparisons, stating that he will never eclipse Maradona's achievements (Planet Football, 2017). While Maradona has sometimes criticized Messi's performances for the national team (Gilpin, 2019), he has never doubted his quality as a football player. However, the topic of this chapter is not the relationship between two of the best players of all time, but how their cultural representations and receptions have influenced each other. To demonstrate the prevailing conception of Messi and Maradona, I first introduce the figure of the double, and then explain how it captures the dynamic between these two cultural legends in Argentina's cultural consciousness.

Following my discussion of Messi and Maradona as figural doubles, with Messi cast as Maradona's doppelgänger, I explain how Maradona may be regarded as the first pure embodiment of another figure, the *pibe*. It was because of Maradona's unprecedented success that he became synonymous with the mythical *pibe*, hence becoming the archetype for the next great Argentinian football players. Instead of rejecting the comparisons to the mythological figure, as Messi does whenever Maradona's name is brought up, Maradona has embraced them, fully accepting the *pibe* persona. Because of that, I pay special attention to the importance of the *pibe* to

Argentinian football, showing how being the double can impact the player's status either positively, in the case of Maradona and the *pibe*, or negatively, as with Messi and Maradona, and what factors may play a part in these popular conceptions.

The Double

In terms of their treatment in Argentinian sporting culture, Lionel Messi has often been relegated to Diego Maradona's shadow, or doppelgänger, forever haunted by his predecessor's achievements. As a specific form of character double, the doppelgänger is produced either by duplication or division. Edward J. Rose writes that "it is not easy to separate the 'double-by-division' and the 'double-by-duplication,' since a double created by division, generally internal, can seem to be a separate being and thus appear to have been the product of duplication rather than division" (1977, p. 128). The double-by-division comes to life through the separation between the body and consciousness. This phenomenon is best explained by Henry David Thoreau, who observes:

> However intense my experience, I am conscious of the presence and criticism of a part of me, which, as it were, is not a part of me, but spectator, sharing no experience, but taking note of it; and that is no more I than it is you. When the play, it may be the tragedy, of life is over, the spectator goes his way. It was a kind of fiction, a work of the imagination only, so far as he was concerned (1854, p. 131).

The psychological dualism that Thoreau is referring to here is reminiscent of a situation when an actor plays a character onstage, allowing that character complete control over their body. This is a common occurrence in sport, as athletes often attribute a game winning shot or a stunning goal to a higher power, as if something would take over their bodies. Such was the case with one of the most infamous football goals of all time, "The Hand of God," which Maradona attributed to God, abdicating responsibility for the clearly illegal play.

Although double-by-division has significance for Messi and Maradona's perceived relationship, my argument primarily focuses on doppelgänger, double-by-duplication, a separate entity mirroring the actions of its predecessor. When it comes to Maradona and Messi, it is clear that both players are separate, but related, beings. Both share the same position, responsibilities on the pitch, and come from the same country. The initial expectations in Argentina regarding players both were also similar; however, it was Maradona's success with the national team that elevated expectations on subsequent players to almost unreasonable heights. Because Maradona was seemingly able to win games by himself, Messi was, and still is, expected to do the same. Consequently, because Messi has failed to win a World Cup with the national team, he will always be regarded as inferior to his elder compatriot, at least in Argentina.

Another foundational aspect of the doppelgänger is that it is always an act, a role performed for an audience. Dimitris Vardoulakis writes that "the doppelgänger is operative in a notion of theatricality that undoes simple presence. The staging suggested by theatricality—the place of the actors and the audience—complicates the distinction between what is on the stage and what is outside the stage" (2010, p. 192). It is only during a particular type of performance(s) that the double appears, as the distinction between the subject and the doppelgänger becomes blurred only under specific circumstances. What happens is referred to as "the mirroring effect," which is "the effect of ideology: reflection positions the subject as either in a state of complete hiddenness or in a state of complete transparency" (Vardoulakis, 2010, p. 195). It is then that the subject and the doppelgänger merge, becoming indistinguishable in the process. In the case of the football game, this applies to the ninety minutes devoted to playing time.

Otto Rank traces the genesis of the double to the relationship between oneself and the shadow, specifically, the superstition that the shadow is one's guardian spirit and the lack of it equals death (1971, p. 49-52). The shadow represents his current successor, no matter who they are. In the case of Maradona, his shadow allows him to remain relevant, to function as a cultural legend in the eyes of many, even among those who have never seen him play live. The search for the next Maradona means that his position in national and world football is still unreachable, and others, no matter how great their individual achievements, will always be assigned the role of doppelgängers.

This shows the impact of Maradona's cultural legend. In many ways, he has set an impossible standard for future players who want to be considered more than human. Mythmaking in modern sports is complicated due to the nature of the sports industry itself, which now makes it harder for legends to be both humanized and immortalized. Grzegorz Kowal writes that "in the past a legend kept the nation together, today it does that as well, but on a much smaller scale, building local and environmental (brand) identity" (2014, p. 11). This is a consequence of the creation of what Mariusz Czubaj, Jacek Drozda and Jakub Myszkorowski call "postfootball," which is the discipline's relationship with economics, marketing, commercialism and sports branding (2012, p. 18).

Maradona, with his cocaine addiction and disregard for conventions would be ill-suited for the postfootball reality. Messi on the other hand is a manifestation of the postfootball ideal, as he does not get involved in scandals and has been loyal to one club throughout his career. For most of his career Messi did not have any tattoos, which also positively affected his marketability. Additionally, the fact that he is perceived as a family man makes it easy for him to be associated with companies like Lay's and Pepsi.

This same status would have been impossible for the hard-partying Maradona to achieve, even though, prior to scandals, he also starred in McDonald's and Coca-Cola commercials. Still, during and after his playing days, Maradona was considered a saint, even earning the moniker "D10s," a spelling of the word *dios* (god) with his shirt number, as well as establishing his own church, *Iglesia Maradoniana*, with over 275,000 registered members. While Messi has experienced commercial success, with billboards endorsing Adidas, Lay's or Pepsi, Maradona is still portrayed on murals in Argentinian *barrios*. Messi is sometimes painted next to him, serving the role of the apostle or prophet, as if he was Maradona's inferior.

The Legend of Maradona

Asif Kapadia's documentary *Diego Maradona* (2019), which explores the myth of Maradona among his contemporaries, shows the player warming up before games. He is seen juggling the ball, bouncing it off his head, shoulders or legs, creating the impression that if he wanted to, he would never allow the ball to touch the ground.

The title screen of the movie perfectly accentuates the dual nature of the player, visually representing the division between "Diego" and "Maradona" not only by showing the two words in two different colors, but also putting a line between them. The discord between the two personas is also commented on in the movie by his personal trainer, Fernando Signorini, who professes unconditional love to Diego and reluctance to side with Maradona, stating: "Diego was a kid who had insecurities, a wonderful boy. Maradona was the character he had to come up with in order to face the demands of the football business and the media. Maradona couldn't show any weakness" (2019, Kapadia). Italian journalist Luciano de Crescenzo described the duality of the player using mythical terms: "The most important characters in mythology were [the Greek gods] Apollo and Dionysus. Apollo represented reason and Dionysus represented emotion. Those who knew Maradona understand that he was the worst of Apollo, but the best of Dionysus" (quoted in Pradeep, 2017). As Bartlomiej Brach puts it, "Maradona is much more than a great player—he is a *vox populi*, who became a transformational mythical hero of the contemporary culture" (2011, p. 424). The mythologization of Maradona in his homeland was made possible because he exhibited the qualities associated with another Argentinian mythical figure: the *pibe*, a poor boy in a man's game, who taught himself how to play football in order to improve his economic situation and uplift his community. Maradona came from a poor background, making it easier for him to be accepted as a man of the people. Maradona openly adopted the mythical figure of the *pibe* and, consequently, created his own myth.

The *Pibe*

Ever since Diego Maradona retired from professional football in 1997, Argentinians have looked for an apparent heir to *El Pibe de Oro*, The Golden Boy, as he was called during his playing days. The player wearing the number ten shirt or serving as the attacking midfielder/second striker is so important to Argentinians, that in the football discourse a rather regular phrase like *la pausa*, the pause, is understood as the moment when the playmaker holds onto the ball long enough so that the team's striker will get into position (Williams, 2018, p. 11). Gus Sanchez writes that in Argentina "the No. 10 is characteristically identified by their mastery of the gambeta, the hyper-stylized form of dribbling that, in turn, prioritizes the individuality of the playmaker" (2017).

Maradona was not the initial reason behind the belief in the importance of that position, as it was historically rooted in *lo criollo*, which refers to the way that the locals played football. *Lo criollo* was identified in opposition to the simplistic, forceful version of football preferred by the English, who brought the sport to the country. The skillful, improvised style filled with trickery was seen as a way of outsmarting the originators of the sport, beating them at their own game, which should, at least to some extent, explain the cultural significance of "The Hand of God" goal scored by Maradona that relied on cunning deception.

There is a certain purity and playfulness to this way of playing, expressed by coach Jorge Valdano when characterizing one of the more notable number tens in Argentinian football history, Juan Roman Riquelme: "he is a player of the time when life was slow and we took the chairs out on the streets to play with the neighbors" (quoted in Wilson, 2008). Like a soloist in an orchestra, the typical Argentinian number ten gets the ball at the opposing half and produces beautiful music against a solid background. Eduardo P. Archetti characterizes that style of play as "'restless, individualistic, less disciplined, based on personal effort, agility and skill'" (1999, p. 60).

In Argentinian football culture, these qualities were most notably exhibited by the *pibe*, the poor boy, who taught himself how to play football to improve his economic situation. He played the game in a particular way because he loved the beauty of it, and he wanted to bring joy to himself and the spectators. The figure has been omnipresent in Argentinian football history, created as a response to the rigorous, organized style preferred by the English. "In 1928 the renowned Argentinian football writer Borocotó, editor of sports magazine *El Gráfico*, proposed a statue in honour of the *pibe*, who he wrote should have 'a dirty face, a mane of hair rebelling against the comb', intelligent, roving, trickster' eyes and a 'rag ball' at his feet" (Williams, p. 14). The figure was equal parts trickster, using all of the means at his disposal to beat stronger or less agile opponents, and a messiah, as the perfect *pibe*'s arrival was awaited for decades. The self-educated, self-made player would lead the national team to victory, a conviction that underlines the childish and naive belief in the powers of this mythical figure.

When it comes to the *pibe* figure, it is not so much what he stands for, but rather what he is up against that is of the utmost importance. This not only applies to his tactically organized opponents, but more so the obstacles associated with his poor upbringing. Archetti writes that "in the Argentinian mythical account of playing, the *pibe*, without any form of teaching, becomes the inventor of the *criollo* style in the *potrero*—a small patch of irregular ground in the city or in the countryside which has not been cemented over. The *pibe* is placed in a mythical territory that inherently empowers those who belong to it" (2001, p. 156). While his opponents operate as a collective, they do not have the pure talent possessed by the *pibe*, which allows him to turn the tides of a particular game with one genius play.

The best, most clear representation of such cunningness occurred during the aforementioned 1986 quarter-final against England, as Maradona scored twice during the game, epitomizing the *pibe* character. Furthermore, he gladly took on the persona of the *pibe*. His boyish features evoked the sense of youthfulness associated with the *pibe*. He even consciously invoked the persona as a promotional tool prior to the 1982 World Cup:

> "The dream of the *pibe*", a tango written in 1943 by Reinaldo Yiso, with music by Juan Puey, illustrates clearly what the figure of the *pibe* has always meant for Argentinian football and the role he has played in the imagination of fans. This particular tango is well known because it was sung on television by Diego Maradona, changing the words to "I will be a Maradona, a Kempes, an Olguín", alluding to the Argentina players about to set off for the 1982 World Cup in Spain (Levinsky).

It was this off-field performance that further contributed to Maradona becoming the real-life representation of the *pibe*.

In later years, as Maradona's star was fading, other players were expected to follow in his footsteps, as it was believed that more *pibes* were waiting in the *porteros* to lead their country to glory. The player that appeared to come the closest to reaching Maradona's status in his beloved club was Juan Román Riquelme, who, like Maradona, joined Boca from Argentinos Juniors and also has a statue in Museo de la Pasión Boquense, the club's official museum. Unlike Maradona though, he enjoyed great club success at Boca, yet failed to positively impact the national team. During the World Cup in 2006 he was praised in Europe, but criticized in his home country for his performances, as he was regarded as too slow and "unhappy" on the pitch to be idolized by his compatriots. He was left out of the 2002 World Cup line-up and also missed out on the 2010 World Cup. A year before the tournament, he had declared on national television that "as long as Maradona is coach, I will not return to the national side" (2009, Brown). The two have never seen eye to eye, as even before Maradona became Argentina's manager, he had marked Pablo Aimar and the young Lionel Messi as his heirs, rather than Riquelme.

There were other players considered for the role of Argentna's new *pibe*, such as Ariel Ortega, Aimar, Marcelo Gallardo, Javier Saviola, Carlos Tevez or Sergio Agüero, but none came close to Lionel Messi. Although Messi has emerged as Argentina's new *pibe*, his casting in the role has been imperfect, drawing attention to the ways he fails to live up to his predecessor. However, although Messi was not born in a *portero* and does not share Maradona's humble origins, he does share many similarities with him. Messi is a short, left-footed, quick dribbler. He plays in a similar way, for the same team Maradona used to play for when he first came to Europe, Barcelona, and wears the same number for the national team. Already by age eighteen, Messi was proclaimed to be Maradona's successor by the "D10s" himself (Reuters 2006). In a 2009 interview with Luca Caioli, journalist Mariano Bereznicki said that people in the country were "all waiting for the day when he becomes Diego's successor" (p. 47). Messi reaching Maradona's level of success, and adopting his mantle as the new *pibe*, was not so much an issue of but when.

There was strong basis for that feeling of certainty as, by age twenty, Messi was already able to repeat two of Maradona's greatest goals, which the legendary player had scored during a four-minute span against England. Messi scored a similar, "illegal" goal to "The Hand of God" in 2006 against Recreativo de Huelva, and repeated Maradona's "Goal of the Century" in 2007 against Getafe C.F. The circumstances in which Messi's goals were scored, —against much inferior competition and on a much smaller stage—highlight the main problem with his legacy, at least as compared to Maradona's. While on the club level he has surpassed his idol, becoming Barcelona's all-time top scorer at just twenty-four years old, it is the performances for *La Albiceleste* that have impeded his ability to overcome Maradona's myth and fully escape his shadow.

Unlike Maradona, Messi plays in a different time and, as a potential superstar, was protected from an early age. As teammate Gerard Pique recounts one youth coach saying: "Don't try to tackle him strong, because maybe you will break him" (2011, Longman). The referees are now perceived to be protective of star players, such as Messi, which was not seen as the case during Maradona's playing days. In the 1982 World Cup game against Italy, Maradona was fouled twenty-three times by the defender Claudio Gentile, who was man marking him up until the final whistle. For further proof of the physicality of play in the '80s, one can look no further than to Kapadia's documentary in which the director shows Maradona battling his opponents, being kicked, tackled and pushed to the ground. The effects of said struggles are emphasized by the amplified sound effects whenever the player comes into contact with his defenders. Consequently, Maradona has been cast in Argentina as a warrior and a hero, who battled physical pain to bring glory to his country.

The different cultural attitudes towards Maradona and Messi may also be explained through their backgrounds. While Maradona came from poverty, Messi's upbringing was middle class. Catherine Addington notes that Maradona

> draws himself as a representative of the popular classes in a world from which they were set up to be excluded. Messi was always meant to be included. Though he is read as perhaps more middle class than he was, given his family's serious financial struggles and his own unusual medical needs, Messi never had to face the life-or-death intensity of slum poverty. (2015, p. 20)

Uprooted from an early age, Messi is seen to be not as relatable as Maradona to fellow Argentinians. Addington elaborates that "if Messi is capable of providing a similar symbolic touchstone [as Maradona] for unity, it is not in Argentina. His personal narrative lacks a compelling 'nativity' but more significantly it does not enter into the moments of suffering that made Maradona's idolization so powerful" (2015, p. 63). Conversely, Maradona's failures, such as the doping and drug scandals, have humanized him and helped to establish him as one of the people, even though his wealth effectively separates him from the material realities of the general population.

Brach shares Addington's view, observing that "Messi is a hybrid many Argentinean fans would prefer to keep at a distance, since his career path undermines the myth of *criollo* football, which was constructed on the premise of the adaptation of Southern European immigrants to the local environment" (2011, p. 422). Even though he plays like a *pibe*, he is not authentically so, due to the fact that he is the product of La Masia, Barcelona's youth academy, which is known for forcing younger players to mirror the style of play of their first team counterparts. This allows for great continuity while simultaneously doing little for the players' flexibility. In a sense, La Masia is a factory of doppelgängers. Because he is perceived in Argentina as the product of a system and his moves, no matter how skillful, bear a strong resemblance to another player that came before him, Messi has not been fully afforded the sacred title of the *pibe* in his home country. Despite his athletic prowess, and international renown, Maradona and the Argentinian shirt bearing the number ten are almost synonymous, so much so that during the broadcast of the 2014 World Cup game between Argentina and Belgium, Polish sportscaster, Dariusz Szpakowski, referred to Messi as "Maradona" three times.

Conclusion

Argentinian idolatry of Maradona has transcended sporting culture, extending to the heights of religious worship. Addington further compares a football game to a religious ritual, a celebration of God, gods or saints, who are canonized on the football pitch. The crowd picks its own gods or saints, celebrates the players by immortalizing them (p. 55). Henri Lefebvre points to the special relationship between the fan and the athlete, as the former "participates in the action and plays sport via an intermediary. He quivers with enthusiasm, he fidgets frenetically, but he never moves from his seat" (1958, p. 36). In a way, the fan triumphs vicariously through the athlete, so a player's triumph becomes the triumph of the community he represents. For many Argentina football fans, Maradona has offered them this transcendental, quasi-religious experience, as both the *pibe* and their sporting messiah. Conversely, despite his exceptional achievements and global renown, Lionel Messi has been relegated to Maradona's doppelgänger: his shadow double-by-duplication.

It is evident that any notable Argentinian player after Diego Maradona's era, even as great as Messi, will be considered inferior to his predecessor, until perhaps winning a World Cup for his country. As Argentina continues to await their new *pibe*, the next Maradona will always be considered a mere copy of the revered original. In 2005, Messi scored two goals in the U-20 World Cup final game. The trophy that his team won was supposed to be the prelude to the success he would enjoy in an *Albiceleste* shirt. His failure to repeat Maradona's achievements positions him in a role supposedly not fitting for a player of his caliber, yet one that perfectly characterizes his status: that of the doppelgänger, the double-by-duplication. An individual seeing a direct copy of himself in the other is one thing, as Maradona did with the emergence of Messi, but the fact that society itself does so as well is crucial in establishing the perception of Maradona as the original and Messi as his mere shadow or doppelgänger.

While Messi has come the closest to mirroring the greatest Argentinian football player ever, whether by wearing the same number, scoring similar goals or putting the team on his back in important games, it currently appears that he will forever be Maradona's shadow within Argentinian sporting culture, his own legacy serving as a continual reminder of Maradona's perceived greatness. The fact that, despite his achievements, Messi is still widely considered inferior to Maradona within Argentinian sport media and fandom, is proof of the latter's impact on world football. While it is possible to claim that, under different circumstances Messi, would have been perceived outside the cultural shadow of Maradona, he would not have been the same player had it not been for the original "D10s," who inspired whole generations of Argentinian footballers to keep the myth of the *pibe* alive.

REFERENCES

Addington, C. (2015). *Dios y los Diez: The Mythologization of Diego Maradona and Lionel Messi in Contemporary Argentina*. MA Thesis.

Ahl, F. (2015). The hand of God: Diego Maradona and the divine nature of cheating in Classical Antiquity. *Archai Journal: On the Origins of Western Thought*. 14. Jan/Jun 2015, 11-19.

Archetti, E. (1999). *Masculinities: Football, Polo and Tango in Argentina*. Oxford: Berg. (2011). The spectacle of a heroic life: the case of Diego Maradona In D. Andrews & S. Jackson (Eds.) *Sports Stars: The Cultural Politics of Sporting Celebrity* (pp. 151-163). London: Routledge.

Brach, B. (2011). Who is Lionel Messi? A comparative study of Diego Maradona and Lionel Messi. *International Journal of Cultural Studies*. 15(4), 415-428.

Britto, Morais and Barreto (2013). The Hand of God, the Hand of the Devil: a sociological interpretation of Maradona's hand goal. *Soccer & Society*. Volume 15, 2015, Issue 5: Heroes, Icons, Legends: Legacies of Great Men in World Soccer, 671-684.

Brown, L. (2009, March 13) Maradona: No Players Have Called Me About Riquelme. Retrieved from:https://www.goal.com/en/news/60/southamerica/2009/03/13/1153733/maradona-no-players-have-called-me-about-riquelme.

Caioli, L. (2009). *Messi: The Inside Story of a Boy Who Became a Legend*. London: Corinthian Books. Copa90 (2017, July 17). The Crazy Day Messi Saved His and Argentina's Legacy / The Real International Break: South America. *Youtube*. https://www.youtube.com/watch?v=pCrsY8ZWC70&t=564s

Czubaj, M, Drozda, J. & Myszkorowski, J. (2012). *Postfutbol. Antropologia piłki nożnej*. Gdańsk: Wydawnictwo Naukowe Katedra.

Dupont, G. & Nedelec, M. & Mccall, A. & McCormack, D. & Berthoin, S. & Wisloff, U. (2010). Effect of 2 Soccer Matches in a Week on Physical Performance and Injury Rate. *The American journal of sports medicine*. 38. 1752-8.

Gilpin, A. (2019, January 9) Lionel Messi slammed by Diego Maradona again over his 'lack of leadership.' *Mirror*. Retrieved from: https://www.mirror.co.uk/sport/football/news/lionel-messi-slammed-diego-maradona-13831641.

Kapadia, A. (Director). (2019). *Diego Maradona* [Motion picture]. Great Britain: On the Corner/Film 4.

Kowal, G. (2014). *Anatomia kulturowej legendy*. Cracow: Universitas.

Lefebvre, H. (1958). *The Critique of Everyday Life. Volume 1*. Trans. John Moore. (1991). London: Verso.

Levinsky, S. (2014, March 1). The Cult of the Pibe. *The Blizzard*. Retrieved from: https://www.theblizzard.co.uk/article/cult-pibe.

Longman, J. (2011, May 21). Lionel Messi: Boy Genius. *The New York Times*. Retrieved from: https://www.nytimes.com/2011/05/22/sports/soccer/lionel-messi-boy-genius.html

Murray, D. (2017, July 28) FourFourTwo's 100 Greatest Footballers EVER: No.1, Diego Maradona.*FourFourTwo*. Retrieved from: https://www.fourfourtwo.com/features/fourfourtwos-100-greatest-footballers-ever-no1-diego-maradona.

Planet Football. (2017, June 22). 16 of the best quotes on Diego Maradona: 'The greatest of all time.' *Planet Football*. Retrieved from: https://www.planetfootball.com/quick-reads/16-best-quotes-diego-maradona-messi-mourinho-gallagher/.

Pradeep, A. (2017, December 1). The Days of Epic Glory—Maradona and Platini (2). Retrieved from: https://www.aclsports.com/7342-2/.

Rank, O. (1971). *The Double. A Psychoanalytic Study*. Trans. Harry Tucker Jr. Chapel Hill: The University of North Carolina Press.

Reuters. (2006, February 25). Maradona proclaims Messi as his successor. *China Daily*. Retrieved from:https://www.chinadaily.com.cn/english/doc/2006-02/25/content_523966.htm.

Rose, E.J. (1977). Blake and the Double: The Spectre as Doppelganger. *Colby Quarterly*. Volume 13, Issue 2 June, 127-139.

Sanchez, G. (2017, June 26). The Shirt, the Playmaker, the Nickname. Retrieved from: http://inbedwithmaradona.com/buenos-aires-blog/2017/6/26/the-shirt-the-playmaker-the-nickname.

Simpson, C. (2018, October 1). Diego Maradona Urges Lionel Messi to Retire from Argentina National Team. *Bleacher Report.* Retrieved from: https://bleacherreport.com/articles/2798469-diego-maradona-urges-lionel-messi-to-retire from-argentina-national-team.

Thoreau, H. (1854) *Walden: A Fully Annotated Edition.* (2004). New Haven: Yale University Press.

Vardoulakis, D. (2010). *The Doppelgänger: Literature's Philosophy.* New York: Fordham University Press.

Williams, T. (2018). *Do You Speak Football? A Glossary of Football Words and Phrases from Around the World.* New York: Bloomsbury.

Wilson, J. (2008, May 6) Modric maps a future for the old-school playmaker. *The Guardian.* Retrieved from: https://www.theguardian.com/sport/2008/may/06/croatiafootballteam.europeanfootball.

Chapter 8

Combating War? Joe Weider, Bodybuilding, and the Korean War

Conor Heffernan, Phillip Chipman, and Nevada Cooke

You Don't Have to Be Weak and Underweight....
—Clarence Ross, *American Manhood,* 1953

Introduction

The average American in the early 1950s was, according to *American Manhood,* weak, underweight, and slovenly (Ross, 1953). They failed to eat correctly, exercise appropriately and, in many cases, act accordingly. The solution? Perhaps unsurprisingly, given the article's appearance in a bodybuilding magazine, was weight training and nutritional supplements. Such actions would improve their health and, it was claimed, help to protect the future of the United States. Previous issues were similarly laden with this message, featuring jingoistic treatises and full-page illustrations of topless, muscular American soldiers. Fueling these messages was the United States' involvement in the Korean War. Nominally depicted as a battle between North and South Korea, the Korean War was an international conflict predicated on international ideologies, and one of the first exhibitions of Cold War hostilities. Shortly after the war began, bodybuilding mogul Joe Weider, owner and publisher of *Mr. America* and *American Manhood,* began to shift the attention of his magazines towards the conflict (Weider et al., 2006).

If 'duelism' is understood as conflict between or within sport, Weider's magazines and the Korean War provide a fine example of this process in action. Weider began publishing his magazines, *Your Physique* and later *Mr. America* and *American Manhood,* to bring health and nutrition information to the reading public. Later reflecting on his successes, Joe Weider claimed that his initial motivation was to bring together a holistic form of bodybuilding, one that encompassed strength training and virtuous eating (Weider et al., 2006). Still trying to establish himself, Weider used the Korean War to increase readership and sales while simultaneously distinguishing himself from contemporary entrepreneurs like Bob Hoffman. What were once magazines aimed at improving one's quality of life became an outlet for celebrating the inherent masculinity in war. The war became a means of differentiating ideal American men from the weak and underweight men previously mentioned. Articles about building a bigger chest were now sandwiched between first-person war stories and puff pieces glorifying the American troops, most notably the Marines and the Air Force. Magazines that advocated, at their core, living a healthier, better life now relied on war, one of history's most indiscriminate takers of life, as their primary driver.

The Korean War and American Masculinity

It was in the Cold War context of fear and proxy war that the Korean conflict took shape. Korea had been a part of the Japanese empire prior to the end of the Second World War and, following Japan's defeat, the Soviets and Americans jointly occupied the Korean Peninsula. Like Germany, it was divided into occupation zones: the 38th parallel demarcated the American-supported Republic of Korea in the south (South Korea) from the communist, Soviet-supported Democratic People's Republic of Korea in the north (North Korea). American Cold War policy of containing the spread of worldwide communism was officially formalized by national security directive NSC 68 in April 1950. Southeast and East Asia were identified by the Soviet Union and the United States as areas either primed for or needing protection from Soviet communism, depending on the point of view, and these areas became primary Cold War battlegrounds where the United States and the Soviet Union sought to exert their influence.

This was, in turn, followed by the beginning of the Korean War. When Joseph Stalin gave North Korea's Kim Il-sung the authority to invade South Korea, he incorrectly gauged the lengths to which America would go to protect East Asia from communism. As Gaddis (2005) notes, the unexpected June invasion of South Korea was "almost as great a shock as the one on Pearl Harbor nine years earlier" (pp. 42-43). This shock created a ripple of fear that would hamstring the United States and lead to the outbreak of another war:

> South Korea in and of itself was of little importance to the global balance of power, but the fact that it had been invaded so blatantly across the 38th parallel, a boundary sanctioned by the United Nations appeared to challenge the entire structure of postwar collective security. (Gaddis, 2005, p. 43)

It took mere hours following the North Korean invasion for the United States to determine it would come to the defense of South Korea.[1]

---

[1] This is a very short summary of the beginnings of the Korean War and the earliest years of the Cold War. Much of it is informed by the work of John Lewis Gaddis, a noted Cold War historian who has spent much of his career researching, writing about, and synthesizing Cold War research. *The Cold War: A New History* is one of his most recent works and attempts to synthesize large chunks of his own research and that of

The Korean War was not the only conflict the United States was embroiled in during the 1950s. In a study investigating the ways that American popular media created a gendered interpretation of the Korean War, Zachary J. Lechner (2014) underlined the "notion of men in danger at home" inherent in the domestic gender panic of the post-Second World War landscape, an "alarmist tract [that] represented a rather pathological response to the political and cultural changes of the post-World War II period" (pp. 316-317). During the Second World War, the male body was shaped both figuratively and physically by the American military, government, and other institutions to convey impressions of national strength and vitality (Jarvis, 2004). The men who would fight in Korea, however, many of whom were too young to participate in the Second World War, were said to have fallen victim to "momism," a plight that left young men coddled and overmothered (Strecker, 1946). The continuing conflict with communism was situated in the language of manliness: cultural commentators argued that men had "gone soft" and would not be able to withstand communist belligerence. Lechner (2014) states that, while the stereotypically manly qualities of strength and endurance were always important in war, the Korean conflict would provide a much greater test of "masculine fortitude" in the gender panicked and anticommunist post-Second World War United States (p. 317).[2] It was in this heavily gendered environment that Weider would first publish *Mr. America* and *American Manhood*.

The Trainer of the Champions

Self-titled "The Trainer of the Champions," Joe Weider was one of the foremost physical culture and bodybuilding entrepreneurs of the twentieth century (Roach, 2011). Born in Montréal in 1920, Joe, along with his brother and business partner, Ben, built a sporting empire that spanned workout courses, magazines, books, nutritional supplements, clothes, and competitions, many of which continue to this day.3 In the past, the Weiders' success, their "rags to riches" story, has been credited to their work ethic, ability to leverage important contacts, and their shrewd eye for promotion (Weider et al., 2006; Fair, 2015). Joe was, in the words of famous

---

other Cold War historians into one concise book. Similarly, Kenneth A. Osgood's "Hearts and Minds" article is itself a meta-analysis of sorts, bookending an analysis of six books on psychological and political Cold War warfare with his own research.

[2] This paragraph is based heavily on the work of Zachary J. Lechner, whose article is itself an examination of the ways in which the American popular media created a gendered interpretation of the Korean War. It has a particularly adroit literature review of related subject material and should be consulted for more information on the subject.

[3] Despite the fact that Joe and Ben Weider were business partners and embarked on many Weider-branded ventures jointly, they did not always split responsibilities evenly, opting instead to devote greater areas of focus to different projects. For example, while Joe was focused on producing Weider-branded magazines, Ben focused on the running and proliferation of the IFBB. Thus, this chapter will focus solely on and mention only Joe Weider, even though everything was undertaken by both Weiders in some capacity.

bodybuilder-turned-actor-turned-governor Arnold Schwarzenegger, one of the most influential men in the popularization of gym culture, first within North America and then, in time, the world (Schwarzenegger, 2012).

At the time of the Korean War, Joe Weider's influence in bodybuilding was small but significant. His first physical culture magazine, *Your Physique*, was founded in Canada in 1940 and by the end of the Second World War had attained a dedicated following in North America (Shurley et al., 2019). Yet in Canada, Weider's path to business hegemony was neither clear nor easy. Phillip Chipman and Kevin Wamsley's (2019) work on Adrien Gagnon's Francophile physical culture magazines during this period stressed the volatile and arbitrary nature of the Canadian market. Gagnon, who predated Weider by several years, relied on a sense of French-Canadian nationalism, devout religious practice, and a belief in Greco-Roman beauty to advance his business interests. Weider, on the other hand, exploited an overt interest in muscular and strong bodies over all else. Where Gagnon linked the strong, muscular, and male bodies to the nation-state or religious piety, Weider focused more on personal health and beauty. It was this more generalised and accessible promotion of the body that explains, somewhat, Weider's ability to attract readers from across North America.

By 1945, the Weiders were Canada's most successful bodybuilding moguls (Roach, 2011). They soon expanded into the United States but were initially relegated to "second-tier" status behind Bob Hoffman, creator of York Barbell and America's most successful entrepreneur of weightlifting materials (Fair, 1999). As the doyen of workout equipment, magazines, and sporting success, he was the coach of America's weightlifting team, Hoffman's rhetoric at this time was steeped in American exceptionalism. A driving force in the revitalization of American weightlifting, Hoffman coached men of different colors and creeds who, he believed, were representative of America's reputation as a cultural mixing pot. John Fair's (1999) extensive biography of Bob Hoffman explains Hoffman's own particularised form of entrepreneurial nationalism, which he used to promote himself. Linking his workout devices to the need to build strong American men and, by proxy, American nationalism, Hoffman presented himself as a key player in American sporting success. Acutely aware of his image as the "Father of American Weightlifting," a title attributed to Hoffman in the mid-1940s, he often attempted to isolate himself from profit-driven motives associated with free-market capitalism. Hoffman often stressed the fact that although he ran a profitable business, his motivations were based first and foremost on expanding the sport of weightlifting (Fair, 1987).

It was for this reason that Hoffman often attempted to work alongside, rather than against, new competitors. This was the case with Joe Weider, whom Hoffman initially helped by including Weider's advertisements in his magazine. Hoffman underestimated Weider's own ambitions, however, and it soon became clear that they would be rivals rather than colleagues. When Weider established Your Physique in 1940, he grew his subscription base by explicitly targeting Hoffman's readers. One of Weider's early tactics was using published lists of Hoffman's readers to send out targeted advertising. Another was to hire writers associated with Hoffman, like the influential British-Canadian physical culturist George Jowett (Fair, 1999). This, Weider later claimed, was the start of the "longest, craziest pissing match in the history of magazine publishing" (Weider et al., 2006, p. 99).

During the Second World War, both men's' interests and profit margins grew. Owing to logistical difficulties, Hoffman was unable to publish his magazine in Canada for several months during the conflict, which helped Weider establish a loyal following (Shurley et al., 2019). Despite the setback, American demand for personalised home exercise equipment increased during the war to the extent that Hoffman emerged richer at the end of the conflict than when he began. As attested by John Fair (1999), Hoffman capitalised on American nationalism to sell products. When the conflict ended and soldiers returned home to the United States, interest in barbell training and personalised fitness grew. Jason Shurley, Jan Todd, and Terry Todd (2019) stressed the importance of demobilized soldiers in the growth of the fitness industry during the late 1940s, many of whom had disposable income through the G.I. Bill. Such men had been introduced to physical training during the war and, on return to the United States, wished to maintain their practice (Fair, 1987). Hoffman, already America's most recognisable exercise entrepreneur, and York Barbell thus thrived.

Still, Weider remained a significant entrepreneur and had, by the end of the War, expanded into America. That the Weiders founded and sustained their first magazine during the War was no easy feat; in a different context, Tawnya Adkins Covert (2003) demonstrated the difficulty faced by some in the print industry during this time. What facilitated Weider's success were the efforts made to distinguish himself from Hoffman. Whereas Hoffman was firmly associated with Olympic weightlifting, Weider sponsored bodybuilding events. The sport of bodybuilding emerged within the United States in the late 1930s through the Mr. America competition hosted by the Amateur Athletic Union (AAU). At that time, the AAU was the sole governing body of Olympic weightlifting. Due to his role in American weightlifting, Hoffman headed the AAU's weightlifting division and, through no desire of his own, bodybuilding (Fair, 2015). The AAU's bodybuilding competitions of the 1940s were marred by Hoffman's insistence that the sport hold a secondary place to weightlifting. AAU physique contests were held directly after weightlifting contests, which often resulted in shows being held in the early hours of the morning (Liokaftos, 2017). Likewise, Mr. America contests were forced to include a weightlifting component to appeal to Hoffman's sensibilities.

In a growing sport, Hoffman's autocratic control caused resentment among competitors. It was this discontent that Weider used to create an opening in the American market. In 1947, the Weiders formed the International Federation of Bodybuilders (IFBB), which served as a governing body for bodybuilding (Dutton & Laura, 1989). IFBB contests, unlike those held by the AAU, solely judged a competitor's physique with no regard for their weightlifting prowess. Likewise, *Your Physique* began focusing more and more on bodybuilding rather than other forms of exercising (Weider et al., 2006). In this way, the fitness landscape of the late 1940s and early 1950s came to be defined by two primary conflicts: bodybuilding versus weightlifting, and Weider versus Hoffman. Despite Hoffman's business sense, he was never known for keeping strict supervision over his workers or, indeed, his finances. In researching his biography of Hoffman, John Fair (1999) found cheque after cheque that Hoffman failed to cash during the height of his success. Weider, on the other hand, has long been noted and praised for his business pragmatism and near-total control over his magazines (Roach, 2011).

A Selling Opportunity? Weider Versus Hoffman

The outbreak of the Korean War gave Weider the opportunity to further distinguish himself from Hoffman through a staunchly jingoistic platform. In 1952, publication of *Your Physique* was formally ended, and it transitioned into a new magazine, *Mr. America*, which became *American Manhood* four issues later. Choosing the title *Mr. America* signaled that this magazine was for the American man who wanted to be *the* American man. Likewise, the blatant use of *American Manhood* undoubtedly provides insight into the way in which Weider sought to utilize this new publication. The editorial policy of the magazines, basically unchanged from *Mr. America* to *American Manhood*, promoted the same lofty ideals. The magazines promised impressive muscular development, good health and vitality, strength of character, education of the youth, success in life, and, perhaps most importantly, becoming a respected citizen: "you will be a diligent, intelligent worker, and in time of war, an asset to your country and a fearless soldier" (Weider, 1952c; Weider, 1953c, p. 1). Where *Mr. America* was as an appeal to the young American male and, as noted by Fair (2015), marked an attempt to dilute the brand importance of Hoffman's Mr. America contest, *American Manhood* was rebranded to appeal to the gay community as well as the average American man (Johnson, 2019). It was through these magazines that the Weiders began to publish and publicize the need for "real Americans" during the Korean War.

Immediately upon publication, *Mr. America* and *American Manhood* began devoting covers and content to the Korean War. In the October 1952 issue, readers were treated to one of several front covers featuring soldiers in action. Shown below (see figure 1), the image featured a heavily muscled sailor loading ammunition; in the background, the faint outline of soldiers loading an artillery cannon. Inside the magazine, Captain Stanley Weston (1952a) warned readers of Korean "death struggles" he had encountered during his time at war. Weston, who incidentally went on to create the popular G.I. Joe action figure in 1963, spoke of the need for strength, vigor, and decisiveness in the most testing of war fronts. The muscular body was not optional in such circumstances, but rather pivotal to one's survival.

The October 1952 issue of *Mr. America* followed the seeming template for *Mr. America* and *American Manhood* issues published throughout the war: muscular, prototypical bodybuilders saving men from drowning, enduring heavy enemy fire, or running through forests angrily firing their weapons (see figure 2). Within the magazine, articles focused on "what you should know about sex," America's "latest public enemies" and, most importantly, the Korean War. Despite a great wave of optimism emanating from the President and the American popular press, the war was a bloody and drawn-out affair (Casey, 2008).

Figure 1: (left), Mr. America, October 1952 and Figure 2: (right). American Manhood, January 1953.[4]

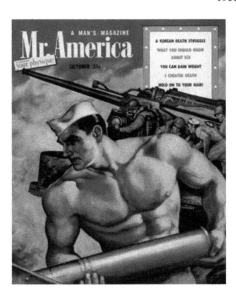 

Major battles and territorial exchanges occurred during the first six months of fighting before coming to a grinding deadlock in early 1951. The next two years saw continued combat with little territorial exchange. In the United States, two pieces of legislation, the Universal Military Training and Service Act and the Armed Forces Reserve Act of 1952, increased America's conscription of troops, creating a new wave of young, male American enlistments in the hope of turning the tide via sheer numerical advantage. Such changes explain why Weider devoted more attention towards the war at this time.

One such example of this was a series of articles entitled "So You're Being Drafted." Focused on the various military and naval outposts for young American men, the articles were firmly situated in discourses of American masculinity. A piece on the Marine Corps, written by Martin Caidin (1953a), exemplified this fact.

---

[4] Photos courtesy of the H.J. Lutcher Stark Center of Physical Culture and Sport Studies, the University of Texas at Austin.

Beginning with the assertion that one was a Marine first before he was a man, the article continued by explaining the guts, courage, and discipline needed to thrive. There was, as the author repeatedly reminded readers, "no place for sissies in this outfit" (p. 48). To prepare for enlisting, Caidin (1953b) spoke of the need to physically strengthen one's body. From a strong body came a strong Marine. Adhering to the magazine's focus, Caidin finished with the assertion that "if you're a marine, you're a man. And a darn good one" (p. 48). Caidin's bravado struck a chord with readers or, at the very least, the editor, as he penned several articles on the draft process. His article on the United States Air Force deviated little from his commentary on the Marines: The Air Force were a group of fit men and joining their ranks necessitated a strong body.

Caidin (1953a; 1953b) also stressed that although a soldier himself, his articles were not intended to be promotional drives for the armed forces but rather an indication of what lay ahead for those enlisted. In this way, Caidin presented himself, and the magazine, as impartial observers who only wished to further the American cause. As a final point, it is worth discussing Caidin's (1953a) article on making the draft "pay off big dividends" for the individual. Here the military was presented as a place wherein one could earn a good wage, develop self-discipline, develop camaraderie, and forge lasting bonds. Most importantly, they could serve their country against a growing communist threat (1953b). Despite Caidin's protestations to the contrary, the articles read like a recruitment drive. Other articles were more impartial. Stanley Weston (1952b) detailed the horrors of war through tell-all stories with titles like "Hell's Hill in Korea." Weston's story, which ended with an American victory, spoke of the importance of strength, skill, and courage in the face of death. In a magazine dedicated to these ideals, or so claimed in the editor's opening remarks at the beginning of an issue, Weston's tripartite recommendations were made in the right arena.

Weider's magazines were positioned as supporters of the American war effort, but also as builders of the men needed to win in Korea. They returned to their by-then-established reputation of building strong male bodies and stronger nerves. Their magazine was unafraid of detailing the horrors of war but offered solace in the fact that their systems of training could prepare one for conflict. This also distinguished them from Hoffman's magazines and his monographs. Where Weider prided himself on the ability to build bodies, Hoffman focused on the help York Barbell provided to the war effort. Still North America's most prolific exercise entrepreneur, Hoffman pivoted some of his factory's output towards war materiel. In this regard, Hoffman wrote of "seventy-hour" working weeks for some engaged in war production. That the company was vital in producing bombs, plane parts, and other combat material was never disputed by Weider and was indeed validated later by John Fair (1999), Hoffman's biographer.

Patriotic though Hoffman's actions may have been, it differentiated Hoffman from Weider. Weider's magazines were explicitly dedicated to the development of a particular kind of American masculinity, predicated on the importance of muscular physiques. Hoffman's own publication, *Strength & Health*, was hamstrung by its association with York Barbell and its long-running commitment to weightlifting. Such constraints explain why, in contrast to Weider, Hoffman's magazines focused on York's efforts to sustain America's materiel production requirements and the international exploits of his weightlifting teams (Fair, 1999). Still coaching the American weightlifting team, Hoffman organised a series of international tours in Soviet and European regions during the 1950s. For Hoffman, American nationalism was born from weightlifting above all else (Schelfhout & Fair, 2018). Hoffman's rigid attachment to his own company and American weightlifting left him in a secondary position when it came to coverage of, and association with, the Korean War. This was certainly evidenced by his profits, which began to drop during this period (Fair, 1999).

The Korean War was not the only way in which Weider differentiated himself from Hoffman. Indeed, several high-profile insults were exchanged between the pair during these years on topics ranging from bodybuilding competitions to nutritional supplements. What the Korean War did do was allow Weider to further popularise himself and present his magazines as those most in touch with current events and political realities. His magazines, unlike Hoffman's, detailed the war from enlistment to engagement. The beginning of the 1950s marked Weider's first major efforts to branch out into the broader public realm and set himself apart from his competition. The Korean War, and how it was dealt with in the magazine, was one obvious example of how this worked. It allowed Weider to produce common-interest stories, position their products as patriotic, and reaffirm their reputation for building patriotically muscular bodies. Where Hoffman prided himself on supporting the war effort, Weider instead glorified the war effort and the bodies that took part in it. It was a subtle change but one that separated the two.

Building Real Soldiers: 'Situational Masculinity' in *Mr. America* and *American Manhood*

With high readership and public visibility brought on by this "patriotic" coverage of the war effort, it is only fitting that Weider, opportunist as he was, seized this occasion to cater his bodybuilding narrative to prevalent military and masculine ideals. When his endeavours as a fitness promoter began in 1940, Weider preached the health benefits of weightlifting and exercising. The first issue of *Your Physique* promised to offer "the proper way to eat for health and strength" while also providing exercises that would ensure the practitioner's access to high-level weightlifting competitions (Weider, 1940, p. 2). In tune with this presentation, penciled-in images of male bodybuilders accompanied the narrative of a healthy lifestyle. In this sense, muscular masculinity[5] was synonymous with health. Years later, in *American Manhood* and *Mr. America*, Weider still preached the benefits of a strict exercise routine and a calculated diet. However, his narrative surrounding fitness and the male body had now grown to include military victory rather than remaining strictly synonymous with health, thus displaying Weider's practice of using world events as a way to push his products and his exercise advice to ultimately expand and legitimize his fitness empire.

In the spirit of 'duelism', we are analyzing how the Korean War shaped Joe Weider's bodybuilding narrative and how, at the same time, Weider's narratives around the male body influenced perceptions of the War itself. Weider capitalized on the war effort to increase sales of magazines and equipment, especially to the detriment of his "archenemy" Bob Hoffman, but he also took the opportunity to cater his bodybuilding narrative to a prevalent ideal of military masculinity. This was apparent in the way the male body was presented in *American Manhood*; the near-nude muscular male being the canvas on which Weider and his staff displayed the benefits of fitness and nutrition, as well as the values relevant to its historical context: bravery, sacrifice, victory, and the will and ability to kill. In this regard, the images and narratives used by Weider were illustrative of this muscular military discourse. The illustration of the near-nude bodybuilder did not differ from earlier (and later) publications, but the text, and the actions some of these men displayed, certainly did. The well-oiled man gazing at his bicep was no longer associated with arm exercises, but rather with guidelines on how to be a successful soldier.

In this sense, the body acted as a text, a mound of flesh on which Joe Weider could imprint his discourse of American military might, and ultimately America's victory, gained strictly through his bodybuilding methods and his nutritional advice. The bodies themselves were passive. While the idea of "passivity" approaches Michel Foucault's (1995) conceptualization of the body as docile and disciplined, with regards to discourse, it does not hold the same connotation in our usage. In Foucault's research, docility and discipline are tied to the actual soldier, the individual fighting for his nation. The body, in this specific work by Foucault, is broken down or psychologically torn apart through methods such as military drills, leading to mental and physical exhaustion. Through this discipline, bodies become docile, and can then be imprinted with military power. It is somewhat paradoxical, as Foucault explains, that such a "docile body" displays so much strength and military meaning (135). In our study, the bodies are viewed as illustrations standing as visual aids for the accompanying text. The individual in question, the hired bodybuilder, has not been torn apart and reconstructed as a disciplined entity. In Weider's case, the bodies are

---

[5] In the construction of gender and masculinity, muscular masculinity refers to a specific way of viewing such a concept. In these terms, the focus is on the shape of the body as a means of defining its masculinity. Muscularity, or possessing a muscular (sometimes overly muscular) physique becomes the norm or the essence for defining what a man is, or for expressing his masculinity.

passive, inanimate images awaiting to be paired with meaningful text to then become, as stated, visual texts themselves. As in Foucault's research, these bodies are surfaces "imprinted by history" (Schilling, 2012, p. 243) on which "the social is inscribed" (Rail & Harvey, 1995, p. 165). The male bodybuilder bodies in Weider's publication were inscribed with a discourse related to war-related values specific to the Korean War. This, in turn, influenced the readers' perception of masculinity. Judith Butler's notion of gender as a "script" (Butler, 1988) is useful in contextualizing masculinity, and by extension, the bodybuilding narrative in Mr. America and American Manhood. According to Butler (1988), gender is constructed, like a script "controlled and constrained by norms and expectations" (p. 520). One's performance, scrutinized by an audience, dictates their embodiment of the "correct" gender. Given that bodybuilding, and more specifically Weider's bodybuilding sphere, is a subculture in a much broader society, we use the term 'situational masculinity' when approaching Weider's conceptualization of masculinity. While Butler maintains that the performance of gender is a "continuous process shaped by pervasive social and cultural norms" (Butler, 1988, p. 519), we argue that situational masculinity is short-lived, restricted to a specific cohort, and shaped by a single group, or in this case, a single individual.

The idea of situational masculinity, especially during a time of conflict, is supported by Joanna Bourke's study of the dismembered male. Bourke (1996) argued that during the First World War, masculinity was defined as "aggressive and stoic" but that these "traits were expressed only because of the exigencies of war" (p. 14). Furthermore, the mangled body reflected this idea of military masculinity. While the body disabled from birth was deemed passive and effeminate, the mutilated was considered manly: "he was the fit man, the potent man [...] both mutilated and mutilator in one" (Bourke, 1996, p. 25). Mutilation, in this sense, reflected male bravery and voluntary heroism, whereas disability was perceived as an error, an image of an undesired oddity. However, once the war ended, the dismembered male became a reminder of a conflict people yearned to forget, rendering what was once considered masculine no longer so, and proving this masculinity to be situational.

Weider's use of the war to shape his magazine's bodybuilding narrative and, by extension, its display, only lasted the length of the Korean War. Masculinity, in Weider's case, is neither mangled nor mutilated; it is blatantly muscular, aggressive, and headstrong. Beginning with the very first *Mr. America* cover in August 1952, and continuing through the transition to *American Manhood*, Weider introduced the readers to his product with images illustrating a mix of violence and blatantly nude virility, characterized by an unfiltered, militaristic masculinity represented by shirtless soldiers in the heat of battle. Upon first glance, the reader is informed of what it takes to be a soldier and is sold the idea that the magazine's content, Joe Weider's narrative, is the means to that end. One of the earliest covers was perhaps the one that blended bodybuilding and war most effectively: a soldier, rifle strapped to his back, is engaged in a dumbbell military press while a plane, likely a bomber, perhaps the iconic Boeing B-52, flies overhead (see figure 3). On another cover, a shirtless sailor heroically rescuing a man, while a naval ship burns in the background, is accompanied by the promise that the reader will "broaden their shoulders" (see figure 4).[6] On another, Weider tells the reader they "don't have to be a skinny weakling," underscored by the inclusion of an image of a muscular, shirtless soldier yelling and firing a rocket launcher (see figure 5). The November 1952 edition of *Mr. America* gives the secret to gaining weight while displaying a shirtless, muscular combatant under fire, mounting a machine gun (see figure 6). Finally, a fearless, armed soldier, unsurprisingly shirtless, running into the fray is accompanied by the assurance that "you can add 10 inches to your chest" (see figure 2).

Figure 3: (left), Mr. America, September 1952 and Figure 4 (right). American Manhood, February 1953.[7]

 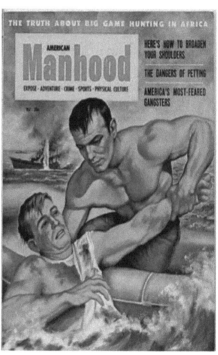

---

[6] As if to run the full gamut of content inclusion, the article on broadening one's shoulders includes the "truth" about big game hunting in Africa as well as the "dangers of petting", the latter, presumably, not relating to the petting of "big game" African animals.
[7] Photos courtesy of the H.J. Lutcher Stark Center of Physical Culture and Sport Studies, the University of Texas at Austin.

It is clear in the way Weider chose to portray the male body, shirtless and in action, that his bodybuilding narrative was undoubtedly influenced by the Korean War. The bodies themselves became texts of militaristic, masculine values. At the same time, Weider, through his displays of this situational masculinity linked to the practice of bodybuilding, such as adding inches to the chest and broadening the shoulders, worked to control the reader perceptions of the war. The covers show the war as violent, deadly, and chaotic. However, in this chaos, we have the triumphant American soldier: the bodybuilder. Relating the notion of 'duelism,' Weider retained similar promises regarding the promotion of a healthy lifestyle, such as lifting weights and eating well, but actively catered his advice to the construction and refinement of a physical weapon in a conflict that definitely inflicted bodily harm: a weapon in the form of a shirtless man, who would ensure America's victory with a rocket launcher nestled atop a well-developed deltoid.

Figure 5: (left), American Manhood, February 1953 and Figure 6 (right). Mr. America, November 1952.[8]

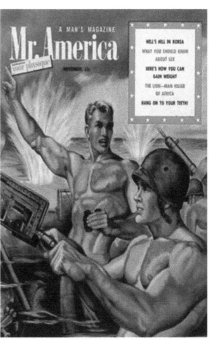

---

[8] Photos courtesy of the H.J. Lutcher Stark Center of Physical Culture and Sport Studies, the University of Texas at Austin.

The content within the magazine reflected the messages portrayed on its covers. A May 1953 article entitled "They Weren't Born That Way" presents the physical hardships of bodybuilder Clarence Ross. According to Joe Weider (1953e), who authored the piece, Ross was a "tall, thin youth" who struggled to gain weight to the point that he became discouraged and "packed away his weights, never to use them again." It was his time as a soldier during the Second World War that persuaded him to return to training with "renewed vigor" and resulted in his winning the prestigious Mr. America title in 1945, shortly after his discharge (p. 23). While Ross' experience stood as an inspirational testimony to dedication, the fact that his story was chosen over all others is telling. Being part of the armed forces provided Ross with the devotion needed to not only to adopt a healthy lifestyle, but to become Mr. America. Here again, we find Weider linking war to bodybuilding success; it was military service that restored his own love of weight training and led to his crowning as the "King of Bodybuilders" (p. 23). Pictures of Clarence Ross posing near-nude stand as testaments to this success: a body developed through commitment to one's country. In the same issue, Barton Horvath (1953) presented Art Gay, a man who, through his participation in the First World War, won a strongman competition. Under the title "Living the Gay Life", we find a muscular, shirtless Art Gay impressing four bikini-clad women with his pullups. Through both Ross' and Gay's testimonies, and their eroticized muscularity, Weider showcases war as a tempting endeavour that pushed readers to exercise and to aspire to gain success in the fitness milieu, by using the latter's methods.

This idea was even more apparent in an article entitled "So You Want to be a Marine," part of the "So You're Being Drafted" series. Sandwiched between advertisements for nutritional supplements and articles promising to improve your sex life, the article outlines what it takes to be a Marine and, ultimately, participate in the conflict at hand. Once again, according to Caidin, it was simple: if "you're a marine then mister, you're a man" (1953c, p. 46). However, this statement prompts a line of questioning: what about those who were not Marines? Were they not men? How does Caidin define masculinity? For starters, a man is "TOUGH" (1953c, p. 47, emphasis in original). His concept of manhood is synonymous with "guts," a "fighting spirit," a "willingness to serve their nation" and the readiness "to stand up and defend the tradition of the Corps [...] with bayonet or fist!" (1953c, p. 46). Later, he reminds readers that "it takes a lot of man" to defend America. A man "must not be lazy" and must show "intelligence" (1953b, pp. 34-35). In the end, "the military wants [someone] with an aggressive, get-ahead determination" (1953a, p. 38). The presence of such articles is telling; as editor-in-chief, Joe Weider actively chose to feature lengthy guidelines, throughout his 1953 publications, that outlined what it took to become a "successful" soldier.

Weider was clearly catering his bodybuilding narrative and, by extension, his idea and concept of masculinity, to the Korean War. By including Caidin's articles, among others, Weider showed that the art of soldiery unquestionably belonged in a magazine aimed at promoting a healthy lifestyle. Interestingly, Caidin's guidelines were not accompanied by the same over-muscular, shirtless men littered throughout the magazine. However, Weider did not shy away from including his idea of the militaristic, sexualized man in other articles pertaining strictly to warfare; the aforementioned series of war stories, entitled "Hell's Hills in Korea," depicts the usual shirtless, well-proportioned soldier in action. Accompanying an exciting depiction of a battle in Korea, written by Captain Weston, was the image of a muscular combatant braving the battlefield against two fully dressed Korean soldiers firing from a machine gun nest. Like Caidin's articles on the art of soldiery, it is our assertion that the "Hell's Hills in Korea" series was included specifically to link the practice of bodybuilding and the Korean War. The display of military manhood braving the fray once again offers Weider's situational masculinity: brave, aggressive, willing to die for his country, and without a doubt, muscular.

In his intertwining of warfare and exercise, Joe Weider's bodybuilding narrative and depiction of the muscular soldier displayed the notion of 'duelism.' While he began his career as a fitness entrepreneur with the promise of aiding people in leading a healthy lifestyle and competing in weightlifting competitions, Weider continues to promote exercise and nutrition (the foundations of health) but with the objective of building soldiers whose goal is to partake in what can be argued is the most physically detrimental event in human history: war. In *Mr. America* and *American Manhood* we find Weider writing a gender "script" regarding the Korean War, which creates a masculinity that is situational. Influenced by this Cold War proxy conflict, Weider caters his narrative to display the muscular male body as resilient in the face of danger and fear and as a tool that can be used to satisfactorily end the war. At the same time, Weider offers his readers a unique perception of the Korean War. Across many articles and graphic covers, the audience is shown that the war is violent and chaotic. But within this chaos, the American soldier, or, more precisely, the Weider bodybuilder, though they are packaged and portrayed as synonymous, will prevail. In this sense bodybuilding, or rather *his* bodybuilding, stands as the solution *par excellence*, in life and in war. As the title indicates, Weider is selling *American Manhood*, at least his idea of what that can and should entail.

Conclusion

As the Korean War broke out, Joe Weider found himself on American soil with new magazines to publish. Coming from Montréal and replacing his first publication, *Your Physique*, with *Mr. America* and *American Manhood*, Weider's promotion of exercise and living a healthy lifestyle continued. However, writing during the Korean conflict, magazines that advocated living a better life also began to rely on war as their primary driver. As shown, Weider not only embraced this shift but orchestrated it in order to increase his readership and, by extension, his sales. We find Weider catering his narrative to include discussions about the war and describe his long-lasting exercises with military lingo. The addition of near-nude soldiers on the covers clearly indicated what the magazine promoted and stood as a contrast to his competition's publications.

Still attempting to differentiate himself from longtime rival Bob Hoffman, Weider positioned his product as patriotic by glorifying the war effort and the bodies that took part in it.

Presenting these muscular bodies as visceral war machines, Weider also took this opportunity to convey a clear message of military masculinity. Understating masculinity as a construct that is superfluid and subjective, we argue that Weider constructed a masculinity that was situational: one that reflected the values propagated during the Korean War but that would only last as long as the fighting continued. While manhood was still synonymous with muscles and strength, Weider's situational masculinity during the Korean War also stressed endurance, bravery, victory, and the will and ability to kill. With regards to the concept of 'duelism,' throughout *Mr. America* and *American Manhood* we clearly see Weider participating in a certain 'duelity.' On one side, we have Weider actively shaping the practice of bodybuilding to conform to the Korean War; on the other, he is using his magazines to create a specific perception of the war. As the fighting continued, bodybuilding became a "patriotic endeavour" that ensured the survival and longevity of the American nation. While bench presses and push-ups still provided a muscular chest, for Joe Weider, in the context of the Korean War, they also ensured victory. While reading about the benefits of protein and ways to improve one's sex life, the audience was told that the war in Korea was exceedingly violent and chaotic. However, among this chaos stood the Weider bodybuilder, and by extension, the American man.

Was Joe Weider "combating war?" In a sense, he was. Through well-written articles, strategically placed images of near-nude muscular athletes, and skillfully drawn shirtless soldiers braving the fray, Weider contributed to the American war effort. In doing so, however, he effectively sold out the good health and vitality that his magazines were trying to sell. By depicting American men as muscular fighters standing victorious on "Hell's Hill" in Korea, it stands to reason that Weider may have contributed to the idea of America being a "naturally" militaristic nation. Weider's magazines were, in essence, "duelism" in both thought and practice.

REFERENCES

Bourke, J. (1996). *Dismembering the Male: Men's Bodies, Britain, and the Great War.* The University of Chicago Press.

Butler, J. (1988). Performative acts and gender constitution: An essay in phenomenology and feminist theory. *Theatre Journal, 40*(4), 519-531. https://doi.org/10.2307/3207893.

Caidin, M. (1953a, February). So, You're Being Drafted. *American Manhood, 18*(5), 38-39.

Caidin, M. (1953b, March-April). So, You're Being Drafted. *American Manhood, 18*(6), 34-35.

Caidin, M. (1953c, May). So, You Want to Be A Marine. *American Manhood, 19*(1), 46-48.

Carver, B. (1953, February). American Manhood Platter Chatter. *American Manhood, 18*(5), 15-17.

Casey, S. (2008). *Selling the Korean War: Propaganda, Politics, and Public Opinion in the United States, 1950-1953.* Oxford University Press.

Chipman, P., & Wamsley, K. B. (2019). Marketing La Survivance in pre-Quiet Revolution Montreal: Adrien Gagnon's physical culture wars with Ben Weider. *Sport History Review, 50*(1), 1-16. https://doi.org/10.1123/shr.2018-0016.

Covert, T. A. (2003). Consumption and citizenship during the Second World War: Product advertising in women's magazines. *Journal of Consumer Culture, 3*(3), 315-342. https://doi.org/10.1177/14695405030033002.

Dutton, K. R., & Laura R. S. (1989) Towards a history of bodybuilding. *Sporting Traditions, 6*(1), 25-41. https://pdfs.semanticscholar.org/e88d/5eb08f79c8a52bba0c9f2680cd77a118cbff.pdf.

Fair, J. D. (1987). Bob Hoffman, the York Barbell Company, and the golden age of American weightlifting, 1945-1960. *Journal of Sport History, 14*(2), 164-188. https://www.jstor.org/stable/43610149.

Fair, J. D. (1999). *Muscletown USA: Bob Hoffman and the Manly Culture of York Barbell.* Penn State Press.

Fair, J. D. (2015). *Mr. America: The Tragic History of a Bodybuilding Icon.* University of Texas Press.

Foucault, M. (1995). *Discipline and Punish: The Birth of the Prison.* Vintage Books.

Gaddis, J. L. (2005). *The Cold War: A New History.* The Penguin Press.

Hovarth, B. (1953, May). Living the Gay Life. *American Manhood, 19*(1), 53-54.

Johnson, D. K. (2019). *Buying Gay: How Physique Entrepreneurs Sparked a Movement.* Columbia University Press.

Jarvis, C. S. (2004). *The Male Body at War: American Masculinity during World War II.* University of Illinois Press.

Lechner, Z. L. (2014). "We Have Certainly Saved Ourselves": Popular Views of Masculinity during the Korean War, 1950-53. *Comparative American Studies, 12*(4), 316-337. https://doi.org/10.1179/1477570014Z.0000000009.

Libasci, M. (1952). What You Should Know About Sex. *American Manhood, 18*(1), 26-27.

Liokaftos, D. (2017). *A Genealogy of Male Bodybuilding: from Classical to Freaky.* Taylor & Francis.

Osgood, K. A. (2002). Hearts and Minds: The Unconventional Cold War. *Journal of Cold War Studies, 4*(2), 85-107. https://doi.org/10.1162/152039702753649656.

Rail, G., & Harvey J. (1995). Body at Work: Michel Foucault and the Sociology of Sport. *Sociology of Sport Journal, 12*, 164-179. https://doi.org/10.1123/ssj.12.2.164.

Roach, R. (2011). *Muscle, Smoke, and Mirrors* (Vol. 2). AuthorHouse.

Ross, C. (1953, May). You Don't Have to be Weak and Underweight. *American Manhood, 19*(1), 20-22.

Schilling, C. (2012). *The Body and Social Theory.* SAGE Publications.

Schwarzenegger, A. (2012). *Total Recall.* Hoffmann und Campe.

Schelfhout, S., & Fair, J. (2018). Lifting 'Round the World': The goodwill weightlifting tours of 1955. *The International Journal of the History of Sport, 35*(10), 1008-1028. https://doi.org/10.1080/09523367.2019.1576637.

Shurley, J., & Todd, J. (2012). Joe Weider, all american athlete, and the promotion of strength training for sport, 1940-1969. *Iron Game History, 12*(1), 4-27. https://www.starkcenter.org/igh/igh-v12/igh-v12-n1/igh1201p04.pdf.

Shurley, J. P., Todd, J., & Todd, T. (2019). *Strength Coaching in America: A History of the Innovation That Transformed Sports.* University of Texas Press.

Strecker, E. A. (1946). *Their Mothers' Sons: The Psychiatrist Examines an American Problem.* Lippincott.

Weider, B. (1953, March-April). Meet America's Most Feared Gangsters. *American Manhood, 18*(6), 40-41.
Weider, J. (1940, August). Editorial. *Your Physique, 1*(1), 2-4.
Weider, J. (1952a, September). Cover. *Mr. America, 17*(6).
Weider, J. (1952b, October). Cover. *Mr. America, 18*(1).
Weider, J. (1952c, October). Our Editorial Policy. *Mr. America, 18*(1), 1.
Weider, J. (1952d, November). Cover. *Mr. America, 18*(2).
Weider, J. (1953a, January). Cover. *American Manhood, 18*(4).
Weider, J. (1953b, February). Cover. *American Manhood, 18*(5).
Weider, J. (1953c, March-April). Our Editorial Policy. *American Manhood, 18*(6), 1.
Weider, J. (1953d, May). Cover. *American Manhood, 19*(1).
Weider, J. (1953e, May). They Weren't Born That Way. *American Manhood, 19*(1), 23-25.
Weider, J. Weider, B., & Steere, M. (2006). *Brothers of Iron.* Sports Publishing LLC.
Weston, S. (1952a, October). A Korean Death Struggle. *Mr. America, 18*(1), 40-41.
Weston, S. (1952b, December). Hell's Hills in Korea. *American Manhood, 18*(3), 46-47.

Chapter 9

'For Both Language Groups to Feel at Home Either as Participants or Sightseers': Sport, Memory, Resistance and Nation at the 1952 Van Riebeeck Sports Festival

Hendrik Snyders

Introduction

There is a persistent myth among some South Africans that sport was one of the few cultural activities "not intrinsically linked to the shame of apartheid" (Dunn, 2009, p. 3). Indeed, Nauright and Black suggest that this 'myth of autonomy' "has shown impressive resilience" and underpins the belief in sport as a trivial and pleasurable form of social recreation that should be free of politics (Nauright & Black, 1998, p. 194). This belief lies at the heart of the narrative that continues to imply that the country's first post-apartheid president, Nelson Mandela, was the first to use sport to achieve political objectives (Carlin, 2008); this is in direct contrast to the fact that all South African sport, especially rugby football, was never a game of innocence but rather "a game [or games] of politics" (Macfarlane & Herd, 1986, p. 132).

The Van Riebeeck Tercentenary Festival, held four years after the implementation of apartheid, was arguably one of the first instances of sport blatantly used to promote a political ideology. There is consensus among South African historians that the event indeed represents a pivotal moment in the life of the nation. Essentially, a "celebration of white supremacy" (Crais, 2004, pp. 523–524) and an exercise in white legitimacy construction (Jörder, 2019, pp. 443–450), it formed an integral part of the country's contested public national history (Rassool & Witz, 1993, pp. 447–468). For Witz (1998/1989, pp. 187–206), the festival and its hosting sites and spaces, its "metaphorical associations with geographical place," have a definite meaning. Within these spaces, "the events associated with the space are themselves ascribed, mapped, labelled and/or contested" as they are harnessed to "promote the idea and images of a racially designated settler nation as the inclusive South African nation." In this process, they became sites of struggle and firmly embedded the partnership between sport and politics.

Although the 'national' sports event, dubbed the Van Riebeeck Sports Festival, formed an integral part of the festivities, historians paid little attention to investigating the role of sport and the complicity of sports administrators in this event and the promotion of their broader political agenda. Although Labuschagne attempted a cultural analysis of the whole event, very little significance was attached to the former programme, despite South Africa's close association with Western sport and its connections with both colonialism and apartheid (Labuschagne, 2017, pp. 106–133). Within the festival's context, with its theme of *Building a Nation*, the organisers framed amateur sports' political role, or partnership, in the 'building of a nation.' The hosting of many sports events, together with some of the other festival offerings, created a situation where the "sights at the fair nearly overshadowed Van Riebeeck" (Witz, 1993, p. 6).

The purpose of this chapter is to investigate the character of the Van Riebeeck Sports Festival, inclusive of the codes and organisations involved as well as those excluded, against the backdrop of colonialism, social segregation, and apartheid. This study, thus, eliminates the persistent myth of the 'innocence' of sport in the pre-democracy days.

Sport and Colonialism

European sport was introduced to South Africa almost as soon as the Dutch and British settlers occupied the southern tip of Africa. Whereas the Dutch introduced several indoor games, such as cards and chess (Bailey, 1991), the Brits introduced competitive outdoor pastimes (De Kock, 1955). One of the first competitive sports, cricket, was played for the first time in 1806, soon after the British occupied the Cape for the second time (Odendaal, Merrett, Winch & Reddy, 2017). Golf or ('Kolf' in Dutch) was played in Cape Town as early as 1843, and at stake was the Silver Kolf or Silver Golf, which was awarded to the colony's white resident golfers (Herman, C.L., Hertzog, W.F. & Van Breda, P., 1843, January 23).

The black colonial elite, who were equally attracted to these games, supported the idea that "good sport, manliness and love of 'fair play'" should be promoted among all classes of society ("Sport on the 'Fields'", 1873, p. 120; "Health and Happiness", 1843, p. 305). They regarded the demonstration of prowess, fair play, and sportsmanship as sufficient indicators of athletes' "fitness to be accepted as full citizens" (Odendaal, 1988, pp. 199–200). As a result, they started to play this and other sports with great enthusiasm and skill. Over a short time, some players, such as cricket player 'Krom' Hendricks, became serious contenders for inclusion in the 'country's' first proto-national teams (Odendaal et al., 2017). The prevailing social custom of social segregation, however, blocked his advancement. The *Cape Argus,* one of Cape Town's oldest newspapers, acted as a propagandist for the notion that "the races are best socially apart, each good in their own way, but a terribly bad mixture" (Bickford-Smith, 1995, p. 149). As a result, social advancement through the demonstration of prowess in 'culturally civilised' sport was curtailed; however, it did not stop the development of significant black sporting traditions in sports such as rugby and cricket during the nineteenth century.

Restricted by racism, black communities throughout the country were forced to form their own clubs and regional or colonial associations and competitions. Most had a broad membership base, consisting of both Africans and so-called 'coloureds,' or people of mixed-race origins. To place their activities on the same, or even higher, moral plane than their white counterparts, and to signal an intention to be forward-looking, integrationist, and universally respected organisations, these bodies further adopted the existing English or other sets of international sport-specific rules (De Beers Archives, 1897). Despite all their efforts to gain entry to international competition, such as the Commonwealth and Olympic Games, most, however, failed (Snyders, 2015, p. 97). Sport, therefore, became an integral part of the black struggle for social justice.

Fear among Afrikaners characterised the period of 1948–1958. As noted by Du Bruyn and Wessels, among others, the prevailing fears were of political domination and economic displacement by blacks, as well as the undermining of their language by English. This fear not only resulted in the emergence of rightist thought and right-wing leanings in their political orientation, but also gave rise to the institutionalisation of a line of fear ('vreeslyn') in their politics. Thus, when they won power, the constituents of the new power bloc insisted on the use of legislation to fashion a socio-political system that combined fundamental values and principles with concrete measures to address both internally and externally-generated fears (Du Bruyn & Wessels, 2007, pp. 86–88).

Preparing to Celebrate, 1946–1952.

In 1946, a few months after South Africa has concluded its participation in the Second World War, the *Cape Times* newspaper called for a proper celebration of the Tercentenary of the landing of the Dutch colonists under Jan Van Riebeeck. It favoured an inclusive event, one that would be:

> representative of all sections of the public, and being entirely non-political, non-sectarian and non-sectional in character, bearing in mind that the proposed celebrations belong to the people of South Africa as a whole and not to any one centre or section ("Riebeeck Landing Tercentenary," 1946).

It was an ambitious call, in the midst of a post war depression. Fear of black domination, racial integration, communist takeover, and perception of failed segregation challenged the Afrikaner community at the time (Du Bruyn & Wessels, 2007, p. 84). Two years later, after the National Party's political takeover, the same publication called for an affordable event and one characterised "by simple services of thanksgiving" ("Should Tercentenary be simple?", 1948). In response to these calls, the City of Cape Town, who generally hosted the annual Van Riebeeck commemorations, invited public bodies, institutions and societies to a wreath-laying ceremony at the Van Riebeeck Statue in Adderley Street ("Commemoration Jan Van

Riebeeck Day," 1948). A large number of organisations, including government representatives, Afrikaans, Dutch and English cultural organisations and several white schools, attended (City of Cape Town, 1948, April 6). This event, and others such as a gala dinner of the Rotary Club of Cape Town, were used as platforms to call on the national government to take the lead concerning an official celebration of what was called the Van Riebeeck Tercentenary, coming in 1952 ("Om Van Riebeeck se aankoms," 1948). The Mayor of Cape Town similarly criticised the lack of celebrations elsewhere and the fact that the event, for all practical purposes, was becoming an 'unnoticed anniversary' ("An Unnoticed Anniversary," 1948). This appeal and others like it encouraged ordinary members of the public to turn to the local media to express their support for straightforward and inexpensive ceremonies (City of Cape Town, 1948, April 6). Member of Parliament, Dirk Mostert, was one of the most vocal supporters of the need of a proper celebration for the arrival of the Dutch settlement in South Africa. He was adamant that one of the inheritances received from Van Riebeeck is the "right of whites to demand the right for their children to remain as such" ("Reg dat kinders Blank moet bly," 1949).

In the aftermath of the 1949 celebrations, several newspapers embarked on a campaign to sway public opinion in favour of a proper Tercentenary celebration. According to the *Cape Argus*, such an event was a fitting honour for "the man who brought civilisation to these shores and laid the foundations of a nation." Furthermore, the newspaper reported how "it is to be supposed that the day will be commemorated with due pomp and ceremony" (City of Cape Town, 1948, April 6). The *Cape Times* similarly criticised what it called the 'lethargic spirit' within government circles ("City plans for Tercentenary," 1949). The leading Afrikaans pro-Afrikaner newspaper, *Die Burger*, supported this position by insisting that the government should take the lead, both in organisational and funding terms ("'n Fees in 1952," 1952). However, the official position, as articulated by the Minister of Defence F.C. Erasmus, was that the government had more urgent priorities, such as passing "legislation this session to place the coloured people on a separate roll and to prohibit mixed marriages" ("Enough Accomplished," 1949). With institutionalising apartheid at the top of the official agenda, the Tercentenary celebrations remained a low priority.

Spurred on by officials' lethargy, a volunteer committee involving significant Afrikaans interest groups, under the chairmanship of Dr E.G. Jansen, Minister of Native Affairs, was started to lobby the government and pursue discussions with Dr T.E. Dönges, Minister of Home Affairs. The sixteen-member Cape Town Committee representative of Afrikaans, English, and Dutch interests, however, excluded blacks or sports administrators. Out of their engagement with state representatives, they formulated a set of proposals ("Groot fees lê voor", 1950), which, among others, included a formal state-decision that the festival would be a 'volksfees' ['people's festival'] and not a 'staatsfees' [state festival] with the latter making a financial contribution ("Volksfees gesteun," 1950). This situation prompted the Afrikaans newspaper, *Die Suiderstem*, to express the hope that the festival, through its "original nature, character-building and internal human energy would excel and provide a lasting national memory" ("Vorder ons?", 1950). Most newspapers reported the official view: that the organisers should take care to prevent the event from degenerating into a fair ('kermis'); this was intended to allow South Africa to give a message, both to itself and the world, and to "show the spiritual values which characterised the South African way of life through the centuries and to indicate the material development in all fields of national life" ("Regeringstandpunt oor Van Riebeeck Fees," 1951; "Cape Town Tercentenary Celebrations," 1951). Importantly, the festival was intended to be a commemorative and pious deed of faith ("Fees in 1952 mag nie kermis wees nie," 1951).

Afrikaans newspapers emphasised that the proposed festival would be a profoundly religious and serious event, stressing that it needed to showcase the true nature of white South African identity. In contrast, the English-language Port Elizabeth *Evening Post* put forward a different view: they appealed to the organisers to, when considering proposed festivities, "steer clear of any pageantry that might offend one or another race group" and preferably use it as "a potent force for unity and improved race relations" while steering away from racial tension ("Van Riebeeck Festival," 1951). Similarly, the *Worcester Standard* called for "separate efforts of the different sectors of the community to form a practicable and satisfactory whole" ("Our part in the Van Riebeeck Festival," 1951). Additionally, in a letter to the *Cape Argus*, Sam Khan, a member of the Communist Party of South Africa in the Cape Town City Council, objected to specific elements of the proposed programme, which he described as 'hurtful to non-Europeans.' In his view, these elements included 'anti-non-European' references, a 'distortion of history,' "depicting Native people in a primitive and barbarous state," and a 'falsification of our history.' As a result, he criticised the exclusion of blacks and urged that they instead spend the money earmarked for the festival on directly improving blacks' lot ("Fees se deure oop vir Nie-Blankes," 1951). He further charged that "the whole slant of the pageant is a vilification of the black people and in contradiction to the admirable slogan selected, namely, 'We build a Nation'" ("Pageant Hurtful to Non-Europeans," 1951). Others, such as the Cape Town branch of the National Council of Women, a campaigner for women's franchise, described the proposed festival as premature and misplaced, and questioned the motivations behind the initiative: "How can we, who have produced so much strife, so little culture, seriously propose to give a message to the world at the 1952 South African Festival." Furthermore, they argued that "the only realistic message we could send and would be to say that we regret our strife and hatred and will try to do better in the next 300 years" ("Regret Should be Union's 1952 Message," 1950).

JC Marais, the organising secretary of the festival committee, strongly contested these sentiments. He felt compelled to issue a public statement declaring that all planning would be free of politics. The central festival committee further addressed a formal written appeal to the government and (white) opposition parties in parliament for a 'political truce' and to "maintain as calm a political atmosphere as possible" during the event "so that members of all parties can enjoy the festival in a spirit of friendship and goodwill" ("Festival Call for Political Truce in S.A.," 1951). In the aftermath of this call, the Cape-based *Die Burger* newspaper asked for politicians "to be vigilant for any harmful words and deeds that may negatively impact on the unifying influence of the proposed festival" ("Politiek en die Fees," 1951).

Sport 'A Unique Manner of Bringing the Tercentenary Celebrations Before the Eyes of the World'

When the national organising committee started its festival planning, the inclusion of sport was not part of the initial ideas raised, ascribed to the fact that the prime motivation behind the event was to establish "clear Afrikaner linkage and ancestry," as opposed to a "direct association with the local, national [political] past" (Labuschagne, 2017, p. 110). In July 1950, the South African Amateur Athletics & Cycling Union requested to be part of the envisaged celebrations, citing it as presenting a unique opportunity to invite overseas athletes in the run-up to the scheduled 1952 Olympic Games to South Africa ("City may see Olympic Champions," 1951). It also saw it as an opportune moment to "represents a unique manner of bringing the Tercentenary celebrations before the eyes of the world as athletes will be coming from countries from all parts of the globe" (Honorary Secretary, 1950, July 20).

    Further approaches along the same lines came from tennis and motor-racing. By October, the Cape Town Committee added as one of their objectives, the "portrayal of the development in the social and religious fields, in agriculture, industry, and mining, defence, communications, youth activities, coloured Malay and Native Customs over the past 300 years" ("1952 Proposals in Detail," 1950). In light of these appeals, a sports sub-committee under the chairmanship of Advocate A.J. 'Sport' Pienaar, president of the South African Rugby Football Board (SARFB), was established to compile a 'festival of South African sport' to cater to all tastes ("Festival of South African Sports," 1951).

    At its first meeting held in Cape Town on the 24 November 1950, the Sports Coordinating Committee (SCC) formally resolved that the sports festival aimed to portray the role of amateur sport in the building of a nation. The Second World War's divisive effect probably motivated this move, seeing a split along linguistic and political lines when those in favour of participation in the war on the side of the British Empire, attempted to use sport as a recruitment tool and as a means of raising funds for the war effort (Smit, 1987, p. 1). Rugby circles, one of the leading sporting codes in the white community, were also split (Dobson, 1989). The treatment of Afrikaner soldiers in the armed forces at the hands of English officers created further divisions, fuelled by the emergence of armed opposition against South Africa's involvement with the war (Grundlingh, 1999, p. 364). Since the point of departure was that amateur sport equalled white sport, including black sportspersons into the programme was not considered. This matter only became relevant when the sub-committee on the participation of coloureds, Malays and Griquas, resolved to include a float representing sport in these communities in the main festival procession. As far as the African population of Cape Town was concerned, the organisers proposed the construction of a 'Bantu Pavilion' for display and that a "definite programme of sports (to keep the function on desirable lines)" would be hosted as a 'local affair' that the Department of Bantu Administration's officials controlled (Secretary for Native Affairs, 1951, November 15).

These developments were consistent with the established segregation practices that characterised organised South African sport since its inauguration in the nineteenth century. It further followed the stipulations of existing legislation, such as the Population Registration Act 30 of 1950, the Prohibition of Mix Marriages Act 55 of 1949, and the Group Areas Act 41 of 1951, passed to institutionalise segregation between the races. This marginalisation further conformed to established practices about events, such as colonial exhibitions that generally hosted stereotypical displays of colonial populations with little regard for the inconsistencies and 'insinuations' of the exhibited reality and the actual experiences of the displayed (Britton, 2010, p. 71). These displays not only generally omitted people classified as native, but also over-emphasised European values and 'civilisation' in distant places (Clendinning, 2006, pp. 81–85, 97). Furthermore, it was common practice to restrict indigenous participation in such events to sideshows and as 'interesting and exotic entertainment' to 'thrill and horrify exhibition audiences' (Clendinning, 2006, p. 103). This 'cultural distance' between the races, according to Coe, "justified legislation that would promote the institutionalisation of that distance" (2001, p. 9). Although no specific legislation was passed up to that point to formalise segregated sport, the existing regulations, policies, and standing practices around separate amenities generally left black sportspeople with the poorest facilities. Similarly, the right to represent South Africa internationally was reserved for white athletes, a situation that forced coloured champion weightlifter, Ron Eland, to compete for inclusion on the Great Britain team that participated in the 1948 London Olympic Games (Atkin, 1948, p. 1; Cleophas, 2018).

Twelve sports associations, including baseball, rugby, football, boxing, bowling, yachting, athletics and cycling, cricket, and women's hockey, attended the follow-up meeting of the sports sub-committee in December 1950. The meeting agreed to the hosting of national events, such as inter-provincial tournaments and championships, that each would finance its participation, and that everything would be done to promote the national character of the main festival (Sports Sub-Committee, 1950, December 8). It further resolved to bring all national bodies together to compile a suitable exhibition programme with the possibility of "making Cape Town the venue for the 1952 Olympic boxing trials and South African championships." The city had to display over three centuries of sport history, including the hosting of sporting codes from the previous century ("Magtige feesplan vir 1952," 1950). In their deliberations, present delegates were unanimous in their decision that the festival should be one in which "both European language groups would feel at home either as participants or sightseers". This objective was directly influenced by what Du Bruyn and Wessels have, in a different context, referred to as a 'line of fear,' especially observable in the late 1940s and early 1950s. Against this background, several organisations signalled their intention to ensure a measure of international involvement in the event and, therefore, continued the practice of using sport as an instrument to foster reconciliation.

The Organising Committee also approached the South African Olympic and British Empire Games Associations (SAOBEGA) to secure optimal involvement from most, if not all, white sports bodies. However, SAOBEGA declined and left the decision to participate to its provincial affiliates, endorsing the original request that sports events be organised 'on a national scale,' in line with the central theme of *S.A. After 300 Years We Build a Nation.* In so doing, they acknowledged sport's undeniable past and ongoing role in the development of the country and nation. It further agreed to the proposal that the "role of sports in the building of a nation might be portrayed by way of exhibits in the national Tercentenary exhibitions, and as part of a pageant or processional exhibition (floats)" (Pauw, J.C. & Getz, H., 1951, January 11).

A Sub-Committee for Non-Whites/Non-Europeans, further subdivided in a sub-committee for Coloureds, Malays, and blacks, under the Chairmanship of Dr I.D. Du Plessis, the commissioner for coloured and Rehoboth Affairs, was established to secure the involvement of blacks in the festivities. The relevant sub-committee initially discussed the hosting of a "traditional Malay pageant," which was "handled as a separate group" for planning to determine the role of the Coloured and Malay population in the festivities ("Jan Van Riebeeck Tercentenary", 1950). For the broader coloured group, the discussion of physical involvement unfolded following the principle of "each one to its nature," as local organisers so eloquently expressed ("Kleurlinge sal ook fees kan vier", 1951). These practices were especially in line with the stipulations of the Population Registration Act 30 of 1950, which had, for governance, sub-divided the South African population along racial lines. According to Breckenridge, this Act was "the bureaucratic cornerstone of the apartheid state, the lynch-pin of the Group Areas Act" (Breckenridge, 2014, p. 225).

The committee invited several high-profile individuals, such as renowned educationist and political activist Richard E. Van der Ross, and others, such as Ibrahiema Schroeder, J.S. Manca, M.A. Regal, Rev. DJA Jordaan, Ms Jean Strapp and a Mr Henry (Silverleaf School, Athlone) to encourage Coloured and Malay participation (Malay and Coloured Sub-Committee, 1951, January 29). Later invitations were extended to other leading luminaries in coloured politics, such as George Golding and George Veldsman, when figures such as Van der Ross were "unable to accept membership" (Malay and Coloured Sub-Committee, 1951, February 15). The attempted inclusion of people such as Van der Ross was particularly significant, since he was a member of the Franchise Action Council (FAC): the lobbying and coordinating group for organising protest action against the Separate Representation of Voters Bill, aimed at removing coloureds from the common voter's roll. Golding was similarly a member of the FAC, but also a representative of the Coloured People's National Union, a moderate political organisation known for its attempts to secure better treatment of coloured people as opposed to blacks (Lewis, 1987, pp. 267–268). There was, therefore, a serious attempt to give legitimacy to the event. On the grassroots level, the sub-committee working through the Department of Coloured and Rehoboth Affairs targeted schools, principals, and teachers to work out a wide-ranging cultural programme involving string band performances, choirs, tableaux, ballet, and folk dances (Malay and Coloured Sub-Committee, 1951, April 30). With this focus, the organisers paid little attention to their involvement in the sports programme, despite the targeted community's significant sporting legacy. Consequently, the final programme only made provision for a float of sportsmen, depicting the Malay in sport (Malay and Coloured Sub-Committee, 1951, November 9). On a community-level, provision was made for a separate sports meeting at Trafalgar Park: swimming baths were designated for Coloured and Malay children, while their white counterparts would have a similar event at Queens Park in Woodstock and Camps Bay ("Children Will Enjoy Themselves," 1951).

The idea of a 'Bantu Pavilion,' propagandised through the media, was proposed to mobilise the African community, with the stated intention "that overtures be made first of all to church bodies closely concerned with Native work" and schools, and that a provisional committee is established (Secretary for Native Affairs, 1951, November 15). This was to be followed by a further media campaign to establish a larger organising committee, which would include Africans. It was further stressed that this non-political event for Africans only, scheduled for the Bantu Sports Ground in Langa, would be open-air to control unpredictability. As far as the sports programme was concerned, it was proposed that it include a children's section with "foot races, three-legged races, sack races, potato races, bottle-on-head races," thread-the-needle races and obstacle races. Additionally, adult sports with three-foot races, three-cycle races, football matches, sack races, three-legged races, and obstacle races would be included, as well as a cultural event with a choir competition, cinema programme and musical items (Secretary for Native Affairs, 1951, November 15). All of these events, including catering, were to be hosted in racially-separated facilities away from the planned festival. The State Information Service would film all events for overseas consumption and to continue the fight against the 'bias against South Africa' ("S.A. Inligtingsdiens," 1950). However, beyond providing for black access to the festival in Pretoria, especially the historical display at the Boom Street Museum on Tuesdays, the Transvaal Festival programme made no provisions for sports participation ("Program vir Transvaalse Fees", 1951). The proposed programme largely ignored almost a century of organised Western sport among black South Africans in sports such as rugby, cricket, athletics, and baseball, and wholly side-lined existing organisations. The omission thereby suggested that blacks in South Africa had no significant sporting tradition (Booley, 1998; Odendaal et al., 2017; Cleophas, 2018).

Black Ambivalence: Rejection and Collaboration

The political objectives behind the Van Riebeeck festival, especially the explicit aim of celebrating European civilisation and colonisation, engendered large-scale dissatisfaction and calls from all sides of the racial divide for blacks to boycott the event. This agitation reached its peak in August to December 1951, when a combination of media outlets, churches, professional organisations, and political organisations strongly articulated their views, each with a different emphasis, in support of a boycott. Leading the charge was the *Cape Argus* newspaper, which, after a further financial allocation from the City of Cape Town, wrote:

> The slogan 'We build a nation' is felt to be a poor and meagre one, more especially when we are told that this is to be a nation from which all non-white persons are to be excluded, and which is to be built by the process of faithfully preserving all the limitations of our ancestors. Nevertheless, even if there is no song in anyone's heart about these celebrations, Cape Town still has a duty to honour its founder, and should bear its share of the cost ("The City and the Festival," 1951).

City councillor Khan voted against the allocation and, yet again, denounced the scheduled event as partisan, discriminatory, and a historical distortion ("Close Voting on £25,000 grant," 1951). His colleague, AZ Berman, called the festival a "tawdry, meretricious interpretation of our history" ("City's Festival Grant," 1951). For the Langa Vigilance Association, based in one of the areas earmarked for the 'Bantu Pavilion,' it was seen as merely a glorification of white domination and "an attempt to launch another 300 years of national oppression and exploitation" ("Will Boycott Festival," 1951). In contrast, the FAC, a broad political front formed to fight the Separate Representation of Voters Act and representative of 125 affiliated organisations, decided not only to boycott the Van Riebeeck Festival but also to stage an alternative event ("Boycotters Plan Their Own Pageant," 1951). It, therefore, called on others to "cooperate in celebrations conceived in a spirit of historical objectivity and dedicated to genuine South African patriotism, based on the recognition that the nation consists of all sections of people" ("To Boycott Festival," 1951; "Rival Van Riebeeck Celebrations Planned," 1951). Their application for a grant from City Council was, however, rejected. The All-African Convention, under the presidency of W.M. Tsotsi, condemned the festival as a 'festival of hate' and one that aimed to celebrate the "subjugation and humiliation of the Native peoples" at their meeting in Bloemfontein ("Africans Condemn Tercentenary," 1951). The African Political Organisation viewed it as merely a "celebration of the domination of the 'Herrenvolk of South Africa' over the non-Europeans" ("Coloured Call for Boycott of Celebrations," 1951). For its part, the African National Congress called on the black population to refrain from participating in the celebration of their subjugation and, according to Labuschagne, used the growing resistance as a "rallying point to express its opposition to the exclusion of blacks" from political rights and the system itself (Labuschagne, 2017, p. 131).

Beyond the political arena, professional groups such as teachers, university students, and some clergy also rejected the proposed Tercentenary celebration, including provision of a float with prominent sportsmen depicting 'Malays in Sport.' The Teachers League of South Africa joined others in opposing what they regarded as a 'glorified celebration of the conquest of the non-white.' It actively opposed the opening of a new coloured-only college in Oudtshoorn, in addition to searching for closer unity with its black counterpart, the Cape African Teachers Association ("Boycott of V. Riebeeck Celebrations," 1951). They called on parents to become educated about the reasons behind the decision and called on all to resist; in the event that force was used, they encouraged everyone to "resolutely refuse to be unwillingly dragged into the celebration of the masters" ("Coloured Teachers to Boycott Van Riebeeck Festival," 1951). They further discouraged students from buying the special festival badges and called on their fellow teachers to "discourage the spreading of sentiment for the celebrations in their schools" ("Boycott of Festival," 1951). In contrast, Phillip Saunders of Zastron in the Free State encouraged coloureds to participate in the festivities, arguing that they as a group had a lot to thank Van Riebeeck for, especially for bringing civilisation to them ("Kleurlinge se dank aan Van Riebeeck," 1951).

The government-supporting newspaper, *Die Burger*, described the opposition's efforts as hard-headedness ("Koppige Kleurlinge Boikot," 1951). Historically liberal white institutions, such as Rhodes University, also supported the call to boycott, denouncing the scheduled event as racially biased. At the same time, the University Players, the Witwatersrand students' dramatic society, declined an invitation to participate in the festival because "the festival programme does not truly represent the roles played by all sections of the population in the building of the nation" ("Wits Players Reply on Festival," 1951). Dr GH Clayton, Anglican Archbishop of Cape, believed that no festival is possible without black people participating and, as this denomination had a large black membership, he was willing to distance himself from the celebrations if the nation was narrowly defined by only white citizens. He further opposed any distortion of South Africa's racial history and past ("Kan nie fees vier sonder Nie-Blankes," 1951). Outlining the dilemma of participating in events "under conditions we deplore," he expressed support for a discussion of the issues and for utilising all opportunities to effect change instead of boycotting the event ("Archbishop's Views of Festival," 1951). A mass mobilisation of the black community and protest meetings against the festival followed these position statements and public declarations.

Against this background, the City of Cape Town's Manager of Native Administration, in a letter to the festival's organising secretary on 12 March 1952, a month before the festivities were due to start, noted that:

I have come to the conclusion that any attempt to arrange for the Natives to participate in the festivities, either at the Festival grounds or at Langa, would be inadvisable, as the of non-cooperation which evinced itself amongst a section of the Native people shortly after the Coloured community had indicated its intention to boycott the festivities, has increased and quite a number of Natives who originally were against the spirit of non-cooperation and were prepared to take an active part in the festivities, have become either disinterested or afraid of being ostracized for not siding with the anti-Festival section (Manager of Native Administration, 1952, March 12).

These and other circumstances undoubtedly contributed to a reluctance on the part of several invited countries to participate in the festivities. Despite these objections, arrangements went ahead as planned.

Willing and Enthusiastic Collaborators: Staging the Van Riebeeck Sports Festival

After the initial enthusiasm from the various sporting codes, the failure of most sports bodies to make good on their initial commitments by September 1951 confronted the organising committee. As a result, it was suggested that the committee should consider the possibility of symbolically representing present-day sports with a float in the main event instead of hosting individual events (Sports Sub-Committee, 1951, September 14). When the organisers reconvened in January 1952, the outlook continued to look bleak with only a small group able to confirm the hosting of individual free-standing events. As a result, the suggestion of float and sketch plans for a symbolic display of sports in South Africa was accepted, and a resolution for an exhibition of sports trophies, photographs and other interesting artefacts to add further weight to the sporting contribution was adopted (Pauw, J.C., 1952, January 21). Against this background, the South African Sports Federation, a newly-established body representative of twenty white national sports codes and federations, offered to assist with festival arrangements as an opportunity to promote their common interests (Meiring, A. & Pauw, J.C., 1952, January 3). This intervention seemingly had the desired effect since, by February, most sports were ready to proceed with hosting their events, either as exhibition matches, contests or tournaments, with entry tickets carrying the official festival emblem (Sports Sub-Committee, 1952, January 9).

When the festivities started at the beginning of April 1952, a significant cross-section of the white sports fraternity participated. Anchored in most cases by the Western Province-based affiliate of the national bodies, sports featured included angling, athletics, baseball, basketball, billiards, bowls, boxing, chess, cricket, cycling, golf, football, jukskei, korfball, lawn tennis, motor racing, polo, snooker, softball, swimming, water polo, and yachting. These events were either hosted as national championships, inter-provincial, invitational or trophy tournaments, festival matches or regattas under the Van Riebeeck banner. After initial reluctance to participate and sacrifice its scheduled national championships, the South African Jukskei Association relented and joined the events, claiming its status as the "only South African-born sport" with the understanding that the festival aimed to give priority to all that "were local and which symbolised the growth of South Africa" (Krüger, D.A. & Pienaar, A.J., 1951, November 17). Proposed individual festival events included a soap-box derby for children, intended to interest young children in careers such as car design and construction. This event was to accompany a proposed *I am a South African* day (Chubbock, E.M.C. & Pauw, J.C., 1951, December 4) and a Robben Island swim for a celebratory Tercentenary medal (Richings, F.G., 1951, May 21). The idea that the sports festival should play a more significant educational role was also emphasised by the swimming fraternity, which aimed to use the tournament by "endeavouring to see that this is of an instructive nature where possible" (Eask, L., 1952, January 12).

For a significant number of participating sports organisations, the festival provided an opportunity for broader exposure: to judge their standards (Jordaan, C.J. & Van Nierop, P.J., 1951, November 7) and to demonstrate their codes to a new pool of potential participants (Hoffa, S.C., 1951, January 8). The event also offered an opportunity to "create a shared cultural heritage in South Africa with the 'old motherland' as part of a more comprehensive nation-building process" (Labuschagne, 2017, p. 117). To this end, several national bodies attempted to secure international participation for the occasion: the SA Baseball and Soft Ball Association envisaged playing an international All-Star team. The SA Billiards Control Association proposed to host a professional billiards and snooker tournament involving two international players, Clark McConachy, runner-up in the 1952 world championships from New Zealand, and Horace Lindrum, world champion from Australia touring the country during the festival (Honorary Secretary, 1952, January 25). Furthermore, the chess fraternity envisaged hosting an 'international telegraphic chess match' featuring the Netherlands and South Africa in which Dr Max Euwe, Dutch Master, and Wolfgang Heidenfeld, a white SA Champion, would represent their respective nations (Pauw, J., 1951, November 2). However, the majority of these initiatives failed due to lack of funding from both private and public sources. Instead, organisations had to be contented with several low-key events, such as the presentation of coaching clinics that renowned American baseball coach John Burrows hosted during this time ("Bofbal afrigter na Stellenbosch", 1952, p. 7; "Goeie nuus vir Bofbal," 1951, p. 8). Although Dutch athletes, Fanny Blankers Koen and Willie Slykhuis, participated in the SA Athletics Championship in March 1952, lack of financial support prevented a larger contingent from participating (Jordaan, C.J. & Van Nierop, P.J., 1951, November 7).

Against the background of the boycott movement's growing influence, most white sports organisations failed to extend an invitation to existing black sports bodies. One of the exceptions was the WP Sea Anglers Association, who proposed a non-white section "if there is enough support" (Honorary Secretary, 1951, December 21). Otherwise, one of the coloured and Malay sub-committee members, N.

Abrahams, promoted a 'coloured' boxing tournament, the only such event on the official festival sports programme (Sports Programme, n.d.). By the start of the festival, the boycott was in full swing, and throughout its hosting, the number of black participants, spectators, and attendees was 'paltry' (Rassool & Witz, 1993, p. 462).

Conclusion

Despite the distraction of a black boycott, the Van Riebeeck Sports Festival, based on the diversity of the number of participating organisations involved, went ahead successfully to visibly demonstrate its undoubted contribution to building and uniting the 'white' nation, as was its original objective. Beyond its symbolic contribution, given the involvement of a significant number of smaller sports, most events did not generate any profit. It therefore demonstrated its embeddedness within the politics of racial discrimination and apartheid, and its opposition to non-racial sport and a common South African identity. Within this context, Afrikaners and white English-speakers collectively transformed the sports arena into a site of struggle and space where the black 'other' is not only reduced to a shadowy marginal figure denoted with a racial identity such as 'native,' 'boy,' and 'non-white,' but also almost exclusively as auxiliary labour, with roles such as caddy, 'water boy,' or a stable hand. These practices, as noted by Nauright (1997, p. 34) in a different context and so accurately demonstrated during the Van Riebeeck Festival, indeed served to "draw whites together as a social collectivity that was different from, and as they viewed it, culturally and morally superior to, blacks."

REFERENCES

1952 Proposals in Detail (1950, November 6). *Cape Times.*
Africans Condemn Tercentenary (1951, December 17). *Cape Argus.*
An Unnoticed Anniversary (1948, April 6). *Cape Argus.*
Archbishop's Views of Festival 'We Build Nation' Slogan Criticized (1951, October 24). *Cape Times.*
Atkin, H. J. (1948, July 1). Ron Eland: Cover Man. *Vigour.*
Bailey, A. (1991). Kaapse Binnenshuise Speletjies. Navorsinge van die Nasionale Kultuurhistoriese Museum/Researches of the National Cultural History Museum, 2, 2. National Museum, Bloemfontein.
De Kock, V. (1955). *The Fun They Had! The Pastimes of Our Forefathers.* Cape Town: Howard B Timmins.
Bickford-Smith, V. (1995). *Ethnic Pride and Racial Prejudice in Victorian Cape Town: Group Identity and Social Practice, 1875–1902.* Cape Town: Cambridge.
Bofbal Afrigter na Stellenbosch (1952, March 1). *Eikestad Nuus.*
Booley, A. (1998). *Forgotten Heroes: A History of Black Rugby, 1882–1992.* Cape Town: Manie Booley Publications.
Boycott of Festival (1951, October 8). *Port Elizabeth Evening Post.*
Boycotters Plan Their Own Pageant (1951, October 4). *Cape Argus.*
Boycott of V. Riebeeck Celebrations (1951, October 9). *Diamond Fields Advertiser.*
Breckenridge, K. (2014). The Book of Life: The South African Population Register and the Invention of Racial Descent, 1950–1980. *Kronos*, 40(1).
Britton, S. (2010). 'Come and See the Empire by the All-Red Route!': Anti-imperialism and Exhibition in Interwar Britain. *History Workshop Journal*, 69 (Spring).
Cape Town Tercentenary Celebrations (1951, February 9). *Cape Times.*
Carlin, J. (2008). *Playing the Enemy: Nelson Mandela and the Game That Made a Nation.* Cape Town: Penguin.
Children Will Enjoy Themselves (1951, December 5). *Cape Argus.*
Chubbock, E.M.C. & Pauw, J.C. (1951, December 4). Mrs EMC Chubbock JC Pauw Organising Secretary Van Riebeeck Festival [Correspondence]. Van Riebeeck Tercentenary Festival, Accessions (A) 709:25, Sport: 19/1, Volume 6. Western Cape Archives and Record Service (KAB), Cape Town.
City May See Olympic Champions (1951, November 17). *Cape Argus.*
City of Cape Town. (1948, April 6). 1952: City of Cape Town: Programme Jan Van Riebeeck Day. [Commemoration Ceremony]. Oudschans Collection: Scrapbook Van Riebeeck. KAB, Cape Town.
City Plans for Tercentenary Government Lead Awaited (1949, July 8). *Cape Times.*
City's Festival Grant to be £25.000 (1951, October 12). *Cape Argus.*
Clendinning, A. (2006). Exhibiting a Nation: Canada at the British Empire Exhibition, 1924–1925. *Histoire Sociale/Social History*, 3(77).
Cleophas, F.J. (Ed.). (2018). *Exploring Decolonising Themes in SA Sport History: Issues and Challenges.* Stellenbosch: African Sun Media.
Cleophas, F.J. (2018, January 18). The Weight of History and the Way it Segregates SA Sport Needs to be Lifted. *Cape Times.*
Close Voting on £25,000 Grant (1951, September 28). *Cape Argus.*
Coe, C. (2001). Histories of Empire, Nation and City: Four Interpretations of the Empire Exhibition, Johannesburg, 1936. *Folklore Forum*, 32(½).
Coloured Call for Boycott of Celebrations (1951, November 1). *The Friend.*
Coloured Teachers to Boycott Van Riebeeck Festival (1951, October 13). *Oudtshoorn Courant.*
Commemoration Jan Van Riebeeck Day (1948, March 20). *Cape Times.*
Crais, C. (2004). Productions of History: The 1952 Van Riebeeck Celebration. *Journal of African History*, 45(3).
De Beers Archives, Kimberley. [General Correspondence]. 9 December 1897.

De Bruyn, D. & Wessels, A. (2007). Vrees as Faktor in die Regse Blanke Politiek in Suid-Afrika Tydens die Eerste Dekade van die Apartheidsera, 1948–1958. *Journal for Contemporary History / Joernaal vir Eietydse Geskiedenis*, 32(2).

Dobson, P. (1989). *Rugby in South Africa: A History 1861–1989.* Cape Town: South African Rugby Football Board (SARFB).

Dunn, J. (2009). Reconciliation and Rugby in Post-Apartheid South Africa. Paper presented at Levitt Summer Research Fellowship summit, 3. Retrieved from https://www.hamilton.edu/documents/Dunn%20Levitt%20paper.pdf.

Eask, L. (1952, January 12). L. Eask: President: WP Amateur Swimming Association Secretary: Van Riebeeck Festival Fair. [Correspondence]. Van Riebeeck Tercentenary Festival, Accessions (A) 709:25, Sport: 19/1, Volume 6. KAB, Cape Town.

Enough Accomplished (1949, April 15). *Cape Times.*

('n) Fees in 1952 (1952, April 7). *Die Burger.*

Fees in 1952 mag nie kermis wees nie (1951, February 9). *Die Burger.*

Fees se deure oop vir Nie-Blankes (1951, November 30). *Die Vaderland.*

Festival Call for Political Truce in S.A. (1951, December 7). *The Friend.*

Festival of South African Sports All Tastes Catered For (1951, November 16). *The Recorder.*

Getz, H. & Van Nierop, P.J. (1951, September 29). Harry Getz Dr PJ van Nierop: MP. [Correspondence]. Van Riebeeck Tercentenary Festival (Accessions (A) 709:25, Sport: 19/1, Volume 6). KAB, Cape Town.

Goeie nuus vir bofbal: Beroemde afrigter kom help (1951, September 21). *Eikestad Nuus.*

Groot fees lê voor vir Suid-Afrika (1950, March 11). *Die Burger.*

Grundlingh, A. (1999). The King's Afrikaners? Enlistment and Ethnic Identity in the Union of South Africa's Defence Force during the Second World War, 1939–45. *Journal of African History*, 40(3).

Health and Happiness: A Lay Sermon (1873, November). *Cape Monthly Magazine.*

Herman, C. L., Hertzog, W. F. & Van Breda, P. (1843, January 23). Memorials Received. [Memorial to Colonial Governor]. Colonial Office (4017: 287). KAB, Cape Town.

Hoffa, S.C. (1951, January 8). S.C. Hoffa: WP Ladies' Hockey Union Secretary Van Riebeeck Festival. [Correspondence]. Van Riebeeck Tercentenary Festival (Accessions (A) 709:25, Sport: 19/1, Volume 6). KAB, Cape Town.

Höglund, K. & Sundberg, R. (2008). Reconciliation Through Sports? The Case of South Africa. *Third World Quarterly*, 29(4).

Honorary Secretary. (1950, July 20). Honorary Secretary: SAAACU Secretary Jan Van Riebeeck Tercentenary Celebration Committee. [Minutes of Meeting]. Van Riebeeck Tercentenary Festival (Accessions (A) 709:25, Sport 19/1, Volume 6). KAB, Cape Town.

Honorary Secretary. (1951, December 21). Honorary Secretary: WP Sea Anglers Association Organising Secretary [Correspondence]. Van Riebeeck Tercentenary Festival (Accessions (A) 709:25, Sport: 19/1, Volume 6). KAB, Cape Town.

Honorary Secretary. (1952, January 25). Honorary Secretary: SA Billiards Control Association Mrs Sell. [Correspondence]. Van Riebeeck Tercentenary Festival (Accessions (A) 709:25, Sport: 19/1, Volume 6). KAB, Cape Town.

Jan Van Riebeeck Tercentenary Committee Plans to Attract Tourists (1950, June 7). *Cape Times.*

Jordaan, C.J. & Van Nierop, P.J. (1951, November 7). CJ Jordaan: Private Secretary Dr PJ van Nierop: MP. [Correspondence]. Van Riebeeck Tercentenary Festival (Accessions (A) 709:25, Sport: 19/1, Volume 6). KAB, Cape Town.

Jörder, K. (2019). Constructing White Legitimacy: The Re-enactment of Jan van Riebeeck's Landing (1952) in Photographs by the Apartheid Regime's State Information Office. In I. Graziani et al. (Eds.), *The Myth of the 'Enemy': The Mutable Faces of the Other and the Construction of European Identities.* Bologna: Minerva.

Kan nie fees vier sonder Nie-Blankes (1951, October 24). *Die Vaderland.*

Kleurlinge sal ook fees kan vier (1951, November 21). *Die Burger.*

Kleurlinge se dank aan Van Riebeeck (1951, October 29). *Die Volksblad.*

Koppige Kleurlinge boikot Van Riebeeckfees en eie opleidingskollege (1951, October 9). *Die Vaderland.*

Krüger, D.A. & Pienaar, A.J. (1951, November 17). DA Krüger: Secretary/ Treasurer: SA Jukskei Association Adv. AJ (Sport) Pienaar. [Correspondence]. Van Riebeeck Tercentenary Festival (Accessions (A) 709:25, Sport: 19/1, Volume 6). KAB, Cape Town.

Labuschagne, P. (2017, July). The 1952 Jan Van Riebeeck Tercentenary Festival: A Political and Cultural Perspective. *South African Journal of Cultural History*, 31(1).

Lewis, G. (1987). *Between the Wire and the Wall: History of South African "Coloured" Politics*. Athlone, Cape Town: David Philip Publishers.

Macfarlane, N. & Herd, M. (1986). *Sport and Politics*. London: Willow Books.

Magtige feesplan vir 1952 Kaapstad sal spil wees (1950, November 6). *Die Burger*.

Malay and Coloured Sub-Committee. (1951, January 29). Minutes of the Malay and Coloured Sub-Committee. [Minutes of Meeting]. Van Riebeeck Tercentenary Festival (Accessions (A) 709, Volume 6). KAB, Cape Town.

Malay and Coloured Sub-Committee. (1951, February 15). Minutes of the Malay and Coloured Sub-Committee. [Minutes of Meeting]. Van Riebeeck Tercentenary Festival (Accessions (A) 709, Volume 6) KAB, Cape Town.

Malay and Coloured Sub-Committee. (1951, April 30). Minutes of the Malay and Coloured Sub-Committee. [Minutes of Meeting]. Van Riebeeck Tercentenary Festival (Accessions (A) 709, Volume 6). KAB, Cape Town.

Malay and Coloured Sub-Committee. (1951, November 9). Minutes of the Malay and Coloured Sub-Committee. [Minutes of Meeting]. Van Riebeeck Tercentenary Festival (Accessions (A) 709, Volume 6). KAB, Cape Town.

Manager of Native Administration. (1952, March 12). Native Participation (NP) Manager of Native Administration City of Cape Town to The Organising Secretary (Mr J.C. Pauw). [Correspondence]. Van Riebeeck Tercentenary Festival (Accessions (A) 709, Sport: 19/1, Volume 41). KAB, Cape Town.

Meiring, A. & Pauw, J.C. (1952, January 3). A. Meiring: Secretary SA Sports Federation JC Pauw: Organising Secretary Van Riebeeck Festival. [Correspondence]. Van Riebeeck Tercentenary Festival (Accessions (A) 709:25, Sport: 19/1, Volume 6). KAB, Cape Town.

Nauright, J. & Black, D. (1998). Sport at the Center of Power: Rugby in South Africa During Apartheid. *Sport History Review*, 29.

Odendaal, A., Merrett, C.E., Winch, J. & Reddy, K. (2017). *Cricket and Conquest: The History of South African Cricket Retold 1795–1914*. Pretoria: Red Press.

Odendaal, A. (1988). South Africa's Black Victorians: Sport and Society in South Africa in the Nineteenth Century. In J. A. Mangan (Ed.), *Pleasure, Profit, Proselytism: British Culture and Sport at Home and Abroad, 1700–1914*. London: Frank Cass.

Om Van Riebeeck se aankoms in S.A. te herdenk (1948, May 19). *Die Burger*.

Our part in the Van Riebeeck Festival (1951, July 13). *Worcester Standard*.

Pageant Hurtful to Non-Europeans (1951, August 1). *Cape Argus*.

Pauw, J.C. & Getz, H. (1951, January 11). JC Pauw Organising Secretary Harry Getz. [Correspondence]. Van Riebeeck Tercentenary Festival (Accessions (A) 709:25, Sport: 19/1, Volume 6). KAB, Cape Town.

Pauw, J. (1951, November 2). Secretary: Chess Federation for Southern Africa J. Pauw Esq. [Correspondence]. Van Riebeeck Tercentenary Festival (Accessions (A) 709:25, Sport: 19/1, Volume 6). KAB, Cape Town.

Pauw, J.C. (1952, January 21). JC Pauw: Organising Secretary Secretary: SA Sports Federation. [Correspondence]. Van Riebeeck Tercentenary Festival (Accessions (A) 709:25, Sport: 19/1, Volume 6). KAB, Cape Town.

Politiek en die Fees (1951, December 7). *Die Burger*.

Program vir Transvaalse Fees (1951, December 7). *Die Vaderland*.

Rassool, C. & Witz, L. (1993). The 1952 Jan Van Riebeeck Tercentenary Festival: Constructing and Contesting Public National History in South Africa. *Journal of African History*, 34.

Reg dat kinders Blank moet bly (1949, April 7). *Die Burger*.

Regeringstandpunt oor Van Riebeeck Fees: G'n Kermis (1951, February 9). *Die Vaderland*.

Regret should be Union's 1952 message (1950, November 15). *Cape Argus*.

Riebeeck Landing Tercentenary Big celebrations in 1952 contemplated (1946, March 21). *Cape Times.*

Richings, F.G. (1951, May 21). FG Richings – Secretary Van Riebeeck Festival. [Correspondence]. Van Riebeeck Tercentenary Festival (Accessions (A) 709:25, Sport: 19/1, Volume 6). KAB, Cape Town.

Rival Van Riebeeck Celebrations planned (1951, October 5). *Pretoria News.*

S.A. Inligtingsdiens het groot planne drie rolprente word vir fees gemaak (1950, July 4). *Die Burger.*

Secretary for Native Affairs. (1951, November 15). Van Riebeeck Festival Fair: Native Participation (NP). [Correspondence]. Van Riebeeck Tercentenary Festival (Accessions (A) 709, Volume 41). KAB, Cape Town.

Should Tercentenary be simple? (1948, January 12). *Cape Times.*

Smit, J. P. J. (1987, July). *Die Ontwikkeling van die Suid Afrikaanse Sportbeleid en sy Politieke Implikasies, 1948–1979.* Unpublished Master of Arts (History) Dissertation, University of the Orange Free State, p. 1.

Snyders, H. (2015). Rugby, National Pride and the Struggle of Black South Africans for International Recognition, 1897–1992. *Sporting Traditions,* 32(1).

Sport on the 'Fields' (1873, November). *Cape Monthly Magazine.*

Sports Programme. (n.d.). Sports Programme Van Riebeeck Festival. [Programme]. Van Riebeeck Tercentenary Festival (Accessions (A) 709:25, Sport: 19/1, Volume 6). KAB, Cape Town.

Sports Sub-Committee. (1950, December 8). Minutes of the Sports Sub-Committee. [Minutes of Meeting]. Van Riebeeck Tercentenary Festival (Accessions (A) 709, Volume 5). KAB, Cape Town.

Sports Sub-Committee. (1951, September 14). Minutes of the Sports Sub-Committee. [Minutes of Meeting]. Van Riebeeck Tercentenary Festival (Accessions (A) 709, Volume 5). KAB, Cape Town.

Sports Sub-Committee. (1952, January 9). Correspondence of the Sports Sub-Committee. [Correspondence]. Van Riebeeck Tercentenary Festival (Accessions (A) 709, Sport: 19/1, Volume 52). KAB, Cape Town.

Sports Sub-Committee. (1950, November 24 – 1952, January 17). Minutes of the Sports Sub-Committee. [Minutes of Meeting]. Van Riebeeck Tercentenary Festival (Accessions (A) 709, Volume 5). KAB, Cape Town.

The City and the Festival (1951, September 28). *Cape Argus.*

To boycott festival (1951, October 5). *Grocott's Daily Mail.*

Van Riebeeck Festival (1951, July 14). *Cape Times.*

Van Riebeeck's Day (1949, April 6). Cape Argus.

Volksfees gesteun deur die staat (1950, April 6). *Die Burger.*

Vorder ons met die Van Riebeeck-feesviering? (1950, May 30). *Die Suiderstem.*

Will Boycott Festival (1951, September 29). *Cape Argus.*

Wits Players Reply on Festival (1951, October 10). *Cape Argus.*

Witz, L. (1993). ''n Fees vir die oog': Looking In on the 1952 Jan van Riebeeck Tercentenary Festival Fair in Cape Town. *South African Historical Journal,* 29(1).

Witz, L. (1998/1999). From Langa Market Hall and Rhodes' Estate to the Grand Parade and the Foreshore: Contesting Van Riebeeck's Cape Town. *Kronos,* 25.

Chapter 10

The Rusedski Affair: Treason, Nationhood, and the Making of a Canadian Tennis Traitor

Andrew Pettit

Introduction: Constructing Sport, Nation, and Narrative

Sports are visceral. Even the most cerebral and emotionally restrained of them, such as tennis, invoke an intensely passionate reaction among its participants and spectators. We cheer when our favourite players and teams do well, we agonize when they fail, and we actively wish for misfortune to befall their, or our, opponents. It is this visceral quality that allows for the boundaries of the playing field to easily become a platform for sports' *dualistic* function as a space for social construction, cohesion, and contestation.

Sport has long been understood as a space where social consciousness and norms are constructed and contested in what Hartmann (2017) calls a "struggle for order, [and] the quest for control and power not hegemony but the *struggle for* hegemony often without the participants being fully aware of the social processes in which they are so clearly implicated" (10). Through sport, social meaning can be continuously realized by individuals and communities who participate in its production (Garneau, 1983; Hargreaves, 1986). Bourdieu (1988) adds that these constructed meanings, which are used to make sense of our lives, are constantly in flux and dependent on sociological and historical forces that are often beyond the control of any one person or group.

In this chapter, I explore the social utility and function of sport as a platform where differing ideas regarding a particular type of community, the nation, are created, performed, and contested by those who identify not only as a member of the nation, but as an *accepted* member of that nation. Canada, and the *Canadian*, is the nation chosen for this endeavour, not only because of the happenstance that the central character in the historical event I present *was* Canadian, but because Canadians have long anguished over the thought of what it is we actually are. Exemplifying such anguish, in an attempt to define what a Canadian is, Thomas Homer-Dixon (2006) shrewdly answered "… almost always unsure of what it means to be a Canadian" (8). It is, indeed, this anxiety riddled 'unsureness' that one must keep in mind when thinking about the Canadian reaction to Greg Rusedski's athletic defection to Great Britain in the mid-1990s.

Nationalism, like sport, has long been associated with visceral appeals to the human condition, which are often intangible and open to interpretation (Koizumi, 1994; Billig, 1995; Allison, 2000). Individual and communal narratives are established and employed in order to interpret and understand the significance of what people witness and in which they participate, both on the playing field and within their broader community. (Kramer, 1997; Hogan, 2009; Gleaves, 2017). The participants in these narratives inevitably become characters in the stories being created. Character-archetypes, such as the hero and the villain, have long been understood as integral elements of a community-member's ability to properly understand and productively participate in their communities (Klapp, 1954). A hero's actions are ideals, to which one should aspire, whereas the villain's actions are to be avoided. Importantly, Morrow (1992) demonstrates that the combative nature of sport allows for the effective production of heroes and villains to be utilized for the purposes of such nation-building narratives.

In this chapter, I focus on a particular type of villain, the traitor, who I argue is an instrumental character in creating national narratives that reinforce cohesive social bonds through discourse and contestation with notions of the outside other. Greg Rusedski rose through the ranks of Canadian Tennis in the late 1980s and early 1990s to become the hockey-mad nation's first shot at international tennis relevance in living memory. In 1995, however, the Montreal-born Rusedski successful petitioned the International Tennis Federation to allow him to play for the more lucrative Great Britain team on account of his mother's British citizenship. My argument is that the Rusedski's defection stands out in Canadian sport history as a ripe example of the intersection between sport and nationhood. Considered the 'Wayne Gretzky of Canadian tennis,' who gave Canadian tennis fans hope for international relevance, Rusedski's perceived treachery demonstrates the central role of the traitor, and treason, in the making and maintenance of the nation.

Defining the Nation and the Social Function of Treason: Interpreting Creative and Internalized Responses of the Nation

Nation and Nationhood

For the purposes of this chapter, I rely on Benedict Anderson's influential definition of the nation as an *imagined community*. Unlike the more stringent Marxist orthodoxy, which emphasised the structural imposition of nationalism onto peoples and societies (Gellner, 1983), Anderson (1983) saw the emergence of the nation and nationhood as a cultural phenomena dependent on the reactions and interplay between all members of various communities in response to historical stimuli (9-46). Anderson's definition of nation is particularly well-suited for the forthcoming analysis of the Rusedski Affair because of his attention paid to its inventive character. Nations are invented, and re-invented, by members who collectively experience and perceive impactful events which occur around them. Nations are, thus, a lens which people use to filter and understand the world, and thus, in a way, it is the nations which creates the world in which the members live.

According to Anderson there are four features that make up the definition of nation: they are imagined, limited, sovereign, and a community. Nations are imagined "because members of even the smallest nation will never know most of their fellow members, meet them, or even hear of them, yet in the minds of each lives the image of their communion" (6). This is a problematic feature, due to its inclination to foster a sense of unknowing and distrust within the community owing to the nation's imagined intangibility. Nations are made up of individuals, each of whom have individual conceptions of what their nation is and should be, and there is no way to be absolutely sure that the others share the same vision of the nation as you. The nation is also limited because "even the most messianic nationalists do not dream of a day when all members of the human race will join their nation" (7). There is a utility to this facet of the nation that seeks to resolve the problem of trust. While no one will ever be sure if all members are thinking of the nation in the 'correct' way, there is always an outside 'other' who helps provide definition for a particular nation.

The sovereign character of the nation is important, in terms of how the nation sees itself. The nation, and its members, must be understood as free and self-determined. The presence of this feature, according to Anderson, is most assuredly due to nationalism's emergence during the age of Enlightenment (7). And finally, the nation is a community. This is important because, according to Anderson, "it is this fraternity that makes it possible for so many millions of people, not so much to kill, as willingly die for such limited imaginings" (7).

Treason and its Creative Function

The intense emotional response to Greg Rusedski's decision not to compete for Canada, the country of his birth, illustrates the important place the traitor, and his or her treachery, inhabits within the fabric of nationhood. Kelly and Thiranagama (2010) note that treason provokes a disturbed, often violent, reaction because it seems to "threaten and destabilize the fragile moral and social relationships that hold us together and bind us to the perhaps otherwise abstract notions of nation, people, or community" (2). Importantly, these reactions may be channelled both externally and internally by the national community. External reactions manifest themselves in the creative actions performed by the community to whom, and in response to, the traitor committed his or her treason against.

Recognizing that the concept of nationhood and nationalism developed parallel with the emergence of modernity, it is generally agreed upon in the literature that the political realization of the modern nation-state was realized through the revolutionary establishment of democratic governments in the 18th and 19th centuries (Kohn, 1944; Anderson, 1983; Greenfield, 1992). However, according to French historian and political philosopher, Claude LeFort, this shift from monarchical to democratic state structures created a "fundamental realignment in the symbolization of power" (Kelly and Thiranagama, 2010, 6). The seat of power for the nation was no longer occupied by a central authority embodied by a King or Queen. In modern democracies, power was possessed, controlled, and wielded symbolically by 'the people.' The politically symbolic social construct of 'the people,' however, can never fully occupy the seat of power as intended because 'the people' are constantly in a state of flux (6).

Remembering the condition of sovereignty as an integral aspect of Anderson's definition of nationhood, and drawing from the work of LeFort, Kelly and Thiranagama (2020) argue that the demand for sovereignty by members of the nation is, thus, paradoxical to the historical rise of modern democracies (6). More importantly, it is through this paradox that the villainous role of the traitor finds its social utility. Through the social act of identifying a traitor, it is always a social act because a traitor's treachery is almost always exposed to the wider group, members of the nation participate in the re-creation and maintenance of modern democratic societies. "The accusation of treachery is socially productive," argues Kelly and Thiranagama, "in that it calls the people into being despite, or even because of their historical absence" (2010, 7). By identifying Rusedski as a traitor for his defection to Great Britain, Canadians we able to tangibly realize themselves as sovereign.

Internalized Reactions to Treason

Treason can also be understood for the internalized emotional responses it provokes, and the resultant actions taken by the community towards the traitor. In an important analysis of the social function of betrayal, Malin Ackerstrom (1991) identifies two significant forms of treachery: telling and leaving (5-11). Telling involves the betrayal of trust through the disclosure of important information considered confidential. Spies are a particularly apt example of this type of treachery. More relevant to this discussion, however, is the treachery of leaving. Ackerstrom notes that the treachery of leaving what she calls the "We" is particularly devastating because of its perceived finality (5). The traitor who makes the decision to leave the We, whether it is known or in secret, is interpreted as having rejected the values of the We (10). The treachery of leaving is, thus, a particularly direct and stringent blow to the We. Whereas the values of the We are reinforced by traitorous telling, if the information being told was not of any worth, it would not be told in the first place, the traitor's leaving forces the We to internalize the act as an indictment against their abilities and values as a society.

Interestingly, Ackerstrom also considers the importance given to the traitor's own internal motivations as perceived by the We. Using the example of Charles de Gaulle's commuting of World War II French collaborators, Ackerstrom states:

> In France after World War II, only de Gaulle could save a collaborator from the firing squad after a Court of Justice sentenced him to death. How did he decide? He commuted 1303 death sentences, notably all of the women, most

minors, and most defendants who had acted under orders and while risking their own life. The 768 rejected appeals concerned persons who de Gaulle felt had acted personally, spontaneously, to kill Frenchmen or serve the enemy (12).

The intent of the collaborator, deemed traitors to France after the war, was an important factor in de Gaulle's ultimate decision for execution. If a person was deemed to have engaged in traitorous acts for personal gain, the punishment was harsher. Perception, whether based on fact or fiction, is an important variable that needs to be considered when understanding the function and utility of treason. For Ackerstrom, this only goes further to show the importance of how a traitor's acts are internalized by the society being victimized.

The Player Who Could Change the Sport in this Country Forever: Rusedski's Roller-Coaster Rise in Canadian Tennis, 1988-1995

On September 6, 1973, three days before the Men's Final of the U.S. Open, Greg Rusedski was born in Montreal, Quebec to Helen and Tom Rusedski making him, by birth, a Canadian citizen. The youngest of three brothers, Greg Rusedski grew up in the English-speaking Montreal suburb of Point Claire in the late 1970s and 1980s. His father, Tom, was a railroad engineer of Ukrainian decent who immigrated to Canada when he was young. A tennis enthusiast, it was he who passed on a love for the game to all three of his sons (Buddell, n.d.). Rusedski's mother, Helen, was born in Yorkshire, England, and immigrated to Canada with her family when she was four-years old. She attended McGill University and eventually became a schoolteacher. A British citizen by birth, it was she who passed on her British citizenship to all three of her sons (Buddell, n.d.).

An English-speaking Quebecor, who played tennis in a country where most boys were skating in rinks with dreams of playing in the NHL, Rusedski was not your proto-typical tennis player. In a sport where the vast majority of players are right-handed, Rusedski swung the racket with his left hand and relied heavily on his strong serve. Additionally, Rusedski bucked traditional coaching practices, opting throughout his career to hire different coaches at different times to focus on individual aspects of his game as needed. According to Tom Tebbutt, however, the coaching carousel was a decision made more by the father than by the player (1993, Nov. 1). By the time Rusedski was entering high school, though, he was quickly distinguishing himself as one of the Canada's most gifted young players. This was much to the delight of his parents, who took on substantial financial debt to fund their son's training and development (Tebbutt, 1993, Nov. 1).

It was in April 1988, when a 14-year-old Rusedski first caught the attention of the Canadian tennis world at the Junior Nationals Under-18 tournament. Qualifying as the previous year's Under-14 champion, Rusedski was unseeded going into the tournament and not expected to advance far against older competition. The 'gangly upstart,' as he was labelled in the media, surprised even himself, however, by reaching the semi-finals with two upsets over top contenders. "I was surprised," Rusedski confessed after beating fourth seeded Phillipe LeBlanc, "I didn't think I was gonna win" (McCabe, 1988, April 9).

Over the next three years, Rusedski continued to improve and develop his game, which increasingly revolved around his hard-hitting serve. In 1991, he turned professional. While not taking the tennis-world by storm, Rusedski did reach as high as No. 138 in the world rankings by August 1992. Beginning with the 1993 Wimbledon Championships, however, Rusedski's play began to capture national attention and raised the hopes of Canadian tennis fans like no other player the sport had seen in the hockey-obsessed country. Unfortunately, while qualifying for Wimbledon was surely a rush for the nineteen-year-old Canadian, Rusedski drew two-time past champion and second seeded Stefan Edberg from Sweden in the first round. Rusedski simply was not yet at the level to pull off the major upset. Nevertheless, the match proved eye-opening. Going into the match a heavy underdog, Rusedski was competitive against the former world No. 1, losing in four strongly contested sets. Afterwards, Rusedski said of his performance: "It was a great experience, I got to go out there with Stefan and I actually had a chance to win the match" (Tebbutt, 1993, July 12). Gracious in victory, Edberg conceded to the media that he "was lucky to win" (Ormsby, 1993, July 25).

Immediately following his exciting, but abrupt, first round exit in England, Rusedski hoped to build off his promising Wimbledon experience by competing at the Hall-of-Fame Open in Newport, Rhode Island in July. The final grass court event on the tour schedule for the year, Rusedski surprised many by winning the tournament, thus becoming the first Canadian to win a pro-tour event since Mike Belkin did so at the Western Open in 1969 (Tebbutt, 1993, July 12). During the press conference after the victory, Rusedski credited his serve for his success throughout the tournament: "all week long my lowest service percentage was 62 percent, which is unbelievable that's what made the difference" (Tebbutt, 1993, July 12).

As a result of the victory at Newport, Rusedski shot up the world rankings to No. 108. The press anointed him Canada's great hope for international tennis relevance. Within Canadian tennis circles, Rusedski was "considered to be the one, the real thing, the player who could change the sport in this country forever" (Ormsby, 1993, July 25). Others were more cautiously optimistic, noting that the competition at Newport was not the strongest owing to its proximity to the most prestigious tennis tournament of the year. Former Canadian national champion, and the organizer of the Canadian K-Swiss Challenger circuit, Dale Power opined: "we're waiting for the one Canadian guy who can make the top 10 and stay there. Will Greg be the one? This is his big test, he's in position, he's on the launching pad to do something great" (Ormsby, 1993, July 25). Yves Boulais, coach for the top ranked Canadian woman, Patricia Hy, observed that "you can tell Greg really feels he belongs out there you can't say that about some other Canadian players" (Tebbutt, 1994, January 18). For his part, Rusedski seemed to be taking it all in stride. In an article for the *Toronto Star*, Rusedski seemed equally pleased by what his success meant for the growth of tennis in Canada as it did for him personally. "I am getting a lot of attention now after Newport but it doesn't bother me," he stated, "I feel that if I'm getting attention, then so is tennis and that is a really good thing for the sport in this country" (Ormsby, 1993, July 25).

If Rusedski put himself on the so-called 'launching pad' in the summer of 1993, his performance on the court in the fall of that same year catapulted him to distances rarely seen by Canadian tennis players. Questions regarding his ability to win against elite competition were silenced in October at the Seiko Super Tournament in Japan. Rusedski defeated three top-20 ranked players, including American world No. 8, Michael Chang, on his way to the semi-finals, where he was ultimately defeated. Later that month, he upset world No. 19 Magnus Gustafson at the Salem Open in Beijing where he reached the tournament final, this time losing to Chang. Rusedski's performance in Asia in the fall of 1993 saw him rocket up the world rankings and reaching as high as No. 48, a mere two places behind the highest ranking ever achieved by a Canadian in the modern era (Tebbutt, 1993, Nov. 1).

Illness and a hip injury in December, however, stopped Rusedski's ascension going into the beginning of 1994. A first round exit at the Australian Open against the 20th-ranked Ivan Lendl did not reap the same admiration and sense of promise that his loss at Wimbledon did the previous summer (Tebbutt, 1994, January 18). More disappointment followed with several first and second round losses in the first quarter of 1994. This caused some in the media to observe: "Greg Rusedski's breakthrough year is close to half over, and so far, no breakthrough" (Ormsby, 1994, May 6). In the month leading up to the French Open, Rusedski had four consecutive first-round exits (Tebbutt 1994, May 26). To some, over-reliance on a dominant serve, while lacking an elite level backhand and proper footwork, were mechanical issues being exploited by his competition (Tebbutt, 1994, January 18). Rusedski, however, was determined to improve the finer aspects of his game, stating to Mary Ormsby (1994, May 6) of the *Toronto Star*: "I've been working hard on my return of serve, my groundstrokes and putting more topspin on my backhand."

Rusedski's renewed focus on the finer elements of the game translated to success at the French Open in May. By defeating the 1993 U.S. Open semi-finalist, and world No. 22, Alexander Volkov from Russia, Rusedski became the first Canadian in the Open era to advance past the second round at Roland Garros (Tebbutt, 1994, May 26). While he did not advance any further on the red clay, Rusedski became the highest ranked Canadian player ever in the modern era, reaching No. 41 in the world. Tennis Journalist for the *Globe and Mail*, Tom Tebbutt (1994, May 26), who had been covering Rusedski from the start of his career, seemed elated by the swelling interest towards the twenty-year old Canadian in the international media. Ukrainian Andrei Medvedev, Rusedski's third round opponent who defeated him after five gruelling sets, praised the young Canadian's skill and mental strength: "you have to give Greg credit, it was the first time he's ever played on the centre court [at a Grand Slam event] and he didn't seem nervous at all" (Tebbutt, 1994, May 28). Both Rusedski and Medvedev seemed certain that the Canadian was equipped for more success as the tour transitioned to its grass-court schedule. "In the locker room after he [Medvedev] told me he didn't want to see me on the grass courts," Rusedski said in the post-match press conference, "I am hoping for a lot at Wimbledon, grass is my favourite surface when I play a good player I feel that I can beat him" (Tebbutt, 1994, May 28).

Unfortunately, the favoured grass at Wimbledon did not provide Rusedski the breaks he needed for a deep run. After a promising straight-sets victory over Nicklas Kulti in the first round, Rusedski was defeated in four sets by the significantly lower ranked Christian Bergstrom of Sweden in the second. Early round losses and frustration continued throughout the rest of the 1994 season. By the end of the year, Rusedski had fallen to No. 117 in the world rankings. Additionally, Rusedski's sometime doubles partner and fellow Canadian, Sebastien Lareau, overtook him as Canada's top ranked player on the tour (Tebbutt, 1994, December 20). Indeed, the 1994 season was certainly emblematic of Rusedski's down and up (and down) career to that point.

This latest experience in Rusedski's early career, however, would be his last such lull as a Canadian. At the 1995 Australian Open, Rusedski advanced to the third round where he succumbed to the finesse of rising American star, Andre Agassi. Going into the match, Tom Tebbutt (1995, January 20) of the *Globe and Mail*, argued that "Rusedski will have to rely on his principle weapon, his serve, if he is to threaten Agassi," but Agassi was able to make the match revolve around the return game which Rusedski struggled with at times. "A year ago, I gave up on the idea that a big serve was what I needed," Agassi told the press, "my game doesn't revolve around that" (*New York Times*, 1995). The big serve, however, continued to be Rusedski's signature on the tour. In February 1995, at a tournament in San Jose, California, Rusedski served a ball reaching 137mph, the hardest recorded serve in history at the time (Tebbutt, 1995, February 23). In April and May 1995, Rusedski competed at the Seoul Open in South Korea and won his second career tour triumph. As a result of the victory, Rusedski climbed back up the world rankings to No. 56 overall.

The Seoul Open, however, was to be Rusedski's last victory as a Canadian. Later in May, without much fanfare, Rusedski successfully petitioned the International Tennis Federation to allow him to play by his British passport attained through his mother. A traitor was born.

Rusedski's Treason: Context, Construction, and Contestation

Context I: The Rusedski Family

Greg Rusedski's treacherous decision to play for Great Britain in May 1995, instead of his country of birth, did not occur unexpectedly, even if some of the reaction in the press and by fans certainly made it seem so. In fact, while Rusedski's intentions and motivations from the beginning may never be completely known, seeds were sewn in the press as far back as 1993 regarding an awareness of the difficulties associated with being an elite-calibre international tennis player from Canada at the time. Chief among these difficulties were the financial realities of competing professionally on the pro-tour. "I'm not from a rich family and you need money to play tennis," Rusedski said in a 1993 interview in the Toronto Star after winning the Hall-of-Fame Open, "It costs $50,000 minimum, minimum, to go on the tour for a year and that's if you're travelling alone. Once you start adding other expenses, like a coach or a special session here and there, the cost goes way up" (Ormsby, 1993, July 25).

The lengths to which the Rusedski family went to assure Greg's financial ability to compete on the professional tour were made apparent in the press. It was reported in several news outlets that Rusedski's parents took out two mortgages on their Pointe Claire home in addition to multiple bank loans and fundraisers to pay the costs associated with their son's training, travel, and play. In sum, it was estimated that the family was in debt upwards of $200,000 (Ormsby, 1993, July 25; Tebbutt, 1993, November 11). Upon hearing this, a sympathetic Walter Gretzky donated hockey memorabilia to Rusedski's father, Tom, to help pay for coaching (Ormsby, 1993, July 25).

By the end of 1993, it was becoming more evident to Tom Tebbutt of the *Globe and Mail* that the risk of Rusedski defecting to Britain was more likely than not. As Tebbutt made aware, a player with as much potential and as accomplished as Rusedski was would not be in such dire financial straits if he were playing under the Union Jack flag (1993, November 11). A nation that took tennis as seriously as Canada did hockey, Great Britain in the 1990s was starving for a real contender on the world stage that could win major tournaments. No British tennis player had won a Grand Slam event since 1977, and not since Fred Perry in 1936 had a Briton won Wimbledon. In the *London Daily Mail*, British sportswriter Mike Dickson stated unequivocally that "the next big British player is going to make a bloody fortune…that's a well-known fact" (Tebbutt, 1993, November 11). In 1995, as it was becoming more probable than not that Rusedski was in the midst of deciding to switch allegiances, Richard Lewis, the director of national training for the British Lawn Tennis Association, coyly stated to press: "we would welcome him, he would be an asset" (Tebbutt, 1995, February 23).

More frustrating, perhaps, for the Rusedskis was that a number of far less accomplished British tennis prospects were benefiting far more from endorsements and sponsorships. For example, Chris Bailey, barely ranked above No. 200, and whose claim to fame was reaching the second round of Wimbledon in 1993, was showered with endorsement offers, employed a full-time travelling coach, and drove a high-priced Lotus car (Tebbutt, 1993, November 11). Great Britain's top-ranked junior player, sixteen-year old Jamie Delgado, had a racquet contract worth over $200,000 which was, according to Tebbutt, ten times what Rusedski could expect in Canada at the time (1993, November 11). Yet, for Rusedski, a top-50 world ranking and a tour victory under his belt were not enough for more than the mere hope "that Canadian companies can help me out" (Tebbutt, 1993, November 11).

Context II: Canadian Cultural Anxiety in the 1990s

In understanding this economic context surrounding Rusedski's eventual decision to play for Britain instead of his birth country, it is important to also consider the broader Canadian socio-political milieu of the late 1980s and 1990s. Greg Rusedski was not the first person who would disappoint Canadian sport fans by abandoning the country in order to play for another. In fact, for Tebbutt, the Rusedski Affair was beginning to feel like déjà vu (1993, November 11). In 1988, after winning an Olympic gold medal in boxing for Canada at the Seoul Olympics, Lennox Lewis, the future two-time heavyweight champion, moved to Britain to compete as a British athlete. Being British-born, Lewis' defection was easier to handle by some in the media, but the parallels between his reasons for leaving Canada and Rusedski's were readily apparent. Reflecting in retirement on his decision to compete under the British flag, Lewis said: "when I turned pro, I had to go to the United Kingdom in order to pursue my career. The infrastructure to develop boxers wasn't in Canada then" (Lankhof, 2015, July 14).

The Lewis and, subsequently, Rusedski defections were evidence used to fuel the fear possessed by many in Canada during the 1990s regarding the country's ability to hold onto its best and brightest. Known then, as it is now, as Brain Drain, the idea that Canadian governments and other institutions were spending vast amounts of resources to train Canadians who would only leave in a mass migration for greener economic pastures has been proven to be an overwhelmingly exaggerated fear. Yet, the fear of such a national crisis was very much a real phenomenon that reached a fever pitch in the 1990s (Helliwell, 1999; Zhao et al., 2000; Kesselman, 2001).

Importantly, however, the fear that Canadian sport was being 'drained' was not confined to athletes who competed in sports that were on the fringe of the national consciousness, such as tennis and boxing. Athletes in sports that were embedded in the Canadian psyche, such as hockey, were also perceived to be leaving Canada for economic gain. The most infamous case where such a narrative took hold was in 1988 when Wayne Gretzky was sent from the Edmonton Oilers to the Los Angeles Kings in a trade that not only shook the hockey world, but most of Canada as well. That Gretzky was traded and did not 'defect' on his own accord, perhaps helped ease the collective shock of a reality that was once considered unimaginable. But to many Canadians, Gretzky was a national resource and the thought of him playing for an American team, let alone a team based in sunny California, in the prime of his career was a hard pill to swallow (Brunt, 2010).

Jackson and Ponic (2002) root fan and media reaction to the trade in the broader socio-political discourse of the period. Their analysis suggests that the reaction to the trade exemplified crisis-discourse that was emblematic of wider national fears relating to the public debate over free trade between Canada and the U.S. and the fear for the continuing loss of Canadian identity. On a *Globe and Mail* radio broadcast, after the news had broken that Gretzky had been traded, one caller, for instance, said, "This is what happens with free trade. We export a national hero to the United States"

(Jackson and Ponic, 2002). A few days later, in an editorial for the *Edmonton Sun*, a reader wrote that "if this is an indication of the free trade between Canada and the U.S., than Canada is in trouble" (Jackson and Ponic, 2002).

To many in Canada, Rusedski was simply another case of a talented home-grown athlete who had outgrown the country's athletic capacity to support him. It was the continuation of a regrettable 'athletic-drain.' This was certainly how the *Globe and Mail*'s Tom Tebbutt understood the situation as it was progressing in 1994 and 1995. In an article published in March 1995, two months before Rusedski began playing for Great Britain, the writer called on Canada Tennis to do more to persuade Rusedski to stay with Canada. "The national association's mandate is to promote the sport," Tebbutt argued, "and Canadian tennis could not be better promoted than by Rusedski's exploits" (1995, March 2). Calling out Tennis Canada for its seemingly defeatist attitude towards Rusedski and the organization's perpetuation of Canadian cultural malaise in protecting national assets, Tebbutt charged, "It's a cop out for Tennis Canada to dig in its heels and argue that one player cannot be treated differently than the others. In an extremely competitive marketplace, sports executives routinely make deals to accommodate exceptional athletes" (1995, March 2). Through this lens, the discourse and narratives used to explain Rusedski's treacherous play for Great Britain in 1995 can be more clearly understood as the manifestation of a national anxiety regarding Canada's ability to be economically attractive in an increasingly competitive and globalized world.

Construction I: The Canadian Reaction to Rusedski in Tennis and the Media

While the financial incentives available for rising tennis players in Great Britain were enough to arouse fears in Canadian tennis fans' minds of a possible defection, it was also Rusedski's hesitation to play for Canada's Davis Cup team in 1994 and 1995 that sparked serious criticism targeting Rusedski's character and manhood. Rusedski was often coy about his desire to play for Canada's national team, which created a vacuum for some in the press to speculate that Rusedski was too focused on improving his tour-ranking to play for his country (Ormsby, 1994, May 6). In 1994, when Rusedski officially declared that he would not be available for the Canadian team's upcoming match against Venezuela in July, intense debate centered on the question of individual needs vs. national duty took place in the press and tennis circles around the country.

For his part, Tom Tebbutt presented a sympathetic argument explaining Rusedski's absence on the national team in the Globe and Mail, citing much needed rest from a grueling tour schedule as well as his vulnerability to criticism in case of a bad performance with little to gain (1994, May 6). Rusedski needed to focus on his pro-tour performance in order to improve his ranking, which equated to more sponsorship dollars, and not worry about a national tournament that would bring him little in tangible/monetary benefits. It was, in fact, his rise in the world rankings that would put a larger spotlight on Tennis Canada in addition to providing financial stability for Rusedski and his family.

Not unexpectedly, such arguments were met with visceral reactions. In a column responding to Tebbutt's argument in favour of Rusedski's absence from Davis Cup qualifying matches, Mark Dake questioned Rusedski's resilience, professionalism, and patriotism. "If Rusedski can't manage to play two Cup matches over three days, he doesn't deserve to be a pro," Dake argued, while continuing to question his mental toughness in the face of potential failure: "since when has an athlete died from negative press anyway" (1994, May 26). Dake went so far as to question Rusedski's manhood, in comparison to his contemporaries on the tour who regularly played in Davis Cup matches: "Tebbutt says Rusedski would be so tired from the tie, he would play dismally the following weeks. As if John McEnroe, Jim Courier and Pete Sampras, Davis Cup Regulars, beg off competing for the U.S. team due to fatigue. Please" (Dake, 1994, May 26).

For Mark Dake, and many others, Rusedski's unwillingness to play for his country at the Davis Cup was simply the selfish act of a person who put his own individual financial interests above the needs of the greater good of the nation. It signaled for many within Tennis Canada that Rusedski was ungrateful for all that the country had given him to get to where he was. The next year, in 1995, when Rusedski again declined to play for Canada in a Davis Cup qualifying match against Colombia, disgust within the Canadian tennis team was expressed in the media. In an interview with the Canadian Press, the national team coach, Louis Cayer, lamented that "in my case, it's pretty frustrating because I was his coach from age eight to 17 and his father accesses me almost on a monthly basis for consulting" (1995, April 3). Martin Laurendeau, a former Canadian tour player then coach for Sebastien Laureau, was also disappointed and lashed out against Rusedski in the media. "I've known Greg for a long time," Laurendeau claimed, "and money has always been the main thing he's interested in" (Tebbutt, 1995, June 20).

In the lead-up to Rusedski's eventual decision to play for Great Britain, narratives in Canadian media smeared his integrity, trustworthiness, and patriotism. He was selfish, a user, and ungrateful. Such narratives and discourse speak loudly to the demand for loyalty that the nation demands from the individual. As Druckman (1994) notes: "people see groups as providing them with security and safety as well as status and prestige in return for their loyalty and commitment (63). Thus, the nation can be considered as a type of social contract. In the minds of many Canadians, Greg Rusedski broke his part of this bargain, loyalty and commitment, and as a result forfeited the right to receive its benefits, such as security, safety, status, and prestige. In fact, by breaking this so-called contract, Rusedski became an easily identifiable outsider that members of the in-group could direct hostility towards. This manifested in the form of personal attacks against his status and prestige as a tennis player as well as his masculinity.

Interestingly, in both the Gretzky and Rusedski episodes, each athlete's wife/girlfriend became unwitting characters in the narratives being sold in the media and gossiped about in the public discourse. In Gretzky's case, his marriage to actress Janet Jones in August 1988 sparked speculation that the lures of Hollywood were tempting Gretzky away from his homeland. Jones was effectively cast as a villain in Gretzky's departure, being called "the next Yoko Ono" (Friedman et al., 1988, August 29). This part of the narrative was engrained to such an extent in Canadians' minds that Gretzky still felt the need to defend his wife's role in the trade in 2014, explaining in an interview that it was, in fact, his father who wanted him to play for Los Angeles (Canadian Press, 2014).

In Rusedski's case, British Lawn Tennis Association rules stipulated that in order to play for Great Britain, Rusedski would have to reside in the country for at least three years, unless he was to marry a Briton, in which case he could play immediately (Tebbutt, 1993, November 1). The fact that Rusedski was dating Lucy Connor, a British citizen, raised suspicions to the point where Rusedski had to defend his motives to the press. "I've been going out with her for 2 ½ years," Rusedski proclaimed, "I'm going out with her because I like her" (Tebbutt, 1993, November 1). Unlike Gretzky's situation, however, it was Rusedski who was the untrustworthy character in his episode. Whereas Janet Jones was said to have lured Gretzky away from Canada, Lucy Connor was being used as a pawn in Rusedski's long con.

Construction II: Rusedski's British and International Reception

This point is made even more apparent when Rusedski finally did apply for, and was granted by the International Tennis Federation, the right to play for Great Britain in May 1995. Upon his arrival in Great Britain, Rusedski's reception by his new teammates, fans, and those in the British media was a mixture of excitement and resentment to say the least. Indeed, the traitor is a particular type of villain who does not neatly fit into the binary us (good) vs. them (evil) structure of national narratives. Their treachery marks them squarely as a villain in the eyes of the group they betrayed, but instead of being wholly welcomed as a hero of sorts to their new group, the traitor is met with uneasy suspicion, if not outright hostility. For if the traitor betrayed their own once before, what is to stop them from doing it again?

When Rusedski agreed to play for the British Davis Cup team, a decision that ruffled many feathers in Canada considering his past refusal, executives for the British Lawn Tennis Association (BLTA) were elated. Great Britain had no players ranked inside the top-100, Rusedski was at the time No. 47, and had lost six consecutive Davis Cup matches, sending the national team to its lowest ever position in the tournament. The Association's chief executive, Ian Peacock, pleasantly stated his position in the press: "I am very pleased the ITF granted Greg's application, he is an exciting young player and I am sure he will be a great credit to British tennis" (Toronto Star, 1995, May 23).

Rusedski's new teammates, however, were not as receptive to his presence on the team. Mark Petchey, the man who Rusedski overtook as the new British No. 1, was an ardent spokesperson for the team's displeasure. Petchey refused to accept the process through which the Canadian was accepted as a member of the national team. "All of us feel he shouldn't become British," Petchey said, "He played all of his tennis in

Canada. He is Canadian. I've played my tennis here. I've come up through the system here. I am British, and he wants to come in at the top end" (Toronto Star, 1995 May 23).

Petchey's rejection of the decision that allowed Rusedski to become British is significant. Not only did Petchey not trust Rusedski, whom he saw as nothing more than a mercenary for hire (Tebbutt, 1995, June 20), but he expressed the opinion that one's sporting nationhood should be determined by some sort of tangible evidence that measures one's own conception of their self and loyalty to the group, in this case, time and effort. In speaking of the sense of betrayal that he felt towards his own national tennis organization, Petchey explained: "It really hurt me. I put in a whole lot of time towards reaching No. 1, then the goalposts were moved 100 yards down the road" (Toronto Star, 1995, June 14).

In addition to the element of time endured as an important marker of one's nationhood, some in the press questioned Rusedski's Britishness as a result of his 'professionalism.' Later in Rusedski's career, Stephen Bayley (2003, June 29) wrote in the *Independent* that "Greg Rusedski is a great professional tennis player, perhaps a tad too professional for some. Our problem is that professionalism is deeply at odds with the English sensibility." Particularly in the press, many British observers and commentators saw Rusedski as the embodiment of a win-at-all-costs attitude that seemed antithetical to the ideal British athlete, who embodied amateur sportsmanship and the elevation of process over results (Black et at., 2020, 9). Rusedski only cared for results, thus exposing his un-Britishness.

This extended to how Rusedski treated those in the press and how they perceived his communication. While the members of the media are naturally drawn towards, and constantly looking for, charismatic colourful characters to write about in their columns, Rusedski projected a stoic-like demeanour that was perceived as robotic. Respectful, Rusedski was very careful not to say too much in the press. One reporter disappointingly remarked, "He sounds like a recording" (Tebbutt, 1995, June 20). Reporters wanted a new British character, what they received instead was a machine-like personality intent on saying the right thing in order to concentrate on winning. "Greg Rusedski won't wash," chided columnist Robert Crampton of *The Times*, "How are we supposed to champion a man so clearly revealed as a foreigner both by his superb dental work and his ability to win games of tennis?" (Guly, 1995, August 6).

Following a rough beginning to his British career, Rusedski found some semblance of success at Wimbledon. Three early-round victories, including one over 16-seed Guy Forget of France, set up a fourth-round match against world No. 2, Pete Sampras. The Wimbledon crowd seemed to warm to Rusedski over the course of the first week of the championships, increasingly cheering him on with fervor. Following his match against Forget, Rusedski said of the crowd: "I had 13,000 people supporting me today. That's what won me the match" (Toronto Star, 1995, June 29). His fellow British tennis players and others, however, were firmly against him. Chris Wilkinson, who had refused to play with Rusedski on the Davis Cup team, declined to walk back his criticism of Rusedski made earlier in the month. "I'm not going back on what I said," Wilkinson said, "I'm not changing my mind, I don't want to talk about Greg Rusedski anymore" (Toronto Star, 1995, June 29).

Rusedski's fourth-round opponent, Sampras, found it necessary to lodge a more subtle protest on the practice court just before the tournament began. It is tradition at Wimbledon that the British No. 1 player, regardless of his world ranking, gets to have a practice court to himself upon request. According to Robin Finn, of the *New York Times*, when Rusedski made the traditional request, Sampras, who was on the court, "expressed reluctance to give up his practice court to 'a British player'" (1995, July 3). After his straight-sets victory over Rusedski, Sampras was more openly vile in expressing his opinion of the new-Brit: "I was trying to wipe the smile off his face," Sampras said when asked about his aggressive play against Rusedski, "If you are able to return [his serve] he is pretty average" (Tebbutt, 1995, July 4).

Contestation: Rusedski Comes 'Home'

The Rusedski Affair came to a head at the Canadian Open in Montreal a few weeks after Wimbledon. Less than two months after he defected, Rusedski was going to compete on 'foreign' soil just a few kilometers aware from where he grew up. Due to the location, Rusedski was not as able to avoid the Canadian press in the lead up to the tournament. Indeed, the fervor seemed to be reaching a fever pitch. In a column in the *Globe and Mail*, Tom Tebbutt called for everyone "to take a valium" (1995, July 24). That did not stop Mary Ormsby, from the *Toronto Star*, from referring to Rusedski as a "professional tennis mercenary" (1995, July 26).

Rusedski was insistent that he meant no offense by his decision to play for Great Britain. "It was strictly a personal decision," he explained, "my girlfriend is in England, I've been living there for the past four years, and I plan a career after tennis in London" (Ormsby, 1995, July 24). In fact, Rusedski said he still felt a connection to Canada. "The people of Canada have been very good to me," he insisted, "I still feel partly Canadian" (Guly (2), 1995, 11). The idea that Rusedski could still be partly Canadian did not play over well in the press. "Greg has spent so little time in Canada," wrote Bruce Wallace in an otherwise sympathetic article for McLean's Magazine, "that he can't even remember the last time he saw snow" (1995, June 26). A salacious story in the British tabloid, *The Sun*, quoted Rusedski's father remembering a 1991 instance where he remembered "Greg looking over at the wonderful green grace on the centre court [at Wimbledon] and saying to me, 'dad, I'll be out there one day and I'll play on centre court under the Union Jack and I'll win'" (Tebbutt, July 24). Rusedski's father denied that he had told that story, and that it did not happen. In any case, the lead up to the event seemed to overshadow the event itself. In the press, an engagement between the two sides of the Affair, Rusedski and Canada, took place over the correct perception of the narrative that was to define Rusedski's place in Canadian tennis.

Canadian tennis fans, and perhaps several non-fans as well, certainly made the most of their opportunity to make Rusedski aware of how they felt about his decision. Facing American Michael Joyce in the first round, Rusedski "was lustily booed from the moment his name was announced until he left centre court. Howls of derision accompanied each Rusedski error (mostly insipid backhands) while his terrific shots and searing aces were booed" (Ormsby, 1995, July 26). Inventive signs were held up for Rusedski to see. The most symbolically significant of which read: "RUEDKI: Le Fou De La Reine" (translated: RUEDKI: The Queen's Pawn) (Tebbutt, 1995, July 26). While Quebec separatism was not significantly injected into the Rusedski Affair, surprising consider it occurred just a few month before the 1995 Quebec Referendum on the issue, this particular sign demonstrates a distinctly Quebecois attitude toward the English-speaking Rusedski.

Joyce was not entirely sure how to react to the crowd's vitriol. "It was tough," he noted, "because they were cheering for me, but not because they like me. They're cheering for me because he's the enemy all of a sudden" (Ormsby, 1995, July 26). Luckily for Rusedski, the most overt and severe act of violence committed against him was when a spectator threw a tennis ball at him just before play was to begin. Unfortunately for the fan, the little green ball missed Rusedski completely, instead hitting the shoulder of a security guard.

Conclusion

The actual tennis tournament turned out to be a rather anti-climactic affair, perhaps for the better. Rusedski lost in the first round in straight sets to 90th-ranked Joyce. After the match, Rusedski was gracious in defeat: "Michael was just better in key situations," Rusedski said, "that's what decided the match" (Tebbutt, 1995, July 26). Joyce seemed sympathetic to Rusedski and congratulated him on his resolves: "I think Greg did a smart thing by coming here. A lot of players were wondering why came they thought the he might hide out or whatever. But I think he needed to get it over with."

Joyce's comments speak to the fleeting nature of the public reaction to Rusedski's treacherous act. While Greg Rusedski, as a character in Canadian sport history, will always be attached to and interpreted through the traitor label, Canadian reaction rapidly dissipated. As a Briton, Greg Rusedski had an eventful career. He held the record for the fastest recorded serve until Andy Roddick broke it in the early 2000s, made the finals of the 1997 U.S. Open, and reached as high as high as No. 4 in the world rankings. Rusedski's treason certainly hit a nerve in the Canadian national consciousness, which spurred a seemingly natural reaction from those concerned with defending their Canadian-ness. The tennis-court became a space where fragile sensitivities regarding Canadian national identity and its global vitality in the mid-1990s were exposed. And through Rusedski's treachery, the tennis court also became a platform for the renewed assertion of national values.

REFERENCES

Books, Chapters, Journal Articles, Reports:

Ackerstrom, M. (1991). *Betrayal and betrayers: The sociology of treachery.* Routledge.

Allison, L. (2000). Sport and nationalism. In Jay Coakley & Eric Dunning (Eds.), *Handbook for Sport Studies* (pp. 345-356). Sage.

Anderson, B. (1983). *Imagined communities: Reflections on the origins and spread of nationalism.* Verso.

Black, J., Fletcher, T., Lake, R.J. (2020). 'Success in Britain comes with an awful lot of small print': Greg Rusedski and the precarious performance of national identity. *Nations and Nationalism.* https://onlinelibrary.wiley.com/doi/epdf/10.1111/nana.12614

Bourdieu, P. (1988). Program for a sociology of sport. *Sociology of Sport Journal*, 5(3), 153-161.

Brunt. S. (2010). *Gretzky's Tears: Hockey, Canada, and the Day Everything Changed.* Vintage.

Druckman, D. (1994). Nationalism, patriotism, and group loyalty: A social psychological perspective. *Mershon International Studies Review*, 37(1), 43-68.

Gellner, E. (1983). *Nations and Nationalism.* Cornell University Press.

Gleaves, J. (2017). Sport as meaningful narratives. *Journal of the Philosophy of Sport*, 44(1), 29-43.

Greenfield, L. (1992). *Nationalism: Five roads to Modernity.* Harvard University Press.

Gruneau, M. (1983). *Class, sports, and social development.* Human Kinetics.

Hargreaves, J. (1986). *Sport, power, culture: A social and historical analysis of popular sports in Britain.* Polity Press.

Hartmann, D. (2017). Sport and social theory. In Robert Edelman & Wayne Wilson (Eds.), *The Oxford Handbook for Sport History* (pp. 15-28). Oxford University Press.

Helliwell, J.F. (1999). Checking the brain drain: Evidence and implications. *Policy Options*, 20, 6-17.

Hogan, P.C. (2009). *Understanding nationalism: On narrative, cognitive science, and identity.* The Ohio State University Press.

Homer-Dixon, T. (2006). In Irvin Studin (Ed.), *What is a Canadian? Forty-three thought provoking responses* (pp. 8-11). MacMillan & Stewart.

Jackson, S.J. & Ponic, P. (2002). Pride and prejudice: Reflecting on sport heroes, national identity, and crisis in Canada. In Steven Wieting (Ed.), *Sport and Memory in North America* (pp. 43-62). Routledge.

Kesselman, J.R. (2001). Policies to stem the brain drain: without Americanizing Canada. *Canadian Public Policy*, 27(1), 77-93.

Kelly, T., & Thiranagama, S. (2010). Introduction: Specters of treason. In Tobias Kelly and Sharika Thiranagama (Eds.), *Suspicion, Intimacy, and the Ethics of State Building* (pp. 1-23). Pennsylvania University Press.

Klapp, O.E. (1954). Heroes, villains and fools as agents of social control. *American Sociological Review*, 19(1), 56-62.

Kohn, H. (1944). *The idea of nationalism: A study in its origins and background.* Routledge.

Koizumi, T. (1994). Nationalism as ideology, nationalism as emotion, and the pitfalls of national development. *Cybernetics and Systems*, 25(6), 747-761.

Kramer, L. (1997). Historical narratives and the meaning of nationalism. *Journal of the History of Ideas*, 58(3), 525-545.

Morrow, D. (1992). The myth of the hero in Canadian sport history. *Canadian Journal of the History of Sport*, 23(2), 72-83.

Zhao, J., Drew, D., & Murray, S. (2000). Brain drain and brain gain: The migration of knowledge workers from and to Canada. *Statistics Canada Education Quarterly Review*, 6(3), 8-35.

Newspaper/Online Articles:

Bayley, S. (2003, June 29). Well played! Or why an English gent should never win at tennis. *Independent.* https://www.independent.co.uk/voices/commentators/stephen-bayley-well-played-or-why-an-english-gent-should-never-win-at-tennis-110838.html.

Buddell, J. (n.d.). *Greg Rusedski: player bio*. ATP tour. https://www.atptour.com/en/players/greg-rusedski/r237/bio.

Canadian Press. (1995, April 3). Canada advances in Davis cup. *Globe and Mail*, D4.

Canadian Press. (2014, October 7). Wayne Gretzky says dad convinced him to pick L.A. in 1988 trade. *CBC.ca*. https://www.cbc.ca/sports/hockey/nhl/wayne-gretzky-says-dad-convinced-him-to-pick-l-a-in-1988-trade-1.2791960.

Dake, M. (1994, May 26). Suspect reasoning. *Globe and Mail*, D2.

Finn, R. (1995, July 3). The newest British star hits it pretty hard, eh? *New York Times*. 29.

Friedman, J. Schiff, V., & Balfour, V. (1988, August 28). Trading places. *People's Weekly*, 38-41.

Guly, C. (1995, August 6). Rusedski comes home to boos. *The Ukrainian Weekly*. 19.

Guly, C (2). (1995, August 6). Canadian turned Briton plays Canadian open. *The Ukrainian Weekly*, 11.

Lankhof, B. (2015, July 14). Lennox Lewis want to make Toronto a boxing city. *Toronto Sun*. https://torontosun.com/2015/07/14/lennox-lewis-wants-to-make-toronto-boxing-city/wcm/b82aee52-983b-42e5-8e5c-f3b5f19eea5b

McCabe, N. (1988, April 9). Gangly upstart upsets Leblanc. *The Globe and Mail*, A16.*New York Times*. (1995, January 21). Agassi chills Canadian and gains fourth round. 34.

Ormsby, M. (1993, July 25). Rusedski serves notice hard hitting left-hander courting tennis stardom. *Toronto Star*, E16.

Ormsby, M. (1994, May 6). Canada's Rusedski is stuck in neutral. *Toronto Star*, B8.

Ormsby, M. (1995, July 26). Rusedski engulfed in sea of boos. *Toronto Star*. B1.

Tebbutt, T. (1993, July 12). Rusedski wins at Newport. *The Globe and Mail*, D2.

Tebbutt, T. (1993, Nov. 1). Tennis father's plans include mortgaging future for son's. *Globe and Mail*, D4.

Tebbutt, T. (1994, January 18). Another early exit served to Rusedski. *Globe and Mail*, C8.

Tebbutt, T. (1994, May 26). Rusedski finds way on clay. *Globe and Mail*, E6.

Tebbutt, T. (1994, May 28). Rusedski earns respect in open loss. *Globe and Mail*, A18.

Tebbutt, T. (1994, December 20). Lareau moves up in ATP rankings, C7.

Tebbutt, T. (1995, February 23). Rusedski said to be seeking greener pastures. *Globe and Mail*, C12.

Tebbutt, T. (1995, March 2). Rusedski burns, Tennis Canada fiddles. *Globe and Mail*, C6.

Tebbutt, T. (1995, June 20). Rusedski titillating British tabloids. *Globe and Mail*, D7.

Tebbutt, T. (1995, July 4). Sampras breaks Rusedski's hopes: Former Canadian overpowered, eliminated from Wimbledon. E2.

Tebbutt, T. (1995, July 24). L'affaire Rusedski running its course. *Globe and Mail*, D5.

Tebbutt, T. (1995, July 26). Boos greet Rusedski's return. *Globe and Mail*, C5.

Toronto Star. (1995, May 23). Rusedski's British courtship sets off tennis controversy: 'He was to play… I don't feel he should.' E5.

Toronto Star. (1995, June 14). No love for Rusedski from Brit conqueror. B7.

Toronto Star. (1995, June 29). Centre court fans adopt Rusedski: Ex-Canadian gets standing ovation after win. D10.

Toronto Star. (1995, July 24). Rusedski defends move to British tennis squad. E4.

Wallace, B. (1995, June 26). The powerhouse defector. *Maclean's*. 42-43.

Chapter 11

England vs Germany in the Sports Press: Mistrust and Glorifying the Past

Christoph Wagner

Introduction

The fixture England versus Germany has caused one of the biggest discussion points in the second half of the twentieth century; the third goal scored by Geoff Hurst in the 1966 World Cup Final has caused debates over whether the ball crossed the line or not. In the end, two English computer scientists from Oxford concluded that the ball had not crossed the line. Besides this encounter, England and Germany provided interesting games over the course of the twentieth century. Reading the press coverage of the games provides an interesting insight into the English mindset regarding people from other countries. The Anglo-German relations of the last century can best be described as difficult, which is largely due to the political history of two disastrous world wars.

This chapter examines how the English sports press has covered football matches, friendlies as well as competitive games between England and Germany. Three games will be looked at more closely: the first match after the war in December 1954 when West Germany, the newly crowned World Champions came to Wembley. The second game in question is the World Cup final of 1966. For the first time in history England would welcome a number of countries to stay more than just a few days, in the case of Germany, more than a month. Finally, thirty years later, England were once more hosting an international tournament: The Euro '96. Once more Germany would stay a prolonged time in England. This time, however, the historical circumstances had changed quite significantly: Germany was no longer divided, raising concerns whether the country at the centre of so much pain and suffering during the twentieth century would steer towards a repetition of history or not.

This study will look at how the Germans were portrayed in press reports before and after matches, allowing conclusions for how the English press reporters saw their own team. All three matches will be examined through the prism of press coverage. Three papers have been chosen for this: *The Daily Express*, *Daily Mirror* and *The Times* and their respective Sunday papers. Further, for each of these three games, the historical framework and the Anglo-German relations will provide the framework for the discussion in the article. This permits a double layered reading of these match reports; one layer describing the matches and informing about the formations and results the other indicating the state and nature of the Anglo-German relations at the time of the match in question.

This will be made possible by treating the match reports as texts that allow two different readings: one is the narration of the mere facts of the matches played. The other is the subtext that indicates wider issues within the Anglo-German relations.

The methods applied to draw conclusions are content analysis and discourse analysis. The former is applied to measure the number of football-related articles in the sports sections of English daily and Sunday newspapers selected to typify representations as they appeared in the quality, middlemarket and downmarket press. Besides the frequency with which they appear the tendency that they display, in terms of representation, has been assessed, in particular whether the content is positive or negative towards either team. As Hill has pointed out a match report in a newspaper is not simply a source of evidence; it is itself a text, and thus a historical source in its own right (Hill, 2006, p.117-130). Discourse analysis will be applied to decipher any meta-narratives and discourses that are transmitted through the banalities of match reports. Heinz Bonfadelli has argued that the aim of discourse analysis is to unveil ideologies embedded in the text that exist to maintain the *status quo*. While this indicates an intention to analyse texts from a Marxist position, it is not intended here to politicize the football coverage in English and German newspapers, but rather to identify and explain the discourses used (Bonfadelli, 2002, p. 134-136).

Football in the Anglo-German Context

Anglo-German relations during the second half of the twentieth century have been difficult, to say the least. Partly this is due to the history of both countries, which could not be more different. England experienced its last invasion in 1066 while Germany, at the heart of Europe, suffered centuries of war, invasion, and destruction. As a consequence of the Second World War, it was effectively occupied and divided. However, in some respects the histories of England and the Federal Republic (West Germany) in the post-war period from 1945 through to the early 1970s were similar. Both countries experienced austerity in the immediate aftermath of the war, though this was more intense in Germany given the extent to which its economic infrastructure had been damaged. However, both countries recovered during 'the long boom' that lasted from the mid-1950s to the mid-1970s, a period of sustained economic expansion for the world economy, which saw most developed industrial countries achieve high rates of growth and their peoples enjoy unprecedented levels of affluence (Hobsbawm, 1999, p. 230-255). At the same time, it was noticeable that British growth rates were slower than those of most of industrial countries, especially West Germany and Japan, over whom military victory had been achieved in 1945. Thus, while the English grew more prosperous in this period, they did not experience the equivalent of the German 'economic miracle.' As its people became more affluent, the British lost ground in relative terms when compared to its major competitors.

Just as it is important to highlight the historical differences between England/Britain and (West-)Germany, the press of either country is equally contrasting. For instance, tabloid newspapers have a stronger presence in England; currently there are five daily tabloids, *The Sun*, *Daily Mirror*, *Daily Express*, *Daily Mail and Daily Star*, whereas in Germany only *Bild-Zeitung* is published in this format. This contrast is also evident in the Sunday papers. Whereas England has ten national Sunday newspapers, four 'quality' and six tabloids, Germany has only three: *Frankfurter Allgemeine Sonntagszeitung* ('quality') section, *Welt am Sonntag* ('middlemarket') and *Bild am Sonntag* (tabloid). Esser contends that British/English journalism has a stronger tendency towards sensationalist stories, while the Germans prefer thoughtful analysis. One reason for the prevalence of rather sober journalism is the high percentage of newspaper subscriptions and home delivery in Germany which in the 1990s accounted for between 75 and 90 per cent of all sales, while British newspapers were mainly sold at newsagents or by street vendors. Arguably, this meant that it was imperative to grasp the attention of readers with their front pages and headlines in order to sell copies (Esser, 1999, p. 291-324).

One more striking difference between the English and German press needs to be pointed out. The British press exclusively have their headquarters in London. Moreover, they were all located on Fleet Street, making this area the press centre of Britain. Although some papers had local editions, the heartbeat of the English Press was Fleet Street. The situation in Germany is again very different in comparison to England. Even before 1945, the press was not concentrated in one city, as it was in Britain, but there was instead a strong regional and local focus due to Germany's federal nature. The English papers chosen in this chapter are meant to represent each market segment: *The Times* and *Sunday Times* for the quality section, the *Daily Express* and *Sunday Express* for the middle market and the *Daily Mirror* and *Sunday Mirror* for the tabloid segment.

Colin Seymour-Ure has pointed out that the ownership of English newspapers has often been highly significant in determining what appears on the page. The press 'barons,' he notes, 'were often supreme egotists: flamboyant, assertive, idiosyncratic, ostentatious, ruthless yet inspiring great loyalty and affection' (Seymour-Ure, 1994, p. 34). Roy Greenslade, in his insider's history of the British press, suggests that Lord Thomson was unusual in giving his editors 'an entirely free hand as long as they didn't come out against God or the monarchy' (Greenslade, 2003, p. 81). As laudable as this may sound it paved the way for football writing and reporting of a very particular nature as we shall see.

Post-War: Anglo-German Football in the 1950s

It is important to establish the broader context in which Anglo-German football relations have taken place. The history of armed conflict between the two nation-states was, of course, an especially important factor. Sports writers often reach for military metaphors to describe the 'battles' that take place on the field and the First and Second World Wars supplied a limitless source of references of which they were to make good use, helping them to frame each match in the context of recent Anglo-German history. War had seen hardship, suffering and loss inflicted by Germany on Britain and vice versa. Many on both sides found it difficult to forgive and forget. The idea that Britain/England was in decline, beginning in the 1950s and lasting well into the 1980s, is as also important, especially as Germany, or West Germany at least, was seen to be more successful, especially in terms of economic performance. The intellectual climate of "declinism," described by Hennessy as "almost a disease of the mind" (Hennessy, 2007, p. 28) dominated Britain/England in the 1970s and 1980s, even though the economy was growing, albeit at a slower rate than that experienced by its rivals including, most importantly, Germany. In a BBC Television documentary broadcast in December 1960 titled *Why are we falling behind?* the programme's producer observed:

> In less than ten years' time the people of Western Germany will be enjoying a standard of living twice as high as they have today. Yet it will be over thirty years before we double our standard unless there is a radical change in British industry. (Kynaston, 2014, p. 121)

To put this in perspective, some figures will highlight the issue. Between 1950 and 1983, Japan's annual growth rate was 7.9% and Germany's was 4.5%, while Britain's was only 2.4%. This suggested a relative decline, rather than actual decline (Supple, 1997, p. 9).

What added to the feeling of decline was that the British Empire was falling apart and Britannia no longer "ruled the waves"; by the end of the 1940s India, the largest territory under British rule, had achieved independence. By the end of the sixties, the Empire had been completely replaced by the Commonwealth of Nations. In contrast, the economic recovery and development of Germany post-1945 was attracting considerable attention in Britain. Prompted by the German challenge to British trade in Asia, a continent where British influence was clearly diminishing after India had won independence in 1947, the *Daily Mirror*, in December 1953, headlined an article by its star columnist "Cassandra" under the headline "Lookout! There is a German close behind!" The article traced the economic progress made by England's former enemy since the war under the further sub-headings "1945: How are the Mighty Fallen!' and '1953: How Mighty are the Fallen!" (Daily Mirror, 1 December 1953).

The feeling of decline was amplified by sporting performances of British athletes. As Martin Polley has suggested in relation to sport in post-war Britain, "Defeats on the playing field represented a kind of litmus test for the nation's decline" (Polley, 1998, p. 36). In reality, there was no logical connection between sport and the end of empire performance or an underperforming British economy but in a climate in which declinism was beginning to establish a foothold, the connection was often made.

International football played a part in this process simply because the game itself was so popular. There were signs of crisis in English football during the 1950s, mainly falling attendances after the boom of the immediate post-war years. The reasons were rising admission fees, as well as other leisure activities that became possible due to higher wages. Between 1949 and 1962 attendances at English league matches fell by a total of 11.25m (Russell, 1997, p. 131-138). The clearest sign that England "weren't the governors anymore" (Kowalski, Porter, 2003-04, p. 30-31) came in November 1953 when England were beaten 6-3 by Hungary at Wembley. Germany, on the other hand, were banned from all sporting events until 1952 when their football team achieved a respectable fourth place and won the football World Cup 1954 in Switzerland, beating Hungary 3-2.

Wembley Stadium, London, 1 December 1954

England and Germany were about to meet on the football pitch for the first time since 1938. Since their last encounter, much had changed in both counties. However, whether or not the game could be regarded as a measure of how the English felt towards Germany remained to be seen. Given the history of Anglo-German relations generally, and the fact that memories of the Second World War were still fresh, it seems reasonable to ask whether this would have reverberations on the pitch, at the stadium, and in the newspapers. Writing before the match in *The Times*, Geoffrey Green's tone was conciliatory, though his assumption that sport and politics in Britain were unconnected now seems a little naïve:

> The appearance of Germany's international football side at Wembley Stadium this afternoon adds its bit to Anglo-German relations. It is true that sport in these islands though not by any means always oversea holds no political significance. (The Times, 1 December 1954)

Would the English let their emotions show at a football match? Would the German national team be treated with sporting respect and fairness? Could England and Germany set the past aside and start a new chapter? Though the Germans were world champions the signs were not promising. The form that had won them the World Cup earlier in the year had slipped and they had been recently defeated by Belgium and France. More than half the team that had played in Berne was unavailable due to injuries or sickness; only three members of the championship winning team, Posipal, Kohlmeyer, and Liebrich, were to play at Wembley. The English press conceded that Germany would not be at full strength, with Green noting that "England to be sure would rather have had it otherwise" (The Times, 1 December 1954). This was regarded with suspicion in the middle market *Daily Express* and the tabloid *Daily Mirror*. Desmond Hackett in the *Express* opened his match preview by suggesting that

Germany have already organised their excuses sickness, injuries and all that in the event of defeat at Wembley this afternoon and, make no mistake England will beat the World Soccer champions. (Daily Express, 1 December 1954)

Hackett in particular showed hostility towards the Germans; he picked up on a story in the *Daily Herald* that had linked the absence of so many of Germany's players to rumours that the world champions' performances had been drug assisted (Downing, 2000, p. 73-74; Kistner, n.d.). He further asked Sepp Herberger, the German team coach, if his team would be given "pep injections as they did before the World Cup final with Hungary" and was told "brusquely" that this was entirely a matter for the German team; Hackett thus labelled Herberger 'the old Herr Hush Hush' (Daily Express, 1 December 1954). Hackett's aggressive questioning typified his approach to journalism; he aimed to sensationalise and place himself at the centre of a story (Glanville, 1999, p. 214; Kowalski and Porter, 2007, p. 78). Hackett and his colleague, Bob Pennington, had been waging a war of words for a few days. Having travelled to the German training camp, Herberger "Herr Hush Hush" had tried to have him (Hackett) removed; the underlying message was that the Germans were secretive and unfriendly (Daily Express, 28 November 1954). He went further by stating that the use of substitutes was unsportsmanlike and described Herberger as Germany's "Football Fuhrer," with obvious negative connotations. In a similar way Pennington stressed the importance of the occasion and the opposition. "They must say 'We are playing for England against Germany. That is enough we must fight until we drop'" (Daily Express, 29 November 1954).

Bob Ferrier, writing in the *Mirror*, took a less aggressive line by focusing on England:

> Poor old England! They never seem to be given a fair and square chance. If it isn't one thing it's the other. Here they are today, going in against West Germany at Wembley and in footballer's language they are on a hiding to nothing. For if England beat Germany they have 'merely beaten a team with eight reserves'. And if England fail to beat Germany, why, they 'couldn't even beat a team with eight reserves' (Daily Mirror, 1 December 1954).

Without a doubt, England took this friendly very seriously and changed its managerial system, placing an emphasis on youth. Though for this game, England prioritized their form above future promise and fielded a starting eleven with an average age of almost thirty. Stanley Matthews, thirty-eight years old, had first played for England against Germany in 1935, while Uwe Seeler, Germany's centre forward in 1954, was not even born at the time (The Times, 2 December 1954).

On the day after the match the *Express* published five photographs on its front page under the headline "England win 3-1 but it should have been 9-1" featuring near misses by the England forwards to back up the claim that England should have scored nine (Daily Express, 2 December 1954). The language in the match reports, at least in the *Daily Mirror* and *The Times*, was generally mild, with few battle metaphors or war references. Peter Wilson's report in the *Mirror* was headed "Massacre Match: But why didn't we finish them off" but in terms of content his main focus was that England should have done better (Daily Mirror, 2 December 1954). His colleagues at *The Times* and the *Daily Express* could not but make references to military conflict. For Geoffrey Green, the German defence had been "a veritable Siegfried Line," he observed, but the reference was intended as a compliment (The Times, 2 December 1954). Inevitably, Hackett's match report struck a slightly different tone, praising Stanley Matthews for his "one-man blitzkrieg against Germany" and abandoning almost all restraint in celebrating England's victory (Daily Express, 2 December 1954). On the same page a series of cartoons depicted their three goal-scorers Bentley, Allen, and Shackleton, writing letters of remorse for having behaved so nicely towards the Germans. The message was clear: England should have won more emphatically.

Thus, the first match after the Second World War brought England a third victory in four matches against Germany since 1930. Evidence gathered from *The Times*, the *Daily Express*, and the *Daily Mirror* suggests that the tone of the reporting was relatively mild; the odd war metaphor was used but not in the excessive fashion that became commonplace, at least in the tabloids, in the 1980s and 1990s.

1966 and all That

After the match at Wembley in December 1954, England travelled to Germany in May 1956 to play another friendly. The venue this time was the Olympiastadion in Berlin and the score was the same as in December 1954. However, the biggest match between the two teams took place twelve years later and, once more, Wembley was the venue. This time though, it was the World Cup final: a turning point in the history of Anglo-German football.

There were significant political changes in both countries in the late 1950s and early 1960s. In Britain, the Conservatives, led by Harold Macmillan, were re-elected in 1959, carried to victory on a wave of unprecedented affluence. After running into difficulties in the early 1960s and replacing Macmillan with Sir Alec Douglas-Home as leader, they were subsequently defeated after the general election of 1963 when Harold Wilson's Labour Party won a narrow victory and this was confirmed when they won by a more comfortable margin in 1966, remaining in office until 1970. There was tension between Britain and West Germany, as the latter did not support sufficiently Britain's application to join the European Economic Community (EEC) in 1963 (Ramsden, 2007, p. 285). There were other factors, however, that were drawing Britain and West Germany closer together, notably the Cold War, especially after the East German government sealed West Berlin off from the surrounding countryside in August 1961 in an attempt to stop the outflow of its citizens to the West. Military co-operation saw German soldiers training in Pembrokeshire from 1961 despite some protests, reported by *The Times* under the heading "Call to keep out Panzers" (The Times, 15 May 1961). In 1965 Queen Elizabeth II embarked on a state visit to Germany and, in a speech made after her arrival, spoke of the many historical links between the two countries that had so recently been enemies, reminding her audience that the British and German people had "for most of their history been friends and often allies" (Daily Express, 19 May 1965). An editorial in the *Sunday Times* hoped that the visit was a sign "that this country has at last re-aligned its views about the Germans and accepts them genuinely as allies and fellow human beings. A new nation is forming, freed from, or at least not over-awed by, the legacies of the past, and it is a nation nurtured on democratic values" (Sunday Times, 16 May 1965).

It is also important to note developments in European football that helped to change attitudes in the late 1950s and early 1960s. The game had become more thoroughly internationalized, not just through the World Cup, but through the European Nations Championship, with a competition taking place every four years after 1960, though England did not enter until the 1968 tournament. The European Champion Clubs Cup, started in 1955, proved very popular and Manchester United became the first English side to enter in 1956. The format was so successful that a European Cup Winners Cup competition was introduced in 1961 and awareness in England was heightened when Tottenham Hotspur F.C. beat Atletico Madrid to win in 1963, and especially when West Ham United beat TSV Munich in the final stage at Wembley in 1965. What helped to make the competition more popular in Britain was Real Madrid's scintillating 7-3 win over Eintracht Frankfurt in 1960 at Hampden Park, Glasgow, "under the noses of the British press, radio and television." It was also important that this was the first football match to be broadcast live across the entire continent of Europe (Porter, 2004, p. 42; Goldblatt, 2007, p. 402). Tony Judt noted that it was football, assisted by satellite television, "that really united Europe," while observing that no one gave a thought to the Treaty of Rome when Germany played England (Judt, 2007, p. 782). All this testifies to the power of football in helping to create identity through collective memory. Indeed, Albrecht Sonntag has argued that it should be recognized as a European *Lieux des Memoires* (Sonntag, 2013, p. 29-33). Clearly, for the English, the World Cup Final of 1966, played against West Germany at Wembley on 30 July 1966, falls into such a category, which is why it has resonated so powerfully in English popular culture ever since. It is important to acknowledge, however, that this "memory" has been subject from the outset to a process of mediation in which the sports pages have played a major part. James Walvin has noted that the 1966 final was "impossible to forget, not least because the media recycled the whole affair whenever it seemed appropriate that is as often as possible" (Walvin, 2001, p. 256-257).

Wembley Stadium, London, 30 July 1966, World Cup Final

The task of finding something new to say about the 1966 World Cup Final is daunting. So much has been written about this particular match. It is, without a doubt, one of the most talked and written-about matches in football history, if not *the* most written about. In placing the World Cup 1966 and the final into the wider frame of the Anglo-German relations, thus does not alter the nature of the position of this one particular match it is after all still the fulcrum of this relation in terms of football yet the significance has been diminished as more than fifty years have passed.

The essence of the match has been captured by *Guardian* journalist Simon Hattenstone:

> In the final England eventually won with Geoff Hurst's hat-trick and a goal from Martin Peters. It might not have been great football (the 1966 finals, unlike the finals in 1970, was not a competition for purists), but the drama was consummate. Germany take the lead. Hurst equalises with a header. Peters gives England the lead. Germany equalise in the final minutes. Extra time. Hurst blasts onto the bar and onto the goal line and possibly over. We'll never know for sure, but it was good enough for the referee. And, in the final second, Hurst's hat-trick screecher into the top corner (Hattenstone, 2006, p. 32).

By this time, however, even the controversy regarding England's third goal, known in Germany as *Das Wembleytor*, seemed to have been resolved. Research by two Oxford University scientists using computer-generated images, which traced the trajectory of Hurst's volley after it hit the crossbar, indicates that the whole of the ball could not have crossed the line and that the referee's decision on the day was incorrect (Reid; Zisserman, 1996, p. 647-658). As has been argued elsewhere the main effect of this research, which could not change the result, was "to take any heat that was left" out of a debate that had been simmering for thirty years (Porter; Wagner, 2014, p. 67-84).

Historians have covered the 1966 tournament and final from many different angles. Martin Polley has set it firmly in the context of diplomatic history using British Foreign Office documentation and other official sources (Polley, 1998, p. 1-18). Fabio Chisari began the exploration of the tournament and final as a media event, which allowed football to attract a new audience, including significant numbers of female viewers (Chisari, 2006, p. 42-54). Richard Weight described the tournament as part of "the Golden Age of the 1960s all the ebullient, meritocratic optimism of the decade" (Weight, 2002, p. 458), while Porter aimed 'to explore the ways in which memories of 1966 have been assimilated into England's popular culture (Porter, 2009, p. 519-539). John Hughson meanwhile places the tournament within the culture of the 1960s and considers it a "moment in modernity" (Hughson, 2016, p. 9). Just like Herbert Zimmermann's radio commentary in 1954, Ken Wolstenholme's commentary for the 1966 World Cup final has created a virtual community amongst the English; both have thus helped shape a sense of identity (Brüggemeier, 2005, p. 610-635).

England's progress to the 1966 final was marked by a slow start but gathered momentum as they progressed. This was very much reflected in the press coverage, which became more supportive with each match. A first climax was reached in the notorious quarter-final against Argentina that ended with Ramsey claiming that his opponents had behaved like 'animals,' followed by the semi-final against Portugal, which justified the praise that it received. At this point the press fell behind Ramsey and the English team.

The newspaper coverage ahead of the final was filled with expectations and optimism in contrast to the usual coverage of the bleak economic performance of Britain, which led to pressure on pound sterling in the summer of 1966. On 14 July the *Daily Mirror* had carried banner headlines with the words "Britain is Deeper in the Red"; two days later it was reporting "The World puts the £ under Siege." Front page headlines such as "Great! England's Glory Boys," after the semi-final against Portugal, no doubt made a welcome change. The *Daily Express* took the view that "too much" was heard about Britain's failures and "too little" about its achievements. It was "time to set the record straight" (Daily Express, 29 July 1966). The sports pages, full of positive stories about England's footballers, pointed to Wembley Stadium as the place where this process might start.

On the day of the match the previews were notable for the absence of military metaphors and references to the war. The emphasis was generally on England and Germany as football rivals who played the game in a similar way. Hackett noted that "these two teams play almost identical games"; England would win "because they play it better" (Daily Express, 30 July 1966). In the same paper, an article attributed to Manchester United's manager Matt Busby, presumably ghosted, celebrated the final as a triumph for Anglo-Saxon methods: "That this final has materialised is a triumph of the Anglo-Saxon style over the Latin. The power play and a system of progression over skillful but less progressive football" (Daily Express, 30 July 1966). The *Daily Mirror* struck a similar chord by adding that England and Germany had adopted the same approach and were "working wisely with the same European techniques" (Daily Mirror, 30 July 1966). Geoffrey Green also focused on what either team had in common: "Both believe in the hard tackle, both go for the ball fairly, and both will play until they drop" (The Times, 30 July 1966). By recognizing that Germany's footballers had similar qualities to their English counterparts, journalists were preparing the ground for labelling Schön's team as worthy opponents, an important consideration whether England won or lost. The negativity that had characterized reports on Germany's semi-final performance against the Soviet Union only a few days before was no longer evident.

As many commentators noted at the time, "what made victory all the sweeter [for England and the English] was that it came after two months of terrible economic and political news culminating in Wilson's drastic austerity package and the six-month wage freeze" (Sandbrook, 2007, p. 324). That the victory was achieved against Germany, which seemed immune to such problems, was an additional cause for celebration. As John Ramsden has noted:

The fact that England reached that pinnacle of success by beating 'Germany' in a battle watched by millions of viewers added a good deal of satisfaction to the process. (Ramsden, 2007, p. 353)

The game ended in a 4-2 victory for England. Thus, the world championship had been decided. Geoffrey Green concluded his match report in *The Times* thusly:

> The matter was decided, dismissed. England's players had proved Ramsey right. The Cup belonged to them and later they belonged to the jubilant, chanting crowds of the capital on what was another VE night. (The Times, 1 August 1966)

Green was not alone in comparing the post-match celebrations to VE (Victory in Europe) night in 1945 though, as McIlvanney pointed out, given the circumstances, "this was not the most tactful analogy" (McIlvanney, 1966, p. 164).

Inevitably, the English press reflected the mood of euphoria. The main feature of the match reports was that England's victory was instantly converted into a victory for Englishness; it had been achieved by players possessing qualities that the English liked to think characterised the English people (Porter, 2004, p. 42). As Alan Hoby put it in his match report for the *Sunday Express* on the day after the match: "It was English nerve and English heart which finally overcame the tenacious resistance of Uwe Seeler and his white-shirted men" (Sunday Express, 31 July 1966) Desmond Hackett, wrote a day later of "the spirit of England and St George" as he described how England fought back to equalize after Haller had given Germany the lead (Daily Express, 1 August 1966). As for Ken Jones in the *Daily Mirror*, the fact that England were now world champions simply proved that "it was right to play to our strengths." In *the Times*, Geoffrey Green put the emphasis on the physical qualities traditionally associated with English, and also German, football. Writing of the England team he observed:

> How some of them found the resilience and the stamina finally to outstay a German side equally powerful physically, equally determined, equally battle-hardened, was beyond belief. (The Times, 1 August 1966)

The English press could afford to be magnanimous towards Germany in victory, especially as their players had behaved so well. Some were even prepared to admit that they were unsure if the ball had crossed the line for England's third goal (Porter; Wagner, 2014, p. 71). Schön's determination that his team should behave well meant that they behaved with great restraint despite the doubts regarding *Das Wembleytor*. Only after the game, at the official banquet, did anyone question the referee's decision. "What is perhaps not so well understood is that Germany did not hold a grudge about the outcome, and the controversial third goal in particular," Uli Hesse has observed. He went on to explain that he had talked to many players in Schön's squad "and their comments all struck similar notes" (Hesse, 2013, p. 185; Porter; Wagner, 2014, p. 78-80). This behaviour meant that they could justifiably be described by *The Times* as "honourable losers" (The Times, 1 August 1966). Inevitably, given the heroic quality of the match that had taken place, battle metaphors were not hard to find. Hurst's ability in the air was a "weapon," Hunt was "England's spearhead," but there is nothing there that would not be found in reports of almost any match. Commenting on the English press coverage in the build-up to the final, Dominic Sandbrook, while quoting isolated examples, has that "there was little of the jingoistic baiting that would be associated with future Anglo-German encounters" (Sandbrook, 2007, p. 316). A rather different tone emerged from the match report for *The Sunday Times* by Brian Glanville. The German supporters, who had behaved so well according to Hackett, were viewed differently by Glanville: "The noise from the terraces was like that of a small Nuremberg rally." Glanville's account of the match is notably less sympathetic towards England's opponents than those in other newspapers (Sunday Times, 31 July 1966). In football, at least, Britain was "once more, among the advance guard, no longer in the wake of others" (Daily Mirror, 1 August 1966).

Reflecting on "Two World Wars and one World Cup," a terrace chant much favoured by English fans when playing Germany in the 1970s and 1980s, Chris Young observes that as English football, along with much of British industry, seemed to be losing ground to foreign rivals:

> What Ramsey, his team's victory and the legacy of 1966 stood for in fact was not the beginning of anything but the end. In hindsight and over the years, it has come to stand not even for the end of a glorious past, but the end of believing there ever had been one (Young, 2007, p. 18).

Thus, it might be argued that the World Cup final of 1966 was an event that the English had to remember while in Germany, subsequent success made it relatively easy to forget. As a cultural reference point that both nations shared, it helped to shape Anglo-German cultural relations in the thirty years that followed. If England and Germany should ever find themselves at war again, Peter Beck has observed, it will be a case of "don't mention the football" (Beck, 2003, p. 408).

Euro 1996

The last match closely considered in this chapter is the semi-final during the European Championship 1996, held in England. While in 1966 the Cold War united both countries, it was the end of this very conflict that seemed to divide them thirty years later. It was fitting that England was able to celebrate the thirtieth anniversary of winning the World Cup in 1966 by hosting a major international tournament. It was also fitting, perhaps, that England should play Germany at Wembley in the semi-finals, a match that went into extra time and was then decided by penalties. In the thirty years since 1966, much had changed, not least the extent of media coverage, both in the press and on television. Besides the changes in the press coverage, the most significant change was evident in the flags waved at Wembley whenever England played there. In 1966, the patriotism for England's football team was "contained within a British identity." In 1996, "Wembley was a sea of St George's crosses and red-and-white painted faces" (Weight, 2003, p. 709). The unofficial anthem for the tournament was not "God save the Queen" but the song "Football's coming home," and the implication was that it was coming home to England. (Weight, 2003, p. 709; Young, 2007, p. 15-16; Porter, 2009, p. 522-523).

These changes relating to national identity are important in providing a context for the press coverage relating to Euro 96 and especially the Anglo-German football rivalry. Coverage for the 1990 World Cup was restrained; in 1996, the tone adopted towards Germany was more aggressive. As Downing observes, "the infantile xenophobia which had marred the tabloids coverage of the 1990 World Cup was back in force" (Downing, 2001, p. 266). This was underlined by the BSE crisis that led to an EU ban of British beef in spring 1996; Britain responded with a policy of non-co-operation, which did not help. An American observer noted: "It did not help from a British perspective that the arch-enemy in the whole drama was its old wartime foe, Germany" (New York Times, 24 June 1996). The so-called 'Beef War' fueled Eurosceptic tendencies in the press, so much so that relations between the two countries had been soured by the affair. Previous press reports about Germany were largely concerned with the "much-vaunted post-war 'economic miracle'" but the end of the Cold War and problems arising from (re-)unification had "left the country sloughed in self-doubt," as Ross Benson has noted in the *Daily Express*. He added that football was less important than another game being played by Chancellor Helmut Kohl and his government: "a football match is over in an evening, Germany is also playing another, longer game. It is this one they are truly determined to win' thus alluding to fears regarding fears of Germany's intentions post-(re-) unification which had first surfaced at the end of the 1980s" (Daily Express, 26 June 1996).

It was difficult for those who shared those anxieties to separate football from politics. On match day *The Times* gave Conservative Eurosceptic John Redwood space to remind readers that the German question had "bedevilled the 20th century." The forthcoming semi-final "stirred deep feelings" and Redwood urged Britain to "stand up to Germany, on and off the field" (The Times, 26 June 1996). In its match-day issue, the *Express* used a leading article in its editorial column to respond to eleven questions posed by *Bild* in response to the *Daily Mirror*, which had emerged as Fleet Street's principal tin soldier in a journalistic pantomime war against the Germans as the semi-final clash approached. Under the heading "The spirit of being English," the *Express* answered such delicate questions as "Why do you drive on the wrong side of the road?," "Why can't you beat your former colonies at cricket?," and "Why are you the only people who still think the Wembley goal went in?" The *Express* acknowledged that *Bild* was trying to be funny, "displaying what actually appears to be a sense of humour. For Germans." It replied in the same fashion, treading clumsily through the minefield of Anglo-German relations.

We drive on the wrong side to make it more difficult for our soldiers to invade other countries. We were never European champions because we are an outward-looking nation that doesn't think Europe is the centre of the universe; we were quite happy with the World Cup. We are sorry that you do not understand that proper beer is served warm: why don't you wear proper trousers? We wear bathing trunks in the sauna, because we're not a boastful people.

At least our former colonies still want to play our national sport with us. Do any of your ex-colonies want to play yours with you? Come to think of it, what is your national sport? We won the 1990 semi-final in spirit. You just scored more penalties, that's all. As for THAT GOAL, we simply abided by the referee's decision.

Perhaps this can be best classified as 'blokey nationalism' or 'the jokey jingoism of the press' (Weight, 2003, p. 709-710). In 1996 it was the *Daily Mirror* that pursued this to a new level, prompting a barrage of criticism and complaints to the Press Complaints Commission. "Reducing the noble art of journalism to a few rancid puns and clichés had paid off for the *Sun*, and for once the *Mirror* was determined not to be left behind," Downing observes. Editor Piers Morgan led from the front on 24 June, two days before the match, with an editorial that parodied the well-known words of Prime Minister Neville Chamberlain's broadcast to the nation announcing the outbreak of war in 1939:

> I am writing to you from the Editor's office at Canary Wharf, London. Last night the *Daily Mirror's* ambassador in Berlin handed the German government a final note saying that unless we heard from them by 11 o'clock that they were prepared at once to withdraw their team from Wembley, a state of soccer war would exist between us. I have to tell you now that no such undertaking has been received and that consequently we are at soccer war with Germany.

Though this was in questionable taste, and unlikely to improve the dismal state of Anglo-German relations with the Beef War controversy fresh in the minds of his readers, it could be defended as an example of the irreverence for which the *Mirror* had once been famous. However, Morgan's editorial must be seen in the context of the features that surrounded it, starting with the infamous front page carrying the headline "ACHTUNG! SURRENDER! FOR YOU FRITZ, ZE 1996 EURO CHAMPIONSHIP IS OVER" and pictures of England players Paul Gascoigne and Stuart Pearce wearing World War II army helmets. Pages 2 and 3 carried a feature headed "The Mirror invades Berlin" written by a reporter sent to spy on the "filthy hun"; the Reichstag was described as burned out "a bit like the German soccer squad." Pages 4 and 5 were ostensibly devoted to Jürgen Klinsmann and his injury, though the *Mirror* had "invaded" the hotel where the German squad were staying and left towels and notes reading "*Auf Wiedersehen*" on the sunbeds by the pool. These pages were framed by a repetitive mantra, saying "Germany's going home" and "They're going home," parodying the England football anthem ("Football's coming home"). On page

6 a famous First World War recruiting poster is referenced with a small boy asking his father "What did you do in 1996, Daddy?" The broader context of current Anglo-German relations is then featured on page 7 with Prime Minister John Major criticized for failing to defend British beef; he had given in "without a fight." Finally, Tony Parsons supplied an article praising "the new England" that Euro 96 had awoken, which pointed out that "to be English is to feel nostalgic be they on the field of battle in 1942 or the field of dreams in 1966."

Parsons concluded his article on the state of the English nation in 1996 by claiming that "Football couldn't be coming home to a better place," not least because it was a country where there was "no place for racism." However, the extensive use of racial stereotyping in the English tabloid press suggested that this assessment was too optimistic. As Hesse has pointed out, "Their prevalent usage of war imagery, to be found in tasteless headlines full of words such as 'Blitzkrieg', and 'Kraut' and 'tanks', at first deeply irritated the Germans' (Hesse, 2013, p. 267). On this occasion, the *Daily Mirror* had taken the lead but it was not alone with headlines in the *Sun* ("BRING ON THE KRAUTS") and the *Star* ("LET'S BLITZ FRITZ") adding fuel to the flames (Weight, p. 709). Piers Morgan was inundated with letters of protest and concerns were raised elsewhere in the press. On the day after the infamous "ACHTUNG!" front page, letters to *The Times* included one from Sigmund Sternberg of London that conceded that the "joyous display of patriotism" in relation to international sport was perfectly acceptable but that "manifestations of xenophobia, racial hatred and the near incitement to violence," which amounted to an attempt to "whip up anti-German fervour," were not. Regretfully a major sporting event had been appropriated for "crude racial ends." Another letter from Mr. A.P. Millard, headmaster of Giggleswick School in North Yorkshire, expressed similar concerns about the use of "warlike terminology," fearing that it could lead to violence and calling for the press to show moral responsibility (The Times, 25 June 1996). Morgan, whose aim was to outmanoeuvre *The Sun* and *The Star*, was forced to climb down as the *Mirror*'s management became concerned about the negative publicity the coverage had generated, especially when advertising customers such as Vauxhall Motors were withdrawing their advertisements from the paper. He had an uncomfortable few days "worried that there might be violence for which the *Mirror* could be blamed" (Ramsden, 2007, p. 401-402). In the *Daily Express*, "Britain's leading philosophers" explained the significance of the England-Germany match and the furor that it had aroused. Dr Gordon Reddiford of the University of Bristol pointed out that "National hopes and stereotypes are centered on the game and players have acquired a moral status as ambassadors for a nation's view of itself." Professor Brenda Almond of Hull University addressed the issues raised by the tabloid's hostility towards Germany more directly: "it is one thing to call on the national pride evoked by key international matches, another to forment racial hatred," she argued (Daily Express, 26 June 1996).

According to Richard Weight, "The national football team had become steadily more important to the English since 1954" and this was very evident in the extensive press coverage of Euro 96. The journalism that caused English embarrassment and German irritation appeared on the front pages, while the sports writers simply continued to use their same style they had developed over the years. Germany's footballers were to be admired, but also feared. They played with "intimidating force" displaying their "traditional Teutonic virtues of planning and precision' but also a 'frightening power" (Daily Express, 10 June 1996).

The *Daily Mirror* became less offensive to Germany as the match drew nearer, placing the emphasis on football history rather than the First and Second World Wars. Sir Alf Ramsey expected Paul Ince to "do a Nobby" on Matthias Sammer while Kenneth Wolstenholme reminded readers that there was "no escaping the past" (Weight, 2003, p. 461; Porter, 2009, p. 520-521). England midfielder Paul Ince was quoted as saying that England had the necessary "battling qualities" to overcome "the ghosts" of 1970, 1972 and 1990 surrounding the event (Daily Mirror, 25 and 26 June 1996). Germans, as Hesse has noted, found this English obsession very strange: "playing England was like playing Italy or Brazil prestigious high-profile games, but nothing to get all fired up about" (Hesse, 2013, p. 268).

The match itself was a stirring contest between two evenly-matched teams, which Germany eventually won via a penalty shoot-out. "This was Turin revisited," observed Steve Curry in the *Daily Express*, yet there were compensations, not least that England were now "a side that played in the modern way, far removed from domestic football." There were reasons, therefore, to be proud and hopeful. As for Germany: "They are not like anyone else in football." Vogts' team was not especially outstanding but possessed "the old identity tags of technical ease and a composure which, at times, seems to belong to another world, such was their proficiency in the penalty shoot-out which finally brought down England" (Daily Express, 28 June 1996). The first three pages of the paper covered the disorder that broke out in London and elsewhere after the match. Despite the violence, Piers Morgan and the *Mirror* were not held accountable and the Press Complaints Commission refused to make a judgement on the paper's coverage (Weight, 2003, p. 710; Greenslade, 2003, p. 657).

The press coverage followed a pattern set in the 1970s: England were seen as technically inferior, relying heavily on traditional virtues, powerful running, and team spirit; the Germans were highly skilled, well-organised and efficient. This had become part of the national stereotype and was represented on the sports pages. Press coverage of Anglo-German football matches were partly shaped by what happened on the pitch, partly by the broader context of Anglo-German history and ongoing political and cultural relations. With a new context emerging in the late 1980s and early 1990s, German (re-)unification, British anxieties of history repeating itself gained traction. At the time Britain experienced a sense of restored national pride after the Falklands War of 1982, which negatively impacted relations with the EU and Germany in particular.

Conclusion

For Euro 96, press coverage was more extensive even than 1966, the last time England had hosted a major international football tournament, and even more than it was in 1954. As we have seen, analysis of the way in which Anglo-German football rivalry has been represented in the English press for these three particular matches has changed significantly. There were different narratives embedded in match reports of the English sports press and other items relating to international matches that were seen to reoccur over time. Principally, these were based on the history of Anglo-German military and political conflict in the twentieth century and on a developing story derived from what happened on the field of play in which, for the English, 1966 featured heavily: in other words, 'two world wars and one World Cup.' In general, English press coverage of Anglo-German football rivalry at the international level suggests a persistent undercurrent of mistrust arising from the unhappy history of the twentieth century when the two nations found themselves engaged in two global military conflicts in which suffering was inflicted on, and suffered by, both sides.

These narratives provided the setting for extensive stereotyping, which could be used positively and/or negatively. The way in which these stories were told, and especially the extent to which they carried an overtly hostile anti-German message that drew on negative experiences, folk memories and prejudices, varied over time. Thus, the context of the Anglo-German political, economic and cultural relationship as it evolved over a period of forty years is very important in explaining the nature of representation at any particular time. Change in the way in which sports news was presented in the press is another contextual factor that must be taken into account. For example, football coverage in 1954 was comparatively thin compared to that of 1996. In part, this can be simply explained by problems regarding the availability of paper (newsprint), which was subject to rationing until 1955. When previewing England-West Germany in 1954 for the *Daily Express*, Desmond Hackett's football story had to share the available space with other popular sports, such as boxing, dog racing and cricket. The inclusion of a column entitled 'Soccer on the Inside' ensured that football dominated the sports section, but that dominance was not so evident as would be the case forty years later when it could be spread over several of the sports pages and even, as with the *Daily Mirror* in 1996, take over the front pages too. Moreover, there were marked differences in style between newspapers that shaped the way in which matches were previewed, reported and analysed. In the *Daily Express* and the *Daily Mirror,* the writers were expected to deliver sensationalist and highly opinionated reports. Their approach, what could be called as "we-coverage," was generally quite different from that of *The Times* where the 'Association Football Correspondent' Geoffrey Green, was writing for a better educated, more literate audience.

It is not uncommon for sports writers to use military terminology to describe team games based on attack and defence but the shared history of the First and Second World Wars means that such references are capable of carrying powerful reminders of the past when reporting on England versus Germany. This pattern continued to prevail after 1966, though it was briefly interrupted as Helmut Schön's team made its way, or rather "marched" as some English newspapers described their progress, to the World Cup final against England at Wembley in 1966. There was some justification for the German accusation that some English football writers became 'tin soldiers,' especially in the interlude between the semi-final and the final. If West Germany had won at Wembley in 1966 it is likely that this kind of criticism would have become more evident.

The 1996 match took place against the backdrop of continuing difficulties between Britain and the European Union during the period of Conservative government under John Major from 1990 to 1997, culminating in the so called "Beef War" of 1996 in which Germany played a major part in securing a ban on British beef exports. This incident was very much at the forefront of the news agenda as Euro 96, the first major football tournament to be held in England since 1966, was accompanied by massive exposure on television and in the press. "Football's coming home" was the slogan of Euro 96, yet foreign journalists and fans alike could only have been alarmed by the xenophobic tone of the English popular press, which was hardly welcoming and took on warlike characteristics.

REFERENCES

Beck, Peter, 'The relevance of the 'irrelevant': football as a missing dimension in the study of British relations with Germany' *International Affairs* 79 (2), 2003, 389-411.

Bonfadelli, Heinz: Medieninhaltsforschung. Grundlagen, Methoden, Anwendungen (Konstanz: UVK Verl.-Ges., 2002).

Brüggemeier, Franz-Josef, 'Eine virtuelle Gemeinschaft. Deutschland und die Fußballweltmeisterschaft 1954' *Geschichte und Gesellschaft* 31 (4), 2005, 610-635.

Chisari, Fabio, "Shouting Housewives!" The 1966 World Cup and British Television' *Sport in History* 24 (1), 2004, 94-108.

Downing, David, The *best of Enemies. England v Germany, a century of football rivalry* (London: Bloomsbury, 2001).

Esser, Frank, "Tabloidization of News": A Comparative Analysis of Anglo-American and German Press Journalism' *European Journal of Communication* 3 (1999)

Goldblatt, David, *the ball is round. A global history of football* (London: Penguin Books, 2007)

Greenslade, Roy, *Press gang. How newspapers make profits from propaganda* (London: Macmillan, 2003).

Hattenstone, Simon, *the best of times: What became of the heroes of 1966?* (London: Guardian Books, 2006).

Hesse, Uli, Tor! *The Sory of German Football.* (London: WSC Books, 2013).

Hill, Jeffrey, *Sport and the Literary Imagination: Essays in History, Literature, and Sport (New York: Peter Lang, 2006)* Hobsbawm, Eric J.; Wrigley, Chris, *Industry and empire. From 1750 to the present day* (London: Penguin Books, 1999).

Hughson, John, *England and the 1966 World Cup. A Cultural History* (Manchester: Manchester University Press, 2016).

Judt, Tony, *Postwar. A history of Europe since 1945* (London: Pimlico, 2007).

Kowalski, Ronald; Porter, Dilwyn, 'England's World turned upside down? Magical Magyars and British Football' *Sport in History* 23 (2), 2003-04, 27-46.

Kynaston, David, *Modernity Britain: A shake of the dice, 1959-62* (London: Bloomsbury, 2014).

McIllvanney, Hugh (ed.), *World Cup '66* (London: Eyre & Spottiswoode Ltd., 1966).

Polley, Martin, *Moving the goalposts. A history of sport and society since 1945* (London: Routledge, 1998)

Polley, Martin, 'The diplomatic background to the 1966 football World Cup' *The Sports Historian* 18 (2), 1998, 1-18.

Porter, Dilwyn, "Your Boys took one hell of a beating!" English football and British decline, c. 1950-80', in Adrian Smith und Dilwyn Porter, *Sport and national identity in the post-war world* (London: Routledge, 2004), 31–51.

Porter, Dilwyn, "Egg and Chips with the Connellys: Remembering 1966," *Sport in History* 29 (3), 2009, 519-539.

Porter, Dilwyn; Wagner, Christoph, 'Over the Line? England, Germany and Wembley 1966', in Anthony Waine und Kristian Naglo (eds.), *On and Off the Field. Fußballkultur in England und Deutschland.* (Wiesbaden: Springer Fachmedien, 2014), 67–84.

Ramsden, John, *Don't mention the war. The British and the Germans since 1890* (London: Abacus, 2007).

Russell, Dave, *Football and the English. A social history of association football in England, 1863-1995* (Preston: Carnegie, 1997).

Sandbrook, Dominic, *White heat. A history of Britain in the swinging sixties 1964 - 70* (London: Little Brown, 2007).

Seymour-Ure, Colin, *The British press and broadcasting since 1945* (Oxford: Blackwell, 1994).

Sonntag, Albrecht, 'Im Parallel-Pantheon des Fussballs', *Der Tödliche Pass*, 68, 2013, 29-33.

Supple, Barry, 'Fear of failing: Economic History and the decline of Britain', in Peter F. Clarke (ed.), *Understanding decline. Perceptions and realities of British economic performance* (Cambridge: Cambridge University Press, 1997), 9-32.

Walvin, James, *The only game: Football in our times* (London: Longman Pearson, 2001).

Weight, Richard, *Patriots. National identity in Britain 1940 - 2000* (London: Macmillan, 2002).

Young, Christopher, 'Two World Wars and One World Cup: Humour, Trauma and the Asymmetric Relationship in Anglo-German Football' *Sport in History* 27 (1), 2007, 1-23.

Reid, Ian; Zisserman, Andrew, 'Goal-directed Video Metrology', in B. Buxton and R. Cipolla, *Proceedings of the Fourth European Conference on Computer Vision* (Berlin: SpringerLink, 1996), 647–658.

CPSIA information can be obtained
at www.ICGtesting.com
Printed in the USA
BVHW021357050321
601819BV00010B/474